D1614305

Multiple
Comparisons
for
Researchers

Multiple Comparisons for Researchers

Larry E. Toothaker

SAGE PUBLICATIONS
The International Professional Publishers
Newbury Park   London   New Delhi

For information address:

SAGE Publications, Inc.
2455 Teller Road
Newbury Park, California 91320

SAGE Publications Ltd.
6 Bonhill Street
London EC2A 4PU
United Kingdom

SAGE Publications India Pvt. Ltd.
M-32 Market
Greater Kailash I
New Delhi 110 048 India

Printed in the United States of America

Library of Congress Cataloging-in-Publication Data

Toothaker, Larry E.
    Multiple comparisons for researchers / Larry E. Toothaker.
        p.   cm.
    Includes bibliographical references (p.   ) and index.
    ISBN 0-8039-4176-5 (c)
    1. Research—Methodology.   2. Multiple comparisons (Statistics)
    I. Title.
    Q180.55.M4T66   1991
    001.4—dc20   91-22011
                                                                        CIP

FIRST PRINTING, 1991

Sage Production Editor: Michelle R. Starika

Contents

Preface

The idea for this book originated with the recognition of a need for a supplemental student text on the subject of multiple comparisons. But I also knew that many applied researchers who already had their Ph.D.s needed a source for accurate and current information on multiple comparison procedures (MCPs). Both a friend in the publishing industry, Henry Staat, and the editors for Sage, Michael S. Lewis-Beck and C. Deborah Laughton, came up with the idea of writing two books. The present book is the first of these two, the book for applied researchers. The student text will be done shortly as part of the Sage University Papers Series, Quantitative Applications in the Social Sciences (QASS).

Multiple Comparisons for Researchers is designed for the applied researcher who uses MCPs in his or her research. Graduate statistics courses are often deficient in their coverage of this subject, and it is rapidly and constantly changing. Applied researchers need a reference book that they can understand and use in doing their research. They have neither the time nor the inclination to attempt to decipher a mathematical statistics text or statistics journal articles, yet they want accurate and current statistical procedures. With this book, they will have such a tool: an applied reference book on MCPs written for the applied researcher.

No book is ever done alone. Those who participated in my graduate training, my colleagues, my students, and my family all contributed to this book. Perhaps more than the others, the students in my graduate MCP seminars have helped shape my thinking on this subject. Also, years of experience in teaching the subject as parts of other courses have been invaluable. Two reviewers read all of the manuscript and offered suggestions that have vastly improved the book: Roger E. Kirk, Baylor University, and Philip H. Ramsey, Queens College of the City University of New York. I thank you all.

I am grateful to the literary executor of the estate of the late Sir Ronald A. Fisher, F.R.S., to Dr. Frank Yates, F.R.S., and the Longman Group Ltd, London, for permission to reprint Table III from their book *Statistical Tables for Biological, Agricultural and Medical Research* (6th edition, 1974).

Finally, for the gift of intelligence, for the desire to be the very best teacher possible, for life, light, and encouragement, I want to thank my Lord. "Commit your works to the Lord, and your plans will be established" (Proverbs 16:3).

—Larry E. Toothaker

1 Introduction

A researcher performing a study with more than two groups would want to compare these groups. Consider these examples: market research that asks which of three lengths of television commercials is most preferred by consumers, psychotherapy research that is interested in comparing four different treatments of depression, and educational research concerned with which of three methods used in teaching introductory statistics yields the best performance.

If the research question is about equality of the means of these groups, then the researcher typically will need multiple comparisons. Any overall test of equality of the means of the groups, such as the one-way ANOVA, will simply answer the question, Is there any difference in the groups? Such overall tests do not address questions about which group is "best" or which groups are different when compared two at a time.

For example, in the psychotherapy research, perhaps the dependent variable was a rating for presence of symptoms of depression—the lower the rating, the better the treatment. The one-way ANOVA on the dependent variable would test for equality of all four means. If the overall F test were significant, the overall null hypothesis of equality of means would be rejected, and the researcher could conclude that some differences existed in the four means. However, the researcher likely wants to know which of the four treatments for depression differs from the others. This could be answered by testing which of the four means differs when the means are compared two at a time, that is, by testing which of the pairwise comparisons are significant.

ANOVA

Linear Model

For $J \geq 3$ groups with n observations in each group, there is a total of $N = nJ$ observations. A linear model for the N scores on the dependent variable, Y, is given by

$$Y_{ij} = \mu + \alpha_j + e_{ij} \tag{1.1}$$

where μ is the common grand mean, $\alpha_j = \mu_j - \mu$ is the fixed treatment effect for the jth group, and $e_{ij} = Y_{ij} - \mu_j$ is the random error for the ith subject in the jth group. Because the treatment effects are fixed and thus defined as a deviation score of the group mean minus the grand mean, the α_j are restricted to sum to zero,

$$\sum_{j=1}^{J} \alpha_j = \sum_{j=1}^{J} (\mu_j - \mu) = 0 \tag{1.2}$$

The e_{ij} are assumed to be normally distributed, to have equal variances in the populations, and to be independent. All three of these assumptions are summarized as

$$e_{ij} \overset{d}{\sim} \text{NID}(0, \sigma_e^2) \qquad \text{for each group} \tag{1.3}$$

where d and the wavy line means distributed as, N stands for normal, ID stands for independent, zero is the mean of the e_{ij}, and σ_e^2 is the constant variance of the e_{ij} for each group.

The linear model shows the scores as a function of treatment and error, and the one-way ANOVA can be used to see if these treatment effects are negligible compared with error. That is, in the same way that the linear model partitions the scores into the parts of treatment and error, the one-way ANOVA partitions the variability on the scores into sums of squares between (treatment) and sums of squares within (error).

Overall F Test

The one-way ANOVA F test is an omnibus test of the overall hypothesis of equality of the J group means in the populations, or equivalently, zero treatment effects. If this hypothesis is rejected, the F test simply says that there is some difference in the J population means without stipulating the location or type of difference. The F ratio is given by

$$F = \frac{MS_B}{MS_W} = \frac{SS_B/df_B}{SS_W/df_W} \qquad (1.4)$$

where $df_B = J - 1$ and is called the between degrees of freedom, $df_W = J(n - 1) = N - J$ and is called the within degrees of freedom,

$$SS_B = \frac{1}{n}\sum_{j=1}^{J}\left(\sum_{i=1}^{n}Y_{ij}\right)^2 - \frac{1}{nJ}\left(\sum_{j=1}^{J}\sum_{i=1}^{n}Y_{ij}\right)^2 \qquad (1.5)$$

and

$$SS_W = \sum_{j=1}^{J}\sum_{i=1}^{n}Y_{ij}^2 - \frac{1}{n}\sum_{j=1}^{J}\left(\sum_{i=1}^{n}Y_{ij}\right)^2 \qquad (1.6)$$

Decision Rules

The hypothesis of equality of the J population means is tested by comparing the observed F statistic to an alpha-level critical value from an F distribution with numerator degrees of freedom $df_B = J - 1$ and denominator degrees of freedom $df_W = N - J$. If the observed F equals or exceeds the critical F, then the hypothesis of equality of means is rejected. Critical values for F can be found in Appendix A, Table A.1.

An alternative decision rule for testing the overall hypothesis of equality of means uses the p value for the observed F statistic. The p value for F is the probability that F is greater than or equal to the observed value of the F statistic, $p(F \geq F_{obs})$. If the p value is less than or equal to the chosen level of significance, α, then the hypothesis of equality of means is rejected. The use of a p-value decision rule has become popularized by increased use of computer packages of programs, such as SAS and SPSS, to compute statistics. Most computer programs give the p value of F, but do not compare F to a critical value. Thus, with the output from statistics packages, the researcher can use the p value to test the hypothesis of equality of means.

Depression Example

Emotional depression is a widespread phenomenon, affecting people in all walks of life. There exist many differing treatments for depression, ranging from psychotherapy to medical administration of antidepressant compounds. Obvious questions include the following: Which of these work? Is there one that works best? Many studies have compared the efficacy of various treatments of depression. These studies have often differed in which treatments were compared, which dependent variable was used, how a placebo control group was defined, and so on.

Several years ago, the National Institute of Mental Health decided to undertake a large, multisite, coordinated study of treatments of depression. One of the major aims of the study was to assess the effectiveness of cognitive behavior therapy (CBT) and interpersonal psychotherapy (IPT) compared with use of imipramine hydrochloride plus clinical management (IMI-CM) and a control group of placebo plus clinical management (PLA-CM). Each treatment was carefully defined and carried out using a detailed manual covering every aspect of the treatment, the theory involved, how to deal with specific problems, and so on. Each of the quotes in the following descriptions is from Elkin et al. (1989):

- CBT: "The cognitive therapist uses strategies and techniques designed to help depressed patients correct their negative, distorted views about themselves, the world, and the future, and the underlying maladaptive beliefs that gave rise to these cognitions."
- IPT: "The IPT therapist seeks to help the patient to identify and better understand his or her interpersonal problems and conflicts and to develop more adaptive ways of relating to others."
- IMI-CM: This treatment was the reference condition for the study. Considerable evidence was available as to the efficacy of imipramine, a standard tricyclic antidepressant drug used in pharmacotherapy. "Medication was administered double blind within the context of a CM session (see placebo condition below)." In this context, "double blind" means that the treatment condition was not known to either the subject or those involved in administering the medications.
- PLA-CM: "The pill-placebo condition was administered double blind, within the context of a CM session. The CM component of both pharmacotherapy conditions was introduced into the study to ensure standard clinical care, to maximize compliance, and to address ethical concerns

regarding use of a placebo with depressed patients." It is important to note that PLA-CM is a control condition for IMI-CM, and not a true absence-of-treatment control. Patients met regularly with staff to manage medication (placebo pill), review the patient's clinical status, and provide "support and encouragement and direct advice if necessary."

Patients were prescreened to exclude those with additional psychiatric disorders or other problems and to include those who had a current episode of depression as measured by standard rating scales for depression. The remaining 250 patients were randomly assigned to the four treatment conditions. Experienced therapists were further trained, were monitored throughout the study, and saw patients according to availability. Multiple outcome measures were used, including a rating scale due to Hamilton (1967) called HRSD. Separate trained clinical evaluators rated all patients on this and other instruments.

Data analyses were done on three samples of patients. The *completer sample* consisted of 162 patients who completed at least 15 of 16 weeks of treatment. The *first end-point sample* had 204 patients who had at least 3.5 weeks of treatment, including the 162 completers. The *second end-point sample* had 239 patients who entered treatment, including all completers and the additional first end-point patients. The completer sample best shows the full effect of treatment, whereas the end-point 239 sample best takes into account possible biases caused by treatments having different attrition rates.

For the data to be used in this example, the outcome variable HRSD was selected for the end-point 239 sample.[1] A computer program was written to simulate data with the same group means and standard deviations as reported by Elkin et al. (1989). The original sample sizes were slightly unequal (59, 61, 57, and 62), but a common sample size of 60 will be used in this example. Table 1.1 gives the simulated data, the means (and standard deviations) rounded to two decimal places, and the ANOVA summary table.

The probability of a Type I error selected for the study was $\alpha = .10$. Thus, according to the α chosen by the researchers, there are significant differences in the four group means. However, the ANOVA is not designed to tell the researchers where those differences are located. These data will be used to illustrate each multiple comparison procedure introduced in Chapter 2.

TABLE 1.1 Depression Example: Data, Means (Standard Deviations), and ANOVA

CBT					IPT					IMI-CM					PLA-CM				
3	13	3	8	6	23	5	4	3	14	9	9	3	4	5	17	8	9	7	14
14	3	11	30	9	3	6	7	12	6	10	3	5	21	14	6	26	9	29	8
14	23	5	12	8	4	9	17	7	6	6	4	38	5	12	6	7	11	8	9
5	20	11	8	25	6	3	2	5	38	4	3	17	6	5	10	36	18	10	21
6	12	3	11	7	9	4	10	15	12	30	8	4	7	18	8	9	12	6	8
7	14	3	21	4	14	16	4	12	5	12	33	5	10	10	20	25	7	8	7
4	12	9	8	5	13	3	13	13	4	8	13	3	3	5	7	8	16	19	14
6	16	7	6	5	34	6	12	8	5	21	7	9	9	8	7	11	9	12	26
5	14	11	4	25	2	6	6	23	18	8	6	17	3	8	14	13	6	11	11
14	9	6	10	17	5	10	30	5	6	3	5	21	8	6	16	17	13	30	7
15	5	5	10	47	3	5	4	4	7	3	27	8	9	4	9	27	7	8	6
11	7	6	3	21	9	20	5	24	4	9	3	18	7	9	32	8	14	30	7
10.70 (7.86)					9.80 (7.88)					9.80 (7.75)					13.23 (7.76)				

Source	df	SS	MS	F	p
Between groups	4	474.20	158.07	2.59	.0536
Within groups	236	14404.53	61.04		

Multiple Comparisons

Definition

A comparison on J means is a linear combination[2] of the means, such as the difference between two of the J means or the difference between one mean and the average of two other means. There can be many different comparisons, hence the name *multiple comparisons*. Another word used in the literature on multiple comparisons is *contrast*. Some authors use *comparison* to refer to a comparison that is a difference between any two means and *contrast* for other differences, such as between one mean and the average of two other means. To avoid confusion, in this book I will use *comparison* and *contrast* interchangeably, and identify each comparison as to how many and which means are being considered. To express the definition symbolically,

$$\psi = c_1 \mu_1 + c_2 \mu_2 + \ldots + c_J \mu_J = \sum_{j=1}^{J} c_j \mu_j \qquad (1.7)$$

where the sum of the weights, the c_j, equals zero, but not all of the c_j are zero. Note that the definition of a comparison is given in terms of population means. The sample statistic that is an estimate of the population comparison is given as

$$\hat{\psi} = c_1 \overline{Y}_1 + c_2 \overline{Y}_2 + \ldots + c_J \overline{Y}_J = \sum_{j=1}^{J} c_j \overline{Y}_j \qquad (1.8)$$

where the c_j are as given for the population comparison. As was the case for the ANOVA, there are n observations in each of J groups. Note that the sample and population comparisons are identical except that sample means are substituted for population means.

Consider these examples of sample comparisons:

$$\hat{\psi}_1 = \overline{Y}_1 - \overline{Y}_2$$

$$\hat{\psi}_2 = \overline{Y}_3 - \overline{Y}_4 \qquad (1.9)$$

$$\hat{\psi}_3 = \overline{Y}_1 - \frac{1}{2} (\overline{Y}_2 + \overline{Y}_3)$$

These are all examples of comparisons on, say, $J = 4$ means. Notice the weights in the first comparison: $c_1 = 1$ and $c_2 = -1$ and the other

cs are zero. Here, as in any comparison, the sum of the weights is zero: $1 + (-1) + 0 + 0 = 0$.

The mean of any sample comparison is given by

$$E(\hat{\psi}) = \psi \qquad (1.10)$$

and, with the usual ANOVA assumption of equal group variances, the variance of a sample comparison is given by

$$\sigma_{\hat{\psi}}^2 = \sigma_e^2 \sum_{j=1}^{J} \frac{c_j^2}{n_j} \qquad (1.11)$$

We estimate the variance of a sample comparison with

$$estimated\ \sigma_{\hat{\psi}}^2 = \hat{\sigma}_{\hat{\psi}}^2 = MS_W \sum_{j=1}^{J} \frac{c_j^2}{n_j} \qquad (1.12)$$

where MS_W is the mean square within from the overall ANOVA. Finally, the sample comparison is normally distributed. We now know the mean, variance, and shape of the sampling distribution of a sample comparison:

$$\hat{\psi} \overset{d}{\sim} N\left(\psi, \sigma_e^2 \sum_{j=1}^{J} \frac{c_j^2}{n_j} \right) \qquad (1.13)$$

Dimensions of Classification

There are many ways to describe multiple comparisons and thus many dimensions on which they could be classified. Note that the following classifications will be describing the comparisons themselves, the types of statistics that could be computed on the comparisons, the types of error rate control, or the different reference distributions to which these statistics could be compared.

All versus some. The first classification dimension is the number of comparisons computed by the researcher.[3] The researcher could do all of the possible comparisons or some subset of all possible comparisons.

Orthogonal versus nonorthogonal.[4] The orthogonality being considered here is between the comparisons themselves: For the comparisons in Equation 1.9, is the first comparison orthogonal to the second comparison? The researcher can do a group of comparisons that are all orthogonal to each other or that have some nonorthogonality. This issue will be discussed more fully below.

Pairwise versus general. Pairwise comparisons are those in which the means are compared two at a time, where the weights are 1 and −1 for two of the J means and zero for all others. Another way of defining a pairwise comparison is that it is simply a difference between two means. Examples are given by the first two comparisons in Equation 1.9. The number of pairwise comparisons that could be computed on J means is given as $J(J - 1)/2$. So for $J = 4$ means, there are $4(4 - 1)/2 = 6$ pairwise comparisons. The type of comparison labeled *general* is any comparison that is not a pairwise comparison. The third comparison in Equation 1.9 is an example of a general comparison.

Planned versus post hoc. Planned (or a priori) comparisons are those the researcher planned to do before the results were obtained. Often planned comparisons are based on predictions from the theory that has led to the research project. Post hoc (or a posteriori) comparisons are those computed after the results were obtained. With post hoc comparisons the researcher can choose comparisons based on the results, such as doing only the largest two comparisons. Post hoc comparisons may or may not have a theory base for their inclusion in the study. Some further discussion of planned comparisons will be given in the section below headed "Orthogonality of Multiple Comparisons."

Stepwise versus nonstepwise. Some multiple comparison methods depend in part upon another statistic. A procedure may allow computation of comparisons only if the overall F is significant, or may make computation of one comparison allowable only if some other comparison is significant. Comparison methods that have such a dependency are called stepwise methods because computation of the comparisons proceeds in steps. Multiple comparison methods that do not have such dependencies are called nonstepwise or simultaneous test procedures (STPs), because all of the comparisons may be computed simultaneously.

Types of statistics. Many of the multiple comparison procedures (MCPs) differ with respect to the statistic and/or the theoretical reference distribution used to make the inference. Indeed, some of the methods differ with respect to the type of inference that can be made, such as tests of hypotheses or interval estimation. These issues will be dealt with in the section below on types of statistics.

Types of error rates. There are two basic types of error rates: α control for each comparison and α control for some group of comparisons. The latter category contains several different subtypes of error rate. Additionally, there are different types of null hypotheses and configurations of population means that could occur. Finally, there are several different ways to define power of multiple comparison procedures. The different types of error rates, hypotheses, mean configurations, and power will be discussed below.

Any of these classification categories can occur together, depending upon the choice of the researcher. There are some popular misconceptions that need to be cleared up, namely, that some combinations of these categories cannot occur. A researcher could choose multiple comparisons that are planned and control error rate for the group of comparisons. A researcher may choose comparisons that are orthogonal and not planned, or do post hoc comparisons controlling error rate for each comparison. Although some of these combinations may be unusual, they are neither impossible nor forbidden.

Some of these classification categories are not open to choice by the researcher simply because the research question dictates the nature of the comparisons themselves. Thus the number of comparisons computed, and whether or not the comparisons will be orthogonal or pairwise, are often dictated by the research question and thus are not open to choice by the researcher. Other issues, such as type of null hypothesis and configuration of population means, are dictated by the populations of data. Often whether the comparisons are planned or post hoc is dictated by the research question, but sometimes the researcher has this choice. The researcher can choose type of error rate and power, type of statistic, and stepwise or nonstepwise, with the type of error rate and power being the most basic and perhaps most important decisions.

Types of Error Rate, Hypotheses, Mean Configurations, and Power

Types of Error Rate

The assignment of error rate can be done in several different ways for multiple comparisons, and each researcher must choose one of them for each research project. Basically, the choice of error rate control is choosing what value of α' to assign to each comparison. Such choice also influences the power of the eventual statistic.

Error rate per comparison. One of the two basic categories of α control is to control error rate for each comparison, which is called error rate per comparison (ERPC). This is accomplished by setting $\alpha' = \alpha$ at the chosen level, typically .05, for each comparison. Then the researcher would choose α-level critical values for the appropriate statistic for each comparison.

One problem with controlling α using ERPC is that the probability of at least one Type I error increases as the number of comparisons (C) increases. That is, if $\alpha' = .05$, then for one comparison the probability of at least one Type I error is .05, but for two comparisons it is closer to .10, for three comparisons it is closer to .15, and so on. For C orthogonal comparisons each at level α', this is shown as

$$p(\text{at least one Type I error}) = 1 - (1 - \alpha')^C \leq C\alpha' \qquad (1.14)$$

where $C\alpha'$ is the approximate upper bound on p(at least one Type I error). If the C comparisons are not orthogonal, then

$$p(\text{at least one Type I error}) \leq 1 - (1 - \alpha')^C \leq C\alpha' \qquad (1.15)$$

Empirical research shows that p(at least one Type I error) is fairly close to $1 - (1 - \alpha')^C$ for comparisons that are not orthogonal.

While the bad news for ERPC is that the probability of at least one Type I error is large, the good news is that the power is also large. Control of error rate using ERPC gives higher power than any other method of error rate control, but at the expense of high p(at least one Type I error).[5] As in basic hypothesis testing, where there is a trade-off between control of α and β, allowing high probability of at least one Type I error (high α) gives high power (low β).

Error rate per family. The second of the two basic categories of α control is to control α for some group of comparisons. Error rate per family (ERPF) is the first of two types of α control that do so for a group or, equivalently, family of comparisons.[6] ERPF is not a probability, as are the other definitions of error rate. ERPF is the average number of erroneous statements (false rejections, Type I errors) made in a group (family) of comparisons. ERPF is accomplished by setting α' at some value smaller than α, and the simplest method for doing this is to set α' such that it adds up to α. For example, if α' is equal

TABLE 1.2 Various Values of Type I Error Rate

Number of Orthogonal Comparisons (C)	α'	ERPC	ERFW	ERPF
5	.01	.01	.049	.05
5	.010206	.010206	.05	.05103
10	.005	.005	.04889	.05
10	.0051162	.0051162	.05	.051162
10	.05	.05	.40	.50

for all comparisons, then for C orthogonal comparisons each at level α', ERPF is equal to $C\alpha'$. This method of controlling error rate appears in the logic of the Dunn/Bonferroni and Dunn/Šidák methods to be discussed in Chapter 2.

Error rate familywise. The second type of α control that functions for some group of comparisons is error rate familywise (ERFW). ERFW is a probability, and is defined as the probability of at least one Type I error, p(at least one Type I error), given in Equation 1.14. Even though ERFW and ERPF differ in definition and concept, in practice if a method accomplishes one of these types of control of α, it usually accomplishes the other. Thus the basic decision a researcher faces with respect to α control is whether to control error rate for each comparison (ERPC) or some group of comparisons (ERPF or ERFW).

The first of several points that help to see the relationships among these three different types of α control is that if α' is used for each of C comparisons, then using ERPC gives $\alpha = \alpha'$, using ERFW gives $\alpha \leq 1 - (1 - \alpha')^C$, and using ERPF gives $\alpha \leq C\alpha'$. Putting these together gives

$$\alpha' \leq 1 - (1 - \alpha')^c \leq C\alpha' \qquad (1.16)$$

which easily leads to

$$\text{ERPC} \leq \text{ERFW} \leq \text{ERPF} \qquad (1.17)$$

For example, if we set $\alpha' = .01$ for $C = 5$ orthogonal comparisons, then ERPC = .01, ERFW = .049, and ERPF = .05 (see Table 1.2).

Consider the other values of α', C orthogonal comparisons, and the corresponding values of ERPC, ERFW, and ERPF. For small α' and reasonable C, ERFW and ERPF are fairly close, thus illustrating that control of one of these two error rates gives control of the other. If we set $\alpha' = .05$ for $C = 10$ orthogonal comparisons, then ERPC = .05, ERFW = .40, and ERPF = .50, illustrating that control of α for each comparison (ERPC) leads to excessive α for a group of comparisons (ERFW or ERPF). Finally, note that ERPF serves as an upper bound for ERFW. In practice, ERPC and ERPF are not often used because most researchers control p(at least one Type I error) using ERFW.

Types of Hypotheses

Types of hypotheses give the configurations that exist in the population means that allow the statistician to examine the different types of error rates. That is, attention is paid to the equality, or equalities, in the means rather than the differences.

Overall null hypothesis is the first type of hypothesis. An overall null hypothesis exists if all of the J means are equal. This is the null hypothesis tested by the overall F test, thus the name *overall null hypothesis*. Some researchers may refer to the overall null hypothesis as the "full" null hypothesis.

Multiple null hypotheses exist if the overall null hypothesis is not true, but more than one subset of equal means do exist. The means must be equal within subsets, but there must be differences between the subsets. Then each of these subsets represents a null hypothesis. If there are M multiple subsets of means with equality within the subset, there are M multiple null hypotheses. For example, if $J = 4$ and means 1 and 2 are equal but different from means 3 and 4, which are equal (see Figure 1.1), then there are $M = 2$ null hypotheses.

Partial null hypothesis is the configuration that exists when the overall null hypothesis is not true, but some population means are equal. For example, examine Figure 1.2. For $J = 4$, if the first three means are equal but the fourth is larger than the first three, there would be a partial null hypothesis in the three equal means.

Types of Population Mean Configurations

When we were examining types of hypotheses, attention was paid to which means were equal. Now we want to attend to which means are unequal.

Minimum range configuration. Means in a minimum range configuration have the first half of the means equal and the second half equal

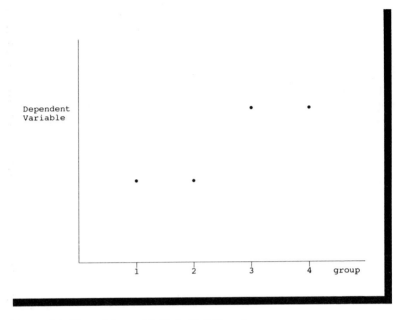

Figure 1.1. Group Means, Multiple Null Hypotheses

but different from the first half (Ramsey, 1978a). For odd J, the first half is defined as means one through $(J + 1)/2$. An example of minimum range means would be if $\mu_1 = \mu_2 = \mu_3 = 50$ and $\mu_4 = \mu_5 = \mu_6 = 70$.

Maximum range configuration. Means in a maximum range configuration have the first mean the lowest, the last mean the highest, and the middle means the average of the first and last (Ramsey, 1978a). An example of maximum range means would be if $\mu_1 = 50$, $\mu_2 = \mu_3 = \mu_4 = \mu_5 = 60$, and $\mu_6 = 70$.

Equally spaced configuration. In this configuration of population means, each succeeding ordered mean is a fixed increment higher than the preceding mean, in a stair-step fashion. An example would be if $\mu_1 = 20$, $\mu_2 = 25$, $\mu_3 = 30$, $\mu_4 = 35$, $\mu_5 = 40$, and $\mu_6 = 45$, with a constant difference of 5 from the preceding mean.

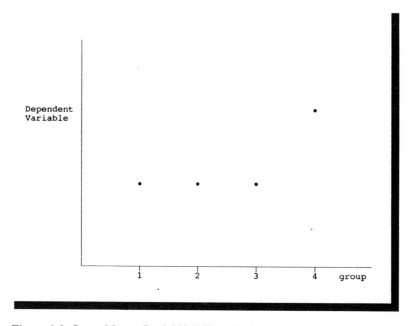

Figure 1.2. Group Means, Partial Null Hypothesis

Types of Power

It stands to reason that if there are different types of Type I error rate for multiple comparisons, there are also different types of power. However, these different types of power do not affect applied researchers as directly in their use of multiple comparison methods as do the different types of error rate. That is, what the researcher practically does when computing a multiple comparison method, such as obtaining a critical value and deciding which comparisons are significant, is not changed by the different types of power.

However, knowledge of the different types of power is essential to an understanding of research on multiple comparison procedures themselves, because different research articles use different definitions of power. Such knowledge also may help the researcher in choosing an appropriate multiple comparison procedure. At least three different types of power have been defined in the literature on multiple comparisons: any-pair power, all-pairs power, and per-pair power.

Any-pair power is the probability of detecting any true mean difference in the J means of the experiment. Any-pair power is most similar to the power of the ANOVA both in value and in definition, because the ANOVA is designed to detect any true difference in the means. It is often very closely related to the power of the multiple comparison method to detect the largest mean difference in the population. However, these two powers are not exactly the same, because the largest mean difference in the population does not always give the largest mean difference in the sample.

All-pairs power is the probability of detecting all true mean differences in the J means of the experiment. All-pairs power is very closely related to the power of the multiple comparison method to detect the smallest mean difference in the population. These two powers will not be the same because the smallest mean difference in the population does not always give the smallest mean difference in the sample.

Per-pair power[7] is the average probability of detecting a true mean difference in the J means in the experiment. For a given set of means, per-pair power will lie somewhere between any-pair power, the largest of the three, and all-pairs power, the smallest of the three. From a different perspective, if the researcher desired power to be some constant value for all definitions, say .90, then the sample size required would be largest for all-pairs power, middle for per-pair power, and lowest for any-pair power, comparable to that for the ANOVA.

One problem with all of these definitions of power is that they ignore the fact that different comparisons will have different power values because of varying values of true differences in the means. Any-pair power ignores all but the largest mean difference, all-pairs power ignores all but the smallest mean difference, and per-pair power gives an average that is appropriate only for those comparisons with "average" mean difference. Note that it is not necessary to present per-pair power as an average, but that it can be presented for any given subset of means. When presented in this way, it is obvious that different comparisons have different power.

A quote from Ramsey (1978b) may provide some help:

Choosing between different criteria of power may not be an easy task. I have suggested that in an exploratory or pilot study one would be interested in a significant overall F test in order to decide whether or not additional investigation is justified. At some point it would seem reasonable to perform a confirmatory study to detect all true differences above some minimal value. In such a case one would want a procedure that maximizes all-pairs power. Many actual studies lie somewhere between these extreme conditions and one would then prefer some criterion such as an average power for all true differences. (p. 487)

Each researcher must decide what type of error rate control and what type of power are desired, and then examine the potential multiple comparison methods that accomplish these goals. Among those methods that give the desired error rate control, it is reasonable to choose the method with the highest power of the type desired.

Types of Statistics

Because of the many different multiple comparison procedures, there has been no universal agreement among the procedures' many authors as to which statistic to use among those that are interchangeable. In fact, some of the MCPs use statistics that cannot be interchanged.

t *Statistic*

For any given comparison, three crucial pieces of information are known about its sampling distribution: the mean, the variance and how to estimate the variance, and that the shape of the sampling distribution is normal. Given this information, it is possible to form a t statistic for any given comparison:

$$t_{\hat{\psi}} = \frac{\hat{\psi} - \psi}{\sqrt{\mathrm{MS_W} \sum_{j=1}^{J} \frac{c_j^2}{n_j}}} \qquad (1.18)$$

For equal sample sizes, the t statistic simplifies to

$$t_{\hat{\psi}} = \frac{\hat{\psi} - \psi}{\sqrt{\frac{\mathrm{MS_W}}{n} \sum_{j=1}^{J} c_j^2}} \qquad (1.19)$$

If there is only a single comparison of interest to the researcher, then, making the usual ANOVA assumptions, the t statistic can be used to test the hypothesis of

$$H_0 : \psi = 0 \qquad (1.20)$$

using a critical value from the t distribution with df = df_W (Appendix A, Table A.2). For multiple comparisons, the t statistics must be referred to appropriate critical values for the MCP selected from those methods given in Chapter 2. Again, the selection of the MCP will depend upon the researcher's choice of error rate and power. Unless otherwise noted, the t statistic can be used for any of the methods discussed in this text.

Range Statistic

One of the basic statistics used in MCPs is referred to as the range statistic, because with equal sample sizes (n), the largest of the differences between group means is distributed as the range of J orthogonal normal variables. When such a difference is divided by an estimate of the standard error of the mean, it is called a Studentized range, and has the following formula:

$$q = \frac{\overline{Y}_j - \overline{Y}_k}{\sqrt{\dfrac{MS_W}{n}}} \qquad \text{for any } j \neq k \qquad (1.21)$$

The Studentized range has two parameters: J = number of means, and df_W. Table A.3 in Appendix A gives the Studentized range for various values of J and df_W for $\alpha = .05$ and $\alpha = .01$.

For pairwise comparisons, there is a very simple relationship between the t and range statistics:

$$t = \frac{\hat{\psi} - \psi}{\sqrt{\dfrac{MS_W}{n} \displaystyle\sum_{j=1}^{J} c_j^2}} = \frac{q}{\sqrt{2}} = \frac{\overline{Y}_j - \overline{Y}_k}{\sqrt{\dfrac{MS_W}{n}}} \frac{1}{\sqrt{2}} \qquad (1.22)$$

The difference in the two formulas is that t has as its denominator the estimated standard deviation of the comparison that includes the Σc_j^2, while q has as its denominator the estimated standard error of one of the means in the comparison. For pairwise comparisons, the Σc_j^2 is always 2, since the weights are 1 and -1 for the two means being compared and zero for the other means. Equation 1.22 expressed in a simple form shows $t = q/\sqrt{2}$. This simple relationship allows the researcher to use the t statistic as a substitute for q with any MCP that has a range statistic. Once the t statistic is computed, it can be compared with a q critical value divided by the square root of 2; that is, compare t to

$$\frac{q_{J,\,df_w}}{\sqrt{2}} \tag{1.23}$$

For example, the q critical value for $J = 4$ and $df_w = 20$ is 3.96, so dividing by the square root of 2 gives 2.80. The t statistic would be compared with 2.80, giving results equivalent to comparing the q statistic with 3.96.

F *Statistic*

Another statistic used for some MCPs is the F statistic for a comparison.[8] This F is related to the t statistic by the formula $t^2 = F$, thus it has only one degree of freedom in the numerator. Since every F statistic is the ratio of two mean squares, an F statistic for a comparison will be a ratio of a mean square for the comparison divided by MS_W. It will be instructive to show the sum of squares and mean square for a comparison by starting with the relationship $t^2 = F$:

$$t^2 = \frac{(\hat{\psi} - \psi)^2}{\dfrac{MS_W}{n} \displaystyle\sum_{j=1}^{J} c_j^2} = \frac{(\hat{\psi} - \psi)^2 / \left[\left(\displaystyle\sum_{j=1}^{J} c_j^2 \right) / n \right]}{MS_W} = F \tag{1.24}$$

Thus, for F,

$$SS_{\hat{\psi}} = MS_{\hat{\psi}} = (\hat{\psi} - \psi)^2 / \left[\left(\sum_{j=1}^{J} c_j^2 \right) / n \right] \tag{1.25}$$

where the MS and the SS are equal because there is only one degree of freedom for the comparison.

An example will be helpful to show the relationships among the three statistics given up to this point. Suppose that there are $J = 4$ groups with $n = 6$ observations in each group. If $MS_W = 12.98$ and the four sample means are computed as

$$\overline{Y}_1 = 54.1, \quad \overline{Y}_2 = 39.8, \quad \overline{Y}_3 = 37.5, \quad \overline{Y}_4 = 29.3 \qquad (1.26)$$

and the researcher wants to compare the first two means, then the weights are 1, −1, 0, 0. With a null hypothesis of the population comparison equal to zero, then the computation of t is given by

$$\hat{\psi} = 54.1 - 39.8 = 14.3, \qquad \psi = 0$$

$$t = \frac{\hat{\psi} - \psi}{\sqrt{\dfrac{MS_W}{n} \displaystyle\sum_{j=1}^{J} c_j^2}} = \frac{14.3 - 0}{\sqrt{\dfrac{12.98}{6}(2)}} = \frac{14.3}{\sqrt{4.3267}} = \frac{14.3}{2.08} \qquad (1.27)$$

$$t = 6.87$$

Computation of q is similar, and is related to t:

$$q = \frac{\overline{Y}_j - \overline{Y}_k}{\sqrt{\dfrac{MS_W}{n}}} = \frac{54.1 - 39.8}{\sqrt{\dfrac{12.98}{6}}} = \frac{14.3}{\sqrt{2.1633}} = \frac{14.3}{1.47}$$

$$q = 9.72 \qquad (1.28)$$

$$t = \frac{q}{\sqrt{2}} = \frac{9.72}{1.4142}$$

$$t = 6.87$$

Thus $t = 6.87$ can be obtained directly or by first computing q and then dividing by the square root of 2. Computation of F is given by

$$F = \frac{MS_{\hat{\psi}}}{MS_W} = \frac{(\hat{\psi} - \psi)^2 / \left[\left(\sum_{j=1}^{J} c_j^2 \right) / n \right]}{MS_W} = \frac{(14.3)^2 / (2/6)}{12.98}$$

$$= \frac{204.49 / .3333}{12.98} = \frac{613.47}{12.98} \tag{1.29}$$

$$F = 47.26$$

$$t = \sqrt{F} = \sqrt{47.26} = 6.87$$

Since t is related to F, the square root of F gives $t = 6.87$, the same value obtained by directly computing t.

Mean Difference

Another form for the statistic on a multiple comparison is what could be called a *mean difference*. Rather than converting the comparison, which is a mean difference for a pairwise comparison, into a t, q, or F statistic, some authors choose to work directly with the mean difference. The mean difference form is shown here as it relates to both t and q:

$$\hat{\psi} = \overline{Y}_j - \overline{Y}_k = t_{crit} \sqrt{\frac{MS_W}{n} \sum_{j=1}^{J} c_j^2}$$

$$\hat{\psi} = \overline{Y}_j - \overline{Y}_k = q_{crit} \sqrt{\frac{MS_W}{n}} \tag{1.30}$$

where t_{crit} and q_{crit} are appropriate critical values that depend upon the MCP selected.

Confidence Intervals

Each of the other statistics given here has been presented primarily as a test statistic appropriate for testing the hypothesis

$$H_0 : \psi = 0 \tag{1.31}$$

for each comparison. All of the MCPs given in this text are able to provide the researcher with a test of this hypothesis. However, if the desire of the researcher is to obtain an interval estimate of the population comparison, then some MCPs are not appropriate. That is, some of the MCPs are used only to test hypotheses and cannot give interval estimates of the population comparisons. For those methods that can give confidence intervals, the interval is given as

$$\hat{\psi} - \text{crit} \sqrt{\frac{MS_W}{n} \sum_{j=1}^{J} c_j^2} \leq \psi \leq \hat{\psi} + \text{crit} \sqrt{\frac{MS_W}{n} \sum_{j=1}^{J} c_j^2} \quad (1.32)$$

where crit is an appropriate critical value, such as t, $q/\sqrt{2}$, or $\sqrt{F}$. The upper and lower values of the interval can also be expressed as

$$\hat{\psi} \pm \text{crit} \sqrt{\frac{MS_W}{n} \sum_{j=1}^{J} c_j^2} \quad (1.33)$$

For those researchers desiring both to test hypotheses and to obtain interval estimates, the confidence interval can be used to test the hypothesis that the comparison is zero by rejecting H_0 if the interval does not contain zero.[9] For example, if an interval has been computed as $(-.42, 3.76)$, then H_0 would not be rejected; if the interval were $(.93, 4.35)$, then H_0 would be rejected.

Use of t

Since all of the statistics presented in this section can be transformed to the t statistic, the MCPs presented in Chapter 2 will use t and transform the appropriate critical values. Use of $t = q/\sqrt{2}$ and $t = \sqrt{F}$ will allow computation of a common statistic, t, and will allow comparison of critical values to determine the most powerful MCP, as will be shown in Chapter 3.

Orthogonality of Multiple Comparisons

Researchers will compute the comparisons that are dictated by their research questions. If the question is, Which of these J means are different? then all possible pairwise comparisons will likely be computed, and they are not all orthogonal to each other. If the question is, Do these two treatment groups differ, on the average, from the control group, and are the two treatments different? then there are two comparisons to be made. One comparison will compare the control mean to the average of the two treatment means and the other will be a pairwise comparison on the two treatment means; these two comparisons are orthogonal. The point to be made is that choice of which comparisons to compute is dictated by the research questions, not by whether or not the comparisons are orthogonal.[10]

Orthogonality of multiple comparisons is considered for pairs of comparisons, two at a time. Thus if there are three comparisons in a group of comparisons, orthogonality is determined for comparisons 1 and 2, comparisons 1 and 3, and comparisons 2 and 3. Orthogonality of any two comparisons is determined by the weights on the means, such that if

$$\sum_{j=1}^{J} \frac{c_{1j} c_{2j}}{n_j} = 0 \qquad (1.34)$$

then comparisons 1 and 2 are orthogonal. Here c_{1j} is a weight for comparison 1 on the jth mean, c_{2j} is a weight for comparison 2 on the jth mean, and n_j is the size of the jth sample. When all the samples have a common size n,

$$\sum_{j=1}^{J} c_{1j} c_{2j} = 0 \qquad (1.35)$$

is used to see if comparisons 1 and 2 are orthogonal. If the sum of the product of the weights is not zero, then the comparisons are nonorthogonal. Consider the following comparisons two at a time and determine which pairs are orthogonal if the ns are equal:

$$\hat{\psi}_1 = \overline{Y}_1 - \overline{Y}_2$$

$$\hat{\psi}_2 = \overline{Y}_1 - \overline{Y}_3 \qquad (1.36)$$

$$\hat{\psi}_3 = \overline{Y}_3 - \overline{Y}_4$$

$$\hat{\psi}_4 = \tfrac{1}{2} \overline{Y}_1 + \tfrac{1}{2} \overline{Y}_2 - \overline{Y}_3$$

First, it is helpful to write down just the c_j for all J means for all of the comparisons in a table, and then compute the sum of products for each pair of comparisons.

	\\jth mean			
	1	*2*	*3*	*4*
comparison 1	1	−1	0	0
comparison 2	1	0	−1	0
comparison 3	0	0	1	−1
comparison 4	½	½	−1	0

So comparison 1 is orthogonal to comparisons 3 and 4, but none of the other pairs have comparisons that are orthogonal. It is possible to have sets of comparisons in which none of the comparisons are orthogonal to each other. In fact, within the set of all possible pairwise comparisons, most of the comparisons are not orthogonal to each other, such as comparisons 1 and 2 above.

$$1 \text{ vs. } 2: \quad \sum_{j=1}^{J} c_{1j} c_{2j} = (1)(1) + (-1)(0) + (0)(-1) + (0)(0) = 1$$

$$1 \text{ vs. } 3: \quad \sum_{j=1}^{J} c_{1j} c_{3j} = (1)(0) + (-1)(0) + (0)(1) + (0)(-1) = 0$$

$$1 \text{ vs. } 4: \quad \sum_{j=1}^{J} c_{1j} c_{4j} = (1)(\tfrac{1}{2}) + (-1)(\tfrac{1}{2}) + (0)(-1) + (0)(0) = 0 \qquad (1.37)$$

$$2 \text{ vs. } 3: \quad \sum_{j=1}^{J} c_{2j} c_{3j} = (1)(0) + (0)(0) + (-1)(1) + (0)(-1) = -1$$

$$2 \text{ vs. } 4: \quad \sum_{j=1}^{J} c_{2j} c_{4j} = (1)(\tfrac{1}{2}) + (0)(\tfrac{1}{2}) + (-1)(-1) + (0)(0) = 1.5$$

$$3 \text{ vs. } 4: \quad \sum_{j=1}^{J} c_{3j} c_{4j} = (0)(\tfrac{1}{2}) + (0)(\tfrac{1}{2}) + (1)(-1) + (-1)(0) = -1$$

The maximum number of comparisons that are all orthogonal to each other is $J - 1$ when the comparisons are on J means. There may exist several sets of comparisons in which all $J - 1$ comparisons are orthogonal to each other, but once such a set is found, there can be no more than $J - 1$ orthogonal comparisons within that set. Here are two examples of such sets of orthogonal comparisons when $J = 4$, illustrating that there are at most $J - 1 = 3$ comparisons in each set:

set one

$$\psi_1 = (1)\,\mu_1 + (-\tfrac{1}{3})\,\mu_2 + (-\tfrac{1}{3})\,\mu_3 + (-\tfrac{1}{3})\,\mu_4$$

$$\psi_2 = (0)\,\mu_1 + (1)\,\mu_2 + (-\tfrac{1}{2})\,\mu_3 + (-\tfrac{1}{2})\,\mu_4$$

$$\psi_3 = (0)\,\mu_1 + (0)\,\mu_2 + (1)\,\mu_3 + (-1)\,\mu_4 \tag{1.38}$$

set two

$$\psi_4 = (1)\,\mu_1 + (-1)\,\mu_2 + (0)\,\mu_3 + (0)\,\mu_4$$

$$\psi_5 = (0)\,\mu_1 + (0)\,\mu_2 + (1)\,\mu_3 + (-1)\,\mu_4$$

$$\psi_6 = (\tfrac{1}{2})\,\mu_1 + (\tfrac{1}{2})\,\mu_2 + (-\tfrac{1}{2})\,\mu_3 + (-\tfrac{1}{2})\,\mu_4$$

Finally, consider some of these topics in combination. Some researchers and authors connect planned comparisons with control of α using ERPC if the comparisons are orthogonal. As indicated earlier, such connection is not necessary. Given that researchers need to emphasize control of α and power, the issues of planned versus post hoc and orthogonality are secondary for most situations, and unimportant in others. When these topics are important in use of a multiple comparison method in later chapters, they will be so noted.

SAS and SPSS

Although many MCPs are relatively simple to calculate without the aid of a computer, some of the more recent methods are relatively computer dependent. For example, Ryan's method can be done with a good calculator, but a computer program makes the task easy instead of tedious. The method due to Peritz is very difficult, if not impossible, to do without a computer program. (Both Ryan's and Peritz's methods are discussed in Chapter 2.) Another reason for showing how MCPs can be done on the computer is that most modern computations of statistics are done with computer programs and many researchers are generally familiar with such programs.

Most packages of statistical programs, such as SAS and SPSS, compute all possible pairwise comparisons as the default when multiple comparisons are requested. Other (general) comparisons are available, but often have some restrictions placed on their use, such as a limitation on which MCPs may be selected.

SAS

Within the package of statistical programs called Statistical Analysis System (SAS), pairwise comparisons may be done on J means from either the PROC ANOVA routine or the PROC GLM routine. Sixteen different MCPs are available and easily implemented with an optional statement that is used the same way in either of the two PROCs:

MEANS *independent variable/mcp names*;

where *independent variable* is the variable used in the *CLASS* statement as the independent (classification) variable by which subjects are grouped, and *mcp names* is a list of the selected MCPs. The user may select as many of the different MCPs as desired by listing the SAS name for the MCP in the MEANS statement, separating each MCP name with blanks.

Here is an example of the SAS code necessary to run an ANOVA with five groups and 10 observations per group, without the specific systems lines that are peculiar to each user's system. The code specifies the MCP that SAS calls TUKEY.

```
(system lines)
DATA EXAMPLE;
INPUT GROUP$;
DO I=1 TO 10;
INPUT Y @@;
```

```
OUTPUT;
END;
CARDS;
CONTROL
45 56 64 47 54 44 51 53 55 60
EXP1
34 45 43 32 28 38 39 32 41 40
EXP2
29 28 30 44 41 28 27 32 33 36
EXP3
35 41 34 32 32 38 39 32 34 31
EXP4
28 27 24 29 31 34 23 31 30 27
PROC PRINT;
PROC ANOVA;
CLASS GROUP;
MODEL Y=GROUP;
MEANS GROUP/TUKEY;
```

The variable names of EXAMPLE, GROUP, I, and Y can be different names chosen by the researcher. These variable names simply indicate and give a name to, in order, the data set, the independent (classification) variable, the subscript for Y, and the dependent variable or score for each subject.

The method of input used in this program assumes that the data are organized by groups with some label for each group on a separate line preceding the data for that group, and the individual scores separated by blanks. In the above code there were five groups, labeled CONTROL, EXP1, EXP2, EXP3, and EXP4, each with 10 scores.

As the data are read, for the variable GROUP the program inputs the value of CONTROL, and then for the variable Y the program inputs the values 45, 56, 64, 47, and so on. It then recycles to the DATA statement and starts over for the next value of GROUP, continuing in this fashion until all the data are read.

The PROC ANOVA; statement must be used as it is given, and the variable GROUP in the CLASS, MODEL, and MEANS statements must agree with the name chosen for the independent variable at the input stage. TUKEY is the name of a multiple comparison method.

```
                          The SAS System
                   Analysis of Variance Procedure
    Dependent Variable: Y
    Source            DF    Sum of Squares    Mean Square    F Value    Pr > F

    Model              4    3490.48000000    872.62000000     34.14     0.0001
    Error             45    1150.10000000     25.55777778
    Corrected Total   49    4640.58000000
                  R-Square              C.V.       Root MSE             Y Mean
                  0.752165         13.582671      5.0554701        37.22000000

    Source            DF         Anova SS    Mean Square    F Value    Pr > F
    GROUP              4    3490.48000000    872.62000000     34.14     0.0001
```

Figure 1.3. SAS Output From PROC ANOVA

Such names are listed following the slash in the MEANS statement, separated by blanks.

The abbreviated SAS output in Figure 1.3 is from the above code. This figure shows the output from the overall ANOVA. The model and "group" both have the same values for df, sum of squares, F value, and probability because the model for a one-way ANOVA contains only the one independent variable. When a two-way ANOVA is done on SAS, the listing under "source" at the bottom of the output contains all of the sources in the model.

The SAS output of MCP results is presented using a vertical "lines" approach, where any means included in the same "line" are not significantly different. The means are arranged in order vertically and the "lines" are given to the left of the means and are "drawn" with letters. So all of the means included in the A line are not significantly different, and the same for the B line and so on. Another output characteristic worthy of mention is that SAS prints the critical value of each MCP, but the user is not warned about the different statistics used. That is, the critical values printed by SAS are not comparable because SAS does not use the same statistic for all MCPs. The Tukey MCP was computed to show the output format used by SAS for MCPs. Figure 1.4 shows the next page of output giving the Tukey results as done by SAS, including the lines approach to denoting significance.

Think of the As and Bs as forming two vertical lines, showing means that are not significantly different. The A line includes only the CONTROL group and the B line shows a cluster of similar means including EXP1, EXP3, and EXP2. The C line shows that

```
                      The SAS System
                Analysis of Variance Procedure
        Tukey's Studentized Range (HSD) Test for Variable: Y
     NOTE: This test controls the type I experimentwise error rate,
           but generally has a higher type II error rate than REGWQ

           Alpha=0.05  df=45  MSE=25.55778
           Critical Value of Studentized Range=4.018
           Minimum Significant Difference=6.4241

     Means with the same letter are not significantly different.

          Tukey    Grouping           Mean     N   GROUP

                       A              52.900   10   CONTROL

                       B              37.200   10   EXP1
                       B
                   C   B              34.800   10   EXP3
                   C   B
                   C   B              32.800   10   EXP2
                   C
                   C                  28.400   10   EXP4
```

Figure 1.4. SAS Output for TUKEY

the means for EXP3, EXP2, and EXP4 cluster together. To see which means are significantly different, find those pairs of means that do not share a common letter. For these data, the CONTROL mean differs significantly from all others, and the EXP1 mean differs significantly from EXP4. There are no other significant differences.

SPSS

Within the package of statistical programs called Statistical Package for the Social Sciences (SPSS), pairwise comparisons may be done on *J* means using the ONEWAY command with the RANGES subcommand. The MCPs available (and their SPSS names) are LSD (LSD), Duncan (DUNCAN), Newman-Keuls (SNK), Tukey (a) (TUKEY), Tukey (b) (TUKEYB) (see Chapter 2), a modified LSD (LSDMOD), and Scheffé (SCHEFFE). The user can also specify ranges, and thus do any MCP for which critical values can be obtained and that uses the same logic as provided by SPSS.

```
- - - - - - - - - - - - - - - O N E W A Y - - - - - - - - - - - -

        Variable   Y
     By Variable   GROUP
                                  ANALYSIS OF VARIANCE

                              SUM OF        MEAN         F        F
        SOURCE        D.F.    SQUARES       SQUARES      RATIO    PROB.

BETWEEN GROUPS         4      3490.4800     872.6200     34.1430  .0000
WITHIN GROUPS         45      1150.1000      25.5578
TOTAL                 49      4640.5800
```

Figure 1.5. SPSS Output for ONEWAY

Here is an example of the SPSS code necessary to run an ANOVA with five groups and 10 observations per group, without the specific systems lines that are peculiar to each user's system. The code specifies the MCP that SPSS calls TUKEY.

```
(system lines)
SET WIDTH 80
DATA LIST FREE/GROUP Y
BEGIN DATA
1 45 1 56 1 64 1 47 1 54 1 44 1 51 1 53 1 55 1 60
2 34 2 45 2 43 2 32 2 28 2 38 2 39 2 32 2 41 2 40
3 29 3 28 3 30 3 44 3 41 3 28 3 27 3 32 3 33 3 36
4 35 4 41 4 34 4 32 4 32 4 38 4 39 4 32 4 34 4 31
5 28 5 27 5 24 5 29 5 31 5 34 5 23 5 31 5 30 5 27
END DATA
VALUE LABELS GROUP 1 'CONTROL' 2 'EXP1' 3 'EXP2' 4 'EXP3' 5
     'EXP4' /
ONEWAY Y BY GROUP (1,5)
/RANGES=TUKEY
FINISH
```

The variable names of GROUP and Y and the value labels of CONTROL, EXP1, EXP2, EXP3, and EXP4 can be different names chosen by the researcher. Additional MCPs may be selected by including more lines of /RANGES=name where *name* is the name

```
- - - - - - - - - - - - - - - - O N E W A Y - - - - - - - - - - - - -
         Variable  Y
     By Variable  GROUP

MULTIPLE RANGE TEST

TUKEY-HSD PROCEDURE
RANGES FOR THE 0.050 LEVEL -

         4.02    4.02    4.02    4.02                                          .

THE RANGES ABOVE ARE TABLE RANGES.
THE VALUE ACTUALLY COMPARED WITH MEAN(J)-MEAN(I) IS..
       3.5748 * RANGE * DSQRT(1/N(I) + 1/N(J))

   (*) DENOTES PAIRS OF GROUPS SIGNIFICANTLY DIFFERENT AT THE 0.050
LEVEL
                              G G G G G
                              r r r r r
                              P P P P P
      Mean        Group       5 3 4 2 1

      28.4000     Grp 5
      32.8000     Grp 3
      34.8000     Grp 4
      37.2000     Grp 2       *
      52.9000     Grp 1       * * * *

HOMOGENEOUS SUBSETS    (SUBSETS OF GROUPS, WHOSE HIGHEST AND LOWEST MEANS
                        DO NOT DIFFER BY MORE THAN THE SHORTEST
                        SIGNIFICANT RANGE FOR A SUBSET OF THAT SIZE)
SUBSET   1

GROUP          Grp 5          Grp 3          Grp 4
MEAN           28.4000        32.8000        34.8000
- - - - - - - - - - - - - - - - - - - - - - - - - -

SUBSET   2

GROUP          Grp 3          Grp 4          Grp 2
MEAN           32.8000        34.8000        37.2000
- - - - - - - - - - - - - - - - - - - - - - - - - -

SUBSET   3

GROUP          Grp 1
MEAN           52.9000
- - - - - - - - - - -
```

Figure 1.6. SPSS Output for TUKEY

SPSS gives to its MCPs (see the above list). The method of input used
in this program assumes that the data are organized with the value of

the variable GROUP followed by the value of the variable Y, with blanks separating the values. Thus the "1 45" in the first line of data indicates 1 for GROUP and 45 for Y. Other pairs of scores also show the pairing of GROUP with Y. Using the FREE type of format, SPSS inputs all of the pairs of GROUP Y scores between the BEGIN DATA and END DATA statements. VALUE LABELS is used to give a label to the values of GROUP, where 1 is labeled HIGH, and so on. The (1,5) tells the program that the researcher has one dependent variable and that GROUP has five levels. Note that the variable names in the DATA LIST command and the ONEWAY command must agree.

The SPSS output shown in Figure 1.5 is for the one-way ANOVA from the above code. Since this output is from ONEWAY, it shows the sources as BETWEEN and WITHIN groups. The Tukey MCP is computed to show the output format used by SPSS, and the results are given in Figure 1.6 for the above code.

SPSS uses the idea of homogeneous subsets to cluster together means that are not significantly different. Note that there can be a pair of means incorrectly declared significantly different in the "(*) DENOTES PAIRS OF GROUPS SIGNIFICANTLY DIFFERENT" part of the output, but correctly grouped into a homogeneous subset. Thus, if there is a discrepancy, the homogeneous subsets are correct. For these data, EXP4, EXP2, and EXP3 means cluster as a homogeneous subset; EXP2, EXP3, and EXP1 means cluster as a homogeneous subset; and the CONTROL mean is in a subset by itself. For these data, the CONTROL mean differs significantly from all others, and the EXP1 mean differs significantly from EXP4. There are no other significant differences.

Notes

1. In the actual analysis, the HRSD scores were adjusted for marital status using analysis of covariance; treatment groups were significantly different. The pretreatment HRSD scores were not used as a covariate due to unequal slopes of the regression lines. In the absence of the original data and to simplify the current example, the simulated data will represent adjusted scores but they will be treated as if they were original raw data from HRSD and an ANOVA will be computed instead of an analysis of covariance. Note that the procedures covered in this book are appropriate for means from an ANOVA and not necessarily so for adjusted means from an analysis of covariance (see Scheffé, 1959, p. 209).

2. That is, this is a weighted sum of the means, where the weights are symbolized as c_js. Note that this weighted sum, or comparison, exists only for fixed means, and thus only for the fixed-effects model ANOVA.

3. Many of the classifications given here are taken from Toothaker (1986).

4. The correct term, *orthogonal*, is being used here in spite of the popular use in multiple comparison literature of the term *independent*. As will be shown in the section on orthogonality of multiple comparisons, what is of concern is if $\Sigma c_{1j}c_{2j}/n_j = 0$, which is orthogonality (see Rodgers, Nicewander, & Toothaker, 1984).

5. A fairly strong argument can be made that examination of powers of methods should take place only for those methods that control α in a similar manner. I agree with this argument, but still recognize the elementary principle that higher α gives higher power.

6. Some authors choose to use the word *experiment* in place of *family* in discussing error rate. Since some experiments will contain more than one family of comparisons, such as a two-way ANOVA, the term *family* is preferred.

7. Some authors use a per-comparison power, which is similar to per-pair power.

8. The F statistic discussed here is not the result of an ANOVA on J means, but a simple transformation on the t statistic. An ANOVA on $J' < J$ means as a multiple comparison statistic is not commonly used by behavioral scientists, but is presented in Chapter 2.

9. Any equivalent word could be used here instead of *contain*, such as *include* or *bracket*.

10. Orthogonality is an important concept in many other areas of statistics, such as its use in two-way and higher ANOVA when equal sample sizes are present. Also, orthogonality of comparisons has utility in consideration of the design matrix for use of the general linear model approach for ANOVA. But for researchers using multiple comparisons in the way discussed in this book, orthogonality of comparisons becomes a secondary issue against the backdrop of the more weighty matters of control of α and power. That is, the researcher should let his or her comparisons be whatever the research dictates, orthogonal or not, and should focus attention on controlling α and choosing a powerful multiple comparison method.

2 Multiple Comparison Procedures

Many different MCPs are available for the one-way ANOVA. Given that the researcher is using a t statistic, and has made a decision about control of error rate, then the choice of MCP is largely a choice of the critical value and thus the theoretical distribution. Unless otherwise noted, the MCPs in this chapter are appropriate for pairwise comparisons for the one-way design with equal numbers of observations per group. MCPs for unequal ns will be covered in Chapter 4. Also, all of the MCPs in this chapter make the usual ANOVA assumptions of normality, equal variances, and independence. They will be organized mainly by the theoretical reference distribution used to obtain the critical value(s) for the procedure. The three principal distributions used are the t distribution, the Studentized range distribution, and the F distribution. The last two sections of this chapter will cover additional methods: those that do not fit cleanly into one of the first three sections, recently introduced methods, and specialized methods.

MCPs Based on the t Distribution

The Usual t

As was mentioned in Chapter 1, the t statistic for a single comparison, either pairwise or general, is given as

$$t_{\hat{\psi}} = \frac{\hat{\psi} - \psi}{\sqrt{\mathrm{MS_W} \sum_{j=1}^{J} \frac{c_j^2}{n_j}}} \qquad (2.1)$$

which for equal sample sizes and pairwise comparisons simplifies to

$$t_{\hat{\psi}} = \frac{\overline{Y}_j - \overline{Y}_{j'}}{\sqrt{\frac{\mathrm{MS_W}}{n}(2)}} \qquad (2.2)$$

These can be used to test the hypothesis

$$H_0 : \psi = 0 . \qquad (2.3)$$

This t statistic has a sampling distribution that is exactly a t distribution with df = $df_W = N - J$ if all of the usual ANOVA assumptions are met. For multiple comparisons, a researcher can choose to control error rate per comparison by setting α' for each comparison at α. That is, the MCP called the *usual t* in this text is given by the decision rule to reject H_0 if

$$| t_{\hat{\psi}} | \geq t_{df_W}^{\alpha} \qquad (2.4)$$

and otherwise fail to reject H_0. The critical value is an α-level value from the t distribution (Table A.2, Appendix A) with df = $N - J$ for each of the C comparisons. Also, the critical value is for a two-tailed test of the nondirectional hypothesis. Note that the *usual t* can be used for either pairwise or general comparisons. Researchers desiring to compute confidence intervals can use the critical value from the *usual t* in combination with Equation 1.32 (Chapter 1) to compute interval estimates of ψ.

Using the depression data from Chapter 1 as an example, the *usual t* is computed on the means of the four groups, PLA for placebo, CBT for cognitive therapy, IPT for interpersonal therapy, and IMI for drug therapy using imipramine. The SAS results for the *usual t* are given in Figure 2.1.

For the *usual t*, the error rate is controlled at α for each comparison (ERPC) and the power is the highest of all MCPs, regardless of which

```
                              SAS
                  ANALYSIS OF VARIANCE PROCEDURE

    T TESTS (LSD) FOR VARIABLE: Y
    NOTE: THIS TEST CONTROLS THE TYPE I COMPARISONWISE ERROR RATE,
          NOT THE EXPERIMENTWISE ERROR RATE

               ALPHA=0.1  DF=236  MSE=61.0362
               CRITICAL VALUE OF T=1.65134
               LEAST SIGNIFICANT DIFFERENCE=2.3554

     MEANS WITH THE SAME LETTER ARE NOT SIGNIFICANTLY DIFFERENT.

          T        GROUPING              MEAN     N    GROUP

                      A                 13.233    60   4_PLA

                      B                 10.700    60   3_CBT
                      B
                      B                  9.800    60   2_IPT
                      B
                      B                  9.800    60   1_IMI
```

Figure 2.1. SAS Output for *Usual t*, Depression Data

type of power is desired. High power is one of the advantages of this procedure; another advantage is simplicity. The *usual t* is easily understood and computed, and critical values are easily obtained. However, there is one principal disadvantage: Control of α using ERPC gives excessive probability of at least one Type I error for any group of comparisons. That is, control of α using ERPC of necessity makes ERPF and ERFW larger than α.

Since an α-level critical value is used for each comparison, for any group of $C \geq 2$ comparisons, p(at least one Type I error) will be larger than α, as shown by

$$\alpha \leq 1 - (1 - \alpha)^C \leq C\alpha \qquad (2.5)$$

However, it should be emphasized that use of this MCP includes the choice of controlling α using ERPC, which gives a resulting large p(at least one Type I error) and high power. That is, all of these characteristics are built into the *usual t*. Selection of the *usual t* includes selection of ERPC, large p(at least one Type I error), and high power.

Dunn and Dunn-Šidák

The MCPs considered in this section are based on use of the t distribution with C comparisons that are planned. Not only is the *number* of comparisons known before the research is done, but also it is known *which* comparisons will be computed. Both of the methods to be discussed here control α for some group of comparisons, and thus maintain low ERPF and ERFW. Also, both of the methods are appropriate for pairwise or general comparisons.

These MCPs share a common idea, that of the division of total α into parts. The simplest application of this idea is to divide α evenly among the C comparisons, by setting the α' for each comparison to $\alpha' = \alpha/C$. This MCP was presented by Dunn (1961) using the Bonferroni inequality, which says that the probability of one or more events is less than or equal to the sum of the probabilities of the separate events. Dunn (1961) contributed a table for t with probabilities α' for various values of C and df_W, which is given as Table A.4 in Appendix A. The decision rule is to reject H_0 if

$$| t_{\hat{\psi}} | \geq t_{df_W}^{\alpha'} \qquad (2.6)$$

otherwise fail to reject H_0. This MCP is known in this text as the Dunn procedure. Dunn's MCP is based on the additive Bonferroni inequality, p(at least one Type I error) $= \alpha \leq \Sigma \alpha'$. When α is divided evenly into C parts of α', this is expressed in the right portion of Equation 2.5. That is, if α' is set as $\alpha' = \alpha/C$, then p(at least one Type I error) $< C\alpha'$ is conservatively bounded by α as shown by

$$C\alpha' = C\frac{\alpha}{C} = \alpha \qquad (2.7)$$

Note that the division of α and calculation of critical values is automatically done for the researcher by choice of critical values from Table A.4.

Another MCP that uses the t distribution and the idea of dividing total α into parts was developed from work done by Dunn (1958) and Šidák (1967). While Dunn's method uses an additive inequality, the Dunn-Šidák procedure uses a multiplicative inequality as its basis.[1] If α'' is set as

$$\alpha'' = 1 - (1 - \alpha)^{1/C} \qquad (2.8)$$

then the following shows α as an upper bound to p(at least one Type I error)

$$\leq 1 - (1 - \alpha'')^C$$

$$= 1 - (1 - [1 - (1 - \alpha)^{1/C}])^C$$

$$= 1 - [(1 - \alpha)^{1/C}]^C \qquad (2.9)$$

$$= 1 - (1 - \alpha)$$

$$= \alpha$$

Notice that the Dunn-Šidák probability is expressed in the middle portion of Equation 2.5. The Dunn-Šidák MCP is given by the decision rule to reject H_0 if

$$| t_{\hat{\psi}} | \geq t_{\mathrm{df_W}}^{\alpha''} \qquad (2.10)$$

and otherwise fail to reject. Critical values for the Dunn-Šidák MCP are given in Table A.5 in Appendix A. As was the case for the Dunn MCP, the critical values in Table A.5 have incorporated into them the computation of α''. The researcher does not have to compute α'', but simply chooses the critical value as a function of the overall α, C, and $\mathrm{df_W}$. Researchers desiring to compute confidence intervals can use a critical value from either Dunn or Dunn-Šidák in combination with Equation 1.32 (Chapter 1) to compute interval estimates of ψ.

A comparison of critical values shows that there is not much difference between tests of H_0 using the Dunn and Dunn-Šidák methods. For $\alpha = .05$, $\mathrm{df_W} = 20$, and $C = 3$, Dunn's critical value is 2.61, while the Dunn-Šidák value is 2.605. If C is 10, the critical values are 3.16 for Dunn and 3.143 for Dunn-Šidák. Since the Dunn-Šidák critical values are always smaller than those for Dunn, the Dunn-Šidák MCP will have slightly higher power. Of course, the *usual t* will have the best power, but at the expense of high p(at least one Type I error).

For the depression example, $\alpha = .10$, $\mathrm{df_W} = 236$, and $C = 6$ for all possible pairwise comparisons on the $J = 4$ means. Results from SAS, in Figure 2.2, show a Dunn critical value of 2.41117 and no significant differences in the four means. The t on the largest difference, $13.233 - 9.8$, is $t = 2.4068$, which is smaller than the critical value.

```
                          SAS
                ANALYSIS OF VARIANCE PROCEDURE

BONFERRONI (DUNN) T TESTS FOR VARIABLE: Y
NOTE: THIS TEST CONTROLS THE TYPE I EXPERIMENTWISE ERROR RATE
      BUT GENERALLY HAS A HIGHER TYPE II ERROR RATE THAN REGWQ

         ALPHA=0.1   DF=236   MSE=61.0362
         CRITICAL VALUE OF T=2.41117
         MINIMUM SIGNIFICANT DIFFERENCE=3.2392

MEANS WITH THE SAME LETTER ARE NOT SIGNIFICANTLY DIFFERENT.

    BON        GROUPING            MEAN      N    GROUP

                  A                13.233    60   4_PLA
                  A
                  A                10.700    60   1_CBT
                  A
                  A                 9.800    60   2_IPT
                  A
                  A                 9.800    60   3_IMI
```

Figure 2.2. SAS Output for Dunn, Depression Data

So Dunn's MCP does not detect any significant differences. Table A.4 cannot be used for this example, because the selected $\alpha = .10$ is not included in the table.

Results from SAS show a Dunn-Šidák (called SIDAK by SAS) critical value of 2.39488 and significant differences in PLA versus IPT and PLA versus IMI (see Figure 2.3). Since IPT and IMI have the same mean, 9.8, the t values for both will be $t = 2.4068$, which is larger than the critical value of 2.39488. Thus both the interpersonal therapy and the drug treatment with imipramine give better relief from depression than the pill-placebo condition. Note that interpolation on values from Table A.5 gives 2.395 to three-decimal-place accuracy, which is comparable to the value from SAS.

Finally, it is helpful to note that both the Dunn and Dunn-Šidák methods use the number of comparisons actually being computed, C, in the selection of critical values. The number of means, J, is not directly used in the critical value choice. Because of reliance on C, both the Dunn and Dunn-Šidák methods will have relatively good power for small sets of planned comparisons and relatively lower power for

```
                              SAS
                 ANALYSIS OF VARIANCE PROCEDURE

SIDAK T TESTS FOR VARIABLE: Y
NOTE: THIS TEST CONTROLS THE TYPE I EXPERIMENTWISE ERROR RATE
      BUT GENERALLY HAS A HIGHER TYPE II ERROR RATE THAN REGWQ

         ALPHA=0.1  DF=236  MSE=61.0362
         CRITICAL VALUE OF T=2.39488
         MINIMUM SIGNIFICANT DIFFERENCE=3.416

   MEANS WITH THE SAME LETTER ARE NOT SIGNIFICANTLY DIFFERENT.

      SIDAK     GROUPING          MEAN     N  GROUP

                    A           13.233    60  4_PLA
                    A
            B       A           10.700    60  1_CBT
            B
            B                    9.800    60  2_IPT
            B
            B                    9.800    60  3_IMI
```

Figure 2.3. SAS Output for Dunn-Šidák, Depression Data

large sets of planned comparisons. As other methods are introduced, relative power will be considered by comparing critical values of the methods covered up to that point.

MCPs Based on the Studentized Range Distribution

Methods based on the Studentized range distribution are among the most well-known and popular MCPs. Like those based on the t distribution, the methods in this section will use the t statistic. The critical values, however, will come from the Studentized range distribution, and will need to be divided by the square root of 2, $q/\sqrt{2}$, to be compatible with the t statistic. As they are presented here, these range methods will be appropriate only for pairwise comparisons. Some of them have been extended for general comparisons, but these extensions will not be discussed in this text. Control of error rate and power will be discussed separately for each MCP.

Tukey

Tukey (1953) presented the MCP that will be referred to here by his name in what may be the most frequently cited unpublished paper in the history of statistics.[2] In a lengthy mimeographed monograph, Tukey introduced a test that controls α using ERFW for all pairwise comparisons on J means. The Dunn and Dunn-Šidák MCPs accomplish ERFW control of α by relying on division of α and use of a t critical value at α' or α''. Unlike those methods, the Tukey method accomplishes α control by using an α-level critical value from the Studentized range distribution for J means. That is, control of α is built into the range critical value at the chosen ERFW α level.

The Tukey MCP is given by the decision rule to reject H_0 if

$$| t_{\hat{\psi}} | \geq \frac{q^{\alpha}_{J, df_{w}}}{\sqrt{2}} \tag{2.11}$$

and otherwise fail to reject. The critical values for the Studentized range are given in Table A.3 in Appendix A. As indicated by the sub- and superscripts on q in Equation 2.11, Table A.3 is entered with $J =$ the number of means, df_w, and the selected overall α. Researchers interested in computing confidence intervals can combine the Tukey critical value with Equation 1.32 (Chapter 1) to compute interval estimates for ψ.

For all possible pairwise comparisons, $C = J(J - 1)/2$, the power for Tukey's method is better than the power for Dunn and Dunn-Šidák. However, if a researcher is doing fewer than all possible pairwise comparisons, and these comparisons are planned, it is possible that Dunn or Dunn-Šidák will give better power than Tukey. This potential power advantage is due to use of C, and not J, in selection of critical values for the Dunn and Dunn-Šidák methods. Since the Tukey critical values pay attention only to J and not to C, the number of comparisons the researcher is actually computing, Tukey has lower power for smaller C.

For example, for $J = 4$ and $n = 6$, there are $(J)(J - 1)/2 = 6$ pairwise comparisons and $df_w = 20$. For $\alpha = .05$, the q critical value for $J = 4$ and $df_w = 20$ is 3.96 and the Tukey critical value is $q/\sqrt{2} = 3.96/\sqrt{2} = 2.80$. If the researcher is doing all six of the pairwise comparisons, then for $C = 6$, $df_w = 20$, and $\alpha = .05$, critical values for Dunn and Dunn-Šidák are 2.93 and 2.918, respectively. Thus, for all possible

```
                              SAS
                   ANALYSIS OF VARIANCE PROCEDURE

  TUKEY'S STUDENTIZED RANGE (HSD) TEST FOR VARIABLE: Y
  NOTE: THIS TEST CONTROLS THE TYPE I EXPERIMENTWISE ERROR RATE
        BUT GENERALLY HAS A HIGHER TYPE II ERROR RATE THAN REGWQ

             ALPHA=0.1  DF=236  MSE=61.0362
             CRITICAL VALUE OF STUDENTIZED RANGE=3.258
             MINIMUM SIGNIFICANT DIFFERENCE=3.2864

  MEANS WITH THE SAME LETTER ARE NOT SIGNIFICANTLY DIFFERENT.

        TUKEY     GROUPING            MEAN     N   GROUP

                     A              13.233    60   4_PLA
                     A
              B      A              10.700    60   1_CBT
              B
              B                      9.800    60   2_IPT
              B
              B                      9.800    60   3_IMI
```

Figure 2.4. SAS Output for Tukey, Depression Data

pairwise comparisons, Tukey is more powerful than Dunn or Dunn-Šidák. However, if the researcher plans to do only three of the pairwise comparisons, the Tukey critical value is still 2.80, the same as for all six pairwise comparisons. Then the critical values are 2.80 for Tukey, 2.61 for Dunn, and 2.605 for Dunn-Šidák. So for three pairwise comparisons that are planned, Dunn-Šidák would be the most powerful of the three MCPs. Again, note that Tukey critical values do not depend on the number of comparisons actually computed, but upon J, the number of means.

For the depression data, the results from SAS show a critical q of 3.258, which, when divided by $\sqrt{2}$, gives a critical t of 2.3038 (see Figure 2.4). SAS shows the same significance results as for Dunn-Šidák, that the placebo group mean differs significantly from the means for interpersonal therapy and drug treatment with imipramine when $\alpha = .10$. The values of t for IPT versus PLA and for IMI versus PLA were 2.4068, larger than the critical value of 2.3038. The value of t for CBT versus PLA was 1.7758, which is not larger than 2.3038.

Newman-Keuls

The MCP due to Newman (1939) and Keuls (1952) is the first of several methods that are stepwise in nature.[3] Stepwise procedures can be either step-down or step-up. Step-down methods start with a test on the largest pairwise difference in ordered means and proceed down to smaller differences. Step-up logic starts with tests on the smallest differences in ordered means, those comparing contiguous ordered means, and proceeds up to the largest difference. The Newman-Keuls method follows the step-down logic.

For the Newman-Keuls MCP, the J means must be arranged in order from the smallest to the largest. For any comparison between two of the means, the concept of *stretch size* must be considered. Stretch size is the number of ordered means between the two means in the comparison, including the two means. Suppose there were five means in the experiment, and the comparison was the largest versus the smallest means. Then stretch size, symbolized by p, would be 5. If the smallest mean were to be compared to the second largest, then $p = 4$. For comparisons on contiguous means in order, $p = 2$. So stretch size, p, ranges between J and 2.

The Newman-Keuls method uses a different q critical value for each stretch size, but keeps α the same for all critical values. Thus for $J = 5$, if .05 is selected, four different q critical values would be selected using $\alpha = .05$ for p of 5, 4, 3, and 2. The value of p is used in place of J in selecting q critical values from Table A.3 (Appendix A).

Now that some of the basics of the Newman-Keuls method are in place, the step-down logic will be considered.

(1) First, for stretch size $p = J$, test the comparison of the largest versus the smallest means. If it is significant, reject H_0 and proceed to the comparisons of stretch size $p = J - 1$. If the test on the largest comparison is not significant, retain all hypotheses for comparisons of stretch size $p \leq J$.

(2) Next, test the two comparisons of stretch size $p = J - 1$. If either of them is significant, proceed to comparisons of the next smaller stretch size. If a comparison of stretch size $p = J - 1$ is not significant, then retain all hypotheses for comparisons that are contained in that stretch.

For example, for five means in order, if the 1 versus 5 (smallest versus largest, $p = 5$) comparison is significant, then do the comparisons for $p = 4$. If the comparison of 1 versus 4 (smallest versus second largest) is not significant, then the hypotheses for 1 versus 4, 1 versus 3, 1 versus 2, 2 versus 4, 2 versus 3, and 3 versus 4 are retained because these comparisons are contained in the nonsignificant 1 versus 4 stretch. Note that these comparisons are not even tested and that the hypotheses they test are said to be retained by implication.

(3) Each comparison down to stretch size 2 is tested in a similar fashion only if the hypothesis it tests has not been retained by implication.

Another way of considering this step-down logic is to realize that a hypothesis for a comparison can be rejected only if two points are both true: The means in the comparison are not contained in a stretch of a previously retained hypothesis and the comparison is significant.

Now it is possible to formalize the Newman-Keuls MCP. For Newman-Keuls, the decision rule is to reject H_0 if the means in the comparison are not contained in the stretch of a previously retained hypothesis and if

$$| t_{\hat{\psi}} | \geq \frac{q_{p, df_w}^{\alpha}}{\sqrt{2}} \qquad (2.12)$$

and otherwise fail to reject. Note that the critical value from Table A.3 is a function of stretch size p and not the total number of means, J. Confidence intervals cannot be computed using the Newman-Keuls method.

Since the Newman-Keuls method sets α for each stretch size, it controls α for each group of p ordered means. The actual error rate is not controlled using ERFW or ERPC, but somewhere in between these two. Because the critical values are a function of p, and are smaller for lower stretch sizes, Newman-Keuls is more powerful than Tukey. Ordinarily, power comparisons between MCPs would be made only between methods that have similar control of α, but because of the popularity of the Newman-Keuls method and the frequent comparison of it to Tukey, relative power will be considered. Remember, Newman-Keuls does not control α using ERFW.[4]

For example, for $\alpha = .05$, $J = 4$, and $df_w = 20$, the Tukey critical value is $q/\sqrt{2} = 3.96/\sqrt{2} = 2.80$. The Newman-Keuls critical value for $p = J = 4$ is the same as that for Tukey, 2.80. For $p = 3$, Newman-Keuls gives $q/\sqrt{2} = 3.58/\sqrt{2} = 2.53$, and for $p = 2$, $q/\sqrt{2} = 2.95/\sqrt{2} = 2.09$. So for stretch size 3 and 2, Newman-Keuls gives lower critical

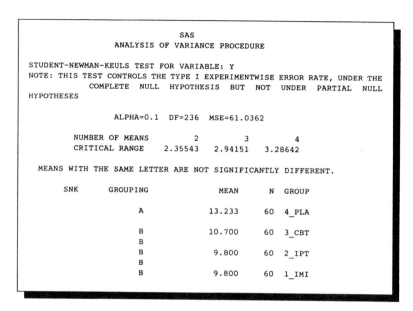

Figure 2.5. SAS Output for Newman-Keuls, Depression Data

values than Tukey and subsequently higher power, although at the expense of increased p(at least one Type I error).

For the depression data, the SAS results for Newman-Keuls (called SNK by SAS, for Studentized Newman-Keuls) show that the placebo mean is significantly different from each of the other three means (see Figure 2.5). That is, CBT versus PLA, IPT versus PLA, and IMI versus PLA are all significant with $\alpha = .10$. The critical values of q from SAS are critical ranges of 3.28642 for $p = 4$, 2.94151 for $p = 3$, and 2.35543 for $p = 2$. To translate these critical ranges into t values, divide each by the square root of MS_W times 2 divided by n, or $\sqrt{61.0362(2)/60} = 1.4264$. The critical values of t are 2.3040 for $p = 4$, 2.0622 for $p = 3$, and 1.6513 for $p = 2$.[5] Whereas the comparison of CBT versus PLA was not significant for Tukey, Dunn, or Dunn-Šidák, the Newman-Keuls MCP finds this difference to be significant. The t statistic had value of 1.7758, which is larger than 1.6513, the critical value for $p = 2$. This difference could be a Type I error for the reason explained in the following paragraph.

If the overall null hypothesis of equality of all J means is true, then the p(at least one Type I error) for Newman-Keuls is α. If multiple null hypotheses are present, then Newman-Keuls does not control p(at least one Type I error) at α, but does control α for each subset of equal means. If there are, say, M of these multiple null hypotheses, then Newman-Keuls will control p(at least one Type I error) at approximately $M\alpha$. For two null hypotheses, p(at least one Type I error) is approximately 2α for Newman-Keuls. Another way to think about this problem is that the Newman-Keuls method allows use of critical values that are too small for stretch sizes $p \leq J - 2$. For example, consider the depression data. The t statistic for CBT versus PLA is 1.7758, which was larger than the critical value of t of 1.6513. The 1.6513 is too small if the researcher wants familywise control of α. Since researchers cannot determine when multiple null hypotheses are present, the Newman-Keuls MCP should not be used. It has been presented here merely to introduce step-down logic and to lead to the MCP due to Ryan.

Ryan (REGWQ)

The MCP that will be called Ryan may be considered a modification of the Newman-Keuls method. Since the Newman-Keuls method changes the number-of-means parameter for each different stretch size, the critical values decrease as stretch size decreases. For the Newman-Keuls method, the critical values for stretch sizes $p \leq J - 2$ decrease too much and are thus too small, allowing more false rejections for these smaller stretches. Of course, the problem is due to control of α for each set of p ordered means, rather than for the whole experiment.

Ryan (1960) proposed modifying the α for each stretch size p to

$$\alpha_p = \frac{\alpha}{J_{/p}} = \frac{p\alpha}{J} \qquad (2.13)$$

where α_p is expressed as a fraction of α. Since the fraction, p/J, decreases as p decreases, α_p decreases as p decreases. By making α_p decrease as stretch size p decreases, the critical values would not be too small for stretch sizes $p \leq J - 2$. Also, the decrease in α_p accomplishes control of p(at least one Type I error) at α.

Ryan's original proposal itself has been twice modified to improve its power without compromise of its ERFW control of α. First, Einot and Gabriel (1975) proposed to let

$$\alpha_p = 1 - (1 - \alpha)^{p/J} \qquad (2.14)$$

This modification also accomplishes a decrease in α_p as stretch size p decreases, but the decrease is not quite as rapid as the original Ryan proposal. Second, Welsch (1977a) proposed to let α_p be equal to α for stretch size $p = J - 1$.[6] Since the comparison for the largest stretch size, $p = J$, has $\alpha_p = \alpha$, the Welsch modification extends this to the next largest stretch size. These two modifications and the step-down logic introduced for the Newman-Keuls MCP give us the current Ryan (REGWQ) method.

For the Ryan MCP, the decision rule is to reject H_0 if the means in the comparison are not contained in the stretch of a previously retained hypothesis and if

$$| t_{\hat{\psi}} | \geq \frac{q_{p, df_w}^{\alpha_p}}{\sqrt{2}} \qquad (2.15)$$

where

$$\alpha_p = \alpha \qquad \text{for } p = J, J - 1$$

$$\alpha_p = 1 - (1 - \alpha)^{p/J} \qquad \text{for } p \leq J - 2$$

otherwise fail to reject. The computer programs in SAS recognize all of the contributions to the current Ryan method by naming it REGWQ: R for Ryan, EG for Einot and Gabriel, W for Welsch, and Q because it uses the range critical value from Table A.3 (in Appendix A). Confidence intervals cannot be computed using the Ryan method.

Comparing the critical values of Ryan, Newman-Keuls, and Tukey will show that Ryan is more powerful than Tukey, but not as powerful as Newman-Keuls. Of course, Ryan will not have the Newman-Keuls problem with lack of control of α. For $\alpha = .05$, $J = 4$, and $df_w = 20$, Table 2.1 shows all of the critical values for each of the three methods as well as α_p for Newman-Keuls and Ryan. For $p = 2$ for Ryan, $\alpha_p = 1 - (1 - \alpha)^{p/J} = 1 - (1 - .05)^{2/4} = .0253205653$, rounded to .0253. Since .0253 is between .05 and .01, the q critical value for $\alpha = .0253$ must be between the q critical values for .05 and .01. Interpolation on the natural logarithms of the αs gives the closest approximation and the value of $q = 2.41$.

Since for $p = J = 4$ and $p = J - 1 = 3$ the value of $\alpha_p = \alpha = .05$, the Ryan critical values are the same as those for Newman-Keuls. How-

TABLE 2.1 q Critical Values

p	Tukey $q/\sqrt{2}$	Newman-Keuls α_p	$q/\sqrt{2}$	Ryan α_p	$q/\sqrt{2}$
4	2.80	.05	2.80	.05	2.80
3	2.80	.05	2.53	.05	2.53
2	2.80	.05	2.09	.0253	2.41

ever, for $p = J - 2 = 2$, α_p for Ryan is .0253 rather than .05, and the Ryan critical value is quite a bit larger than that for Newman-Keuls. This larger critical value circumvents the problem with multiple null hypotheses for the Ryan method. For $J = 4$ ordered means, the only possibility for multiple null hypotheses is for the contiguous pairs of 1,2 and 3,4 to be equal within each pair, but unequal between the pairs. The 1 versus 4 comparison (stretch size $p = 4$) would not be within one of these null sets of means. The same is true for the stretch size $p = 3$ comparisons of 1 versus 3 and 2 versus 4. Thus the critical values for these comparisons do not need to be larger. However, the stretch size $p = 2$ comparisons of 1 versus 2 and 3 versus 4 could be contained in the multiple null hypotheses, if they exist. Thus for $p = 2$ the critical values need to be large enough to protect against Type I errors if the multiple null condition exists.

For the depression data, SAS gives results in Figure 2.6 for Ryan (REGWQ) that show that the mean for the placebo group differs significantly ($\alpha = .10$) from the means for the interpersonal therapy and drug treatment with imipramine. Since Ryan controls α for even multiple null hypotheses, the difference of CBT versus PLA is not significant in contrast to the findings for Newman-Keuls. The Newman-Keuls critical value of t for $p = 2$ was 1.6513, but for Ryan it is 1.9588. The t value of 1.7758 for CBT versus PLA is not significant.

Since two is the maximum number of multiple null hypotheses that could exist when $J = 4$, the upper bound of p(at least one Type I error) can be computed as

$$1 - (1 - \alpha_p)^2 = 1 - (1 - .0253205653)^2 = 1 - .95 = .05$$

The Ryan MCP accomplishes control of α using ERFW, even for the condition of multiple null hypotheses.

```
                        SAS
            ANALYSIS OF VARIANCE PROCEDURE

RYAN-EINOT-GABRIEL-WELSCH MULTIPLE RANGE TEST FOR VARIABLE: Y
NOTE: THIS TEST CONTROLS THE TYPE I EXPERIMENTWISE ERROR RATE

            ALPHA=0.1  DF=236  MSE=61.0362

          NUMBER OF MEANS       2        3        4
          CRITICAL RANGE   2.79394  2.94151  3.28642

   MEANS WITH THE SAME LETTER ARE NOT SIGNIFICANTLY DIFFERENT.

      REGWQ      GROUPING          MEAN    N   GROUP

                    A             13.233   60  4_PLA
                    A
             B      A             10.700   60  1_CBT
             B
             B                     9.800   60  2_IPT
             B
             B                     9.800   60  3_IMI
```

Figure 2.6. SAS Output for Ryan q (REGWQ), Depression Data

Earlier it was mentioned that the Dunn and Dunn-Šidák MCPs have relatively good power for small C, the number of planned comparisons. Also, it was shown that Tukey has better power than Dunn or Dunn-Šidák when all possible pairwise comparisons are computed. However, if $C < J(J - 1)/2$, then Tukey might not have the best power. Comparing critical values for any given situation will show which is most powerful. Now the Ryan method adds a new complexity to our previously simple idea of comparing critical values and knowing that the MCP with the smallest critical value would give the highest power. For a given J associated with the experiment, the Ryan method gives different critical values for different p. So comparing Ryan to Dunn or Dunn-Šidák might give a less than clear answer to the question, Which is most powerful? For example, for $\alpha = .05$, $J = 4$, and $df_W = 20$, if $C = 3$ planned comparisons are used, then the Dunn-Šidák critical value is 2.605. This value is lower than the $p = 4$ Ryan critical value of 2.80, but higher than the $p = 3$ and $p = 2$ critical values of 2.53 and 2.41. Thus, for this situation, Dunn-Šidák is more powerful for the largest stretch size, but Ryan is more powerful for the remaining stretch sizes.

When conflicting answers such as these are given as to which MCP is most powerful, the researcher must make the choice of method based on which particular comparison is important to the research. Suppose it is predicted that the difference between the means of two specific groups will be the largest difference. If this largest difference is crucial to the research, if it is one of three planned comparisons, and if the other conditions are the same as the example, then Dunn-Šidák would be the choice. If, on the other hand, all three of the planned comparisons are of equal importance to the research, then Ryan would be better. Note that the choice must be made before the data are collected and that comparing critical values gives the researcher the basis for choosing the most powerful MCP.

MCPs Based on the F Distribution

One of the procedures discussed in this section, the Scheffé method, will be reasonably well known to most applied researchers, while the others likely will be totally new. Part of the reason for this disparity in familiarity is the length of time since development of these methods, but part is simplicity of use. All of the methods in this section are available on SAS.

Scheffé

The method due to Scheffé (1953, 1959) is among the most widely recognized of all MCPs. However, it also is among the least used of the widely known methods. It is widely known partly because it is one of the earliest developed methods, partly because it has appeared in a number of prominent textbooks on statistics, and partly because it is simple to use. It is among the least used of these widely known methods because it is known to be conservative for pairwise comparisons with respect not only to α but also to power.

Like the Tukey method, the Scheffé MCP has a constant critical value for all comparisons on J means. Unlike the Tukey method, the Scheffé method is appropriate for all possible comparisons, not just pairwise comparisons. Infinitely many comparisons can be done with the Scheffé method while maintaining control of p(at least one Type I error) at α using ERFW: pairwise comparisons, general comparisons, orthogonal polynomials, and so on.

The decision rule for Scheffé is to reject H_0 if

$$| t_{\hat{\psi}} | > \sqrt{(J-1) F^{\alpha}_{J-1, df_W}} \qquad (2.16)$$

otherwise fail to reject. The critical value depends on J, the number of means, rather than C, the number of comparisons actually computed. Note that the F in the right portion of Equation 2.16 is the α-level critical value of F with numerator degrees of freedom of $J - 1$ and denominator degrees of freedom of df_W, from Table A.1, Appendix A. This is the same critical value as used for the overall F test, and not the observed value of F. Researchers interested in computing confidence intervals can use the Scheffé critical value in combination with Equation 1.32 (Chapter 1) to compute interval estimates for ψ.

A comparison of critical values shows the Scheffé conservatism relative to other methods. For $\alpha = .05$, $J = 4$, and $df_W = 20$, the F critical value is 3.10. Remember to use $df_B = J - 1 = 3$ for the numerator degrees of freedom, not the number of means parameter, J, used in obtaining q critical values. The Scheffé critical value is

$$\sqrt{(J-1) F^{\alpha}_{J-1, df_W}} = \sqrt{(3)(3.10)} = \sqrt{9.3} = 3.05 \qquad (2.17)$$

compared with 2.80 for Tukey, 2.93 for Dunn, and 2.918 for Dunn-Šidák. Of course, the Ryan critical values are equal to or smaller than those for Tukey. So for all pairwise comparisons, the Scheffé MCP would be conservative relative to the other methods discussed so far.

For the depression data, SAS results show no significant differences (see Figure 2.7). The largest difference gives a t of 2.4068, while the Scheffé critical value for $df_W = 236$ is $\sqrt{(3)(2.10713)} = 2.5142$. The conservatism of Scheffé for pairwise comparisons is apparent here, even with $\alpha = .10$.

Scheffé may fare better for general comparisons than for pairwise comparisons. For $J = 4$ means, there are 25 comparisons of the general type: pairwise, one versus the average of two, one versus the average of three, and the average of two versus the average of two others. The $\alpha = .05$ Dunn-Šidák critical values for $df_W = 20$ for values of C of 25, 20, 15, 10, 9, and 8 are 3.541, 3.445, 3.320, 3.143, 3.097, and 3.045, respectively. Thus, with $J = 4$ means and the critical value of 3.05, Scheffé would be more powerful than Dunn-Šidák (and

```
                          SAS
              ANALYSIS OF VARIANCE PROCEDURE

SCHEFFE'S TEST FOR VARIABLE: Y
NOTE: THIS TEST CONTROLS THE TYPE I EXPERIMENTWISE ERROR RATE
      BUT GENERALLY HAS A HIGHER TYPE II ERROR RATE THAN REGWF
      FOR ALL PAIRWISE COMPARISONS

         ALPHA=0.1  DF=236  MSE=61.0362
         CRITICAL VALUE OF F=2.10713
         MINIMUM SIGNIFICANT DIFFERENCE=3.5862

  MEANS WITH THE SAME LETTER ARE NOT SIGNIFICANTLY DIFFERENT.

      SCHEFFE  GROUPING          MEAN    N   GROUP

                    A          13.233    60  4_PLA
                    A
                    A          10.700    60  1_CBT
                    A
                    A           9.800    60  2_IPT
                    A
                    A           9.800    60  3_IMI
```

Figure 2.7. SAS Output for Scheffé, Depression Data

consequently Dunn) if there were more than eight planned comparisons of the general type. Dunn-Šidák would be more powerful for eight or fewer planned general comparisons. If the comparisons were not planned, then, of the methods discussed so far in this text, only Scheffé would be appropriate to control α using ERFW for general comparisons regardless of how many were computed.

Newman-Keuls F

Like the Newman-Keuls method using the Studentized range distribution, this MCP has a problem with α control and is introduced to pave the way for a Ryan test. Unlike the Newman-Keuls method using $q/\sqrt{2}$ critical values, the Newman-Keuls F does not use the t statistic. This is the first of only two MCPs in this text that do not use the t statistic, and this fact alone makes it an unusual MCP. The t and q logic of examining the difference between two means is not only simple but has an intuitive appeal. This simplicity and intuitive appeal likely has had much to do with the popularity of MCPs that use the t (or q) statistic.

MCPs using the F statistic described in the next paragraph lack not only simplicity but also intuitive appeal. If any subset of means of size $p \geq 3$ is found to be significant, "then generally no statement can be made about the significance of its subsets without going through the full hierarchy of tests on those subsets" (Hochberg & Tamhane, 1987, p. 111). For example, suppose the researcher has five means ABCDE in order, and has found the subset ABCD to be significant. The researcher cannot proclaim the A-D difference to be significant until all subsets containing A and D are found to be significant, including the AD subset. Note that the language has shifted from discussion of stretch and stretch size to subset and subset size. The symbol p will be used as the size of a subset in addition to its meaning of stretch size.

The statistic used for any subset of p means is the F statistic given as

$$F_p = MS_p / MS_W \tag{2.18}$$

where

$$MS_p = SS_p / (p - 1)$$

$$SS_p = \frac{1}{n} \sum_{j \in p} \left(\sum_{i=1}^{n} Y_{ij} \right)^2 - \frac{1}{np} \left(\sum_{j \in p} \sum_{i=1}^{n} Y_{ij} \right)^2$$

and MS_W is the usual mean square within from all J groups. Note that the numerator of F, MS_p, uses only the observations from the p groups in the subset tested by the F. Methods using the F statistics are sometimes called *multiple F procedures*.

The Newman-Keuls F uses critical values from the F distribution but the same step-down logic of the Newman-Keuls q. The decision rule is to reject H_0 if the means in the comparison are not in a subset that was previously retained and if

$$F_p \geq F^{\alpha}_{p-1, df_W} \tag{2.19}$$

for every subset that contains the two means in H_0, and otherwise fail to reject H_0. Confidence intervals cannot be computed using the

Newman-Keuls F. Of course, this Newman-Keuls test has the problem of controlling α for each set of p ordered means rather than for all J means. For this reason, it is not recommended for use, but is included because it is necessary to introduce the Ryan F.

Ryan F (REGWF)

The Ryan F MCP uses the same α_p as the Ryan q method, but the same statistic and logic as the Newman-Keuls F. The decision rule is to reject H_0 if the means in the comparison are not in a subset for which the hypothesis was previously retained and if

$$F_p \geq F_{p-1, df_w}^{\alpha_p} \qquad (2.20)$$

where

$$\alpha_p = \alpha \qquad \text{for } p = J, J - 1$$

$$\alpha_p = 1 - (1 - \alpha)^{p/J} \qquad \text{for } p \leq J - 2$$

for every subset that contains the two means in H_0, and otherwise fail to reject H_0. SAS recognizes all of the contributions made to the Ryan F method by naming it REGWF: Ryan, Einot and Gabriel, Welsch, and the F statistic. This MCP controls p(at least one Type I error) at α using ERFW. Confidence intervals cannot be computed using the Ryan F.

Since the Ryan F method uses the F_p statistic, the only other MCP that uses a comparable critical value is Newman-Keuls F. Because of this, critical values cannot be used to compare its power with that of any of the other MCPs covered thus far in this text. Table 2.2 presents a comparison of critical values for Ryan F and Newman-Keuls F for $\alpha = .05$, $J = 4$, and $df_w = 20$. Since the Ryan critical value for $p = 2$ is larger than that for Newman-Keuls, the Ryan MCP controls p(at least one Type I error) at α using ERFW, but the Newman-Keuls is more powerful. More information regarding the power of the Ryan F will be given in Chapter 3, where results from research on MCPs are examined.

For the depression data, results from SAS for the Ryan F show the same significance pattern as was found using the Ryan that uses the q statistic (see Figure 2.8). The mean for the placebo group is found to

TABLE 2.2 *F* Critical Values

| | Newman-Keuls | | Ryan | |
p	α_p	$F_{p-1,\,20}$	α_p	$F_{p-1,\,20}$
4	.05	3.10	.05	3.10
3	.05	3.49	.05	3.49
2	.05	4.35	.0253	5.94

be significantly different from the means for the interpersonal therapy group and the group getting drug treatment with imipramine.

Concerning MCPs using the *F* statistic, Miller (1981) finds a disadvantage in the amount of computation involved: "The appeal of simplicity and ease is gone" (p. 97). Of course, a researcher would likely use a computer program such as SAS to compute the Ryan *F*. One advantage to the Ryan *F* is that it is more sensitive than the Ryan *q* to a minimum range configuration of group means. On the other hand, the Ryan *F* is not as sensitive as the Ryan *q* to a maximum range configuration of population means. Miller (1981) notes as an advantage the fact that *F* statistic methods tolerate unequal sample sizes, unlike MCPs that use the *t* or range statistic. The subject of unequal sample sizes will be addressed in more depth in Chapter 4.

Protected Tests

Most of the MCPs presented up to this point do not need a significant overall *F* test before they are computed. In fact, except for the use of MS_W, a researcher would not even need to run the ANOVA. This section introduces two MCPs in which the actual tests on the comparisons are not computed if the overall *F* test is not significant. Because each of these methods uses two distributions, the *F* and either the *t* or *q*, these MCPs do not fit cleanly into one of the previous three sections. None of the protected tests can be used to compute confidence intervals.

Protected t Test (Fisher's LSD)

One of the most popular MCPs is the protected *t* test, which is attributed to Fisher (1935) and often called the *least significant*

```
                              SAS
                ANALYSIS OF VARIANCE PROCEDURE

   RYAN-EINOT-GABRIEL-WELSCH MULTIPLE F TEST FOR VARIABLE: Y
   NOTE: THIS TEST CONTROLS THE TYPE I EXPERIMENTWISE ERROR RATE

              ALPHA=0.1  DF=236  MSE=61.0362

        NUMBER OF MEANS        2        3         4
        CRITICAL F        3.83681  2.3252  2.10713

   MEANS WITH THE SAME LETTER ARE NOT SIGNIFICANTLY DIFFERENT.

       REGWF     GROUPING            MEAN    N   GROUP

                         A          13.233   60  4_PLA
                         A
                  B      A          10.700   60  1_CBT
                  B
                  B                   9.800   60  2_IPT
                  B
                  B                   9.800   60  3_IMI
```

Figure 2.8. SAS Output for Ryan F (REGWF), Depression Data

difference (LSD). Its popularity is unfortunate because it does not control p(at least one Type I error) at α using ERFW for any situation other than the full null hypothesis. That is, if all of the J means are equal, then the LSD controls α. If there is any inequality of any of the J means, then the LSD has α control closer to ERPC.

The decision rule for LSD has two steps: First, test the overall H_0 with the ANOVA F. If the F is significant, go on to the second step. If the F is not significant, then fail to reject H_0 for all comparisons. The second step is to reject H_0 for a comparison if

$$| t_{\hat{\psi}} | \geq t_{df_w}^{\alpha} \tag{2.21}$$

otherwise fail to reject H_0. This MCP is appropriate for pairwise and general comparisons and does not require equal sample sizes. Even though the LSD uses the t as its statistic, comparison of its critical values with those of other MCPS does not yield useful information about relative power due to the first step depending on a significant

F. The LSD is available on SAS, but is not correctly computed because SAS proceeds to do the *t* tests even if *F* is not significant. For the depression data, the SAS results for the LSD are identical to those given for the *usual t* in Figure 2.1.

This method is called the protected *t* test because the usual *t* test is computed only if the overall ANOVA *F* test is significant. Thus the *F* is seen as "protecting" the usual *t* tests. The "least significant difference" is due to the fact that the α-level *t* critical value is the smallest critical value that the *t* statistic must exceed in order to be significant when considering only a single comparison.

The first step of the LSD has good power and control of α. However, once the researcher proceeds to the second step, α is no longer controlled ERFW. There is no adjustment of α and no step-down logic once the researcher is in the second step. All comparisons are compared with the same α-level *t* critical value. As Miller (1981) has pointed out, "However, when, in fact, the null hypothesis is false and likely to be rejected, the second stage of the LSD gives no increased protection to that part (if any) of the null hypothesis which still remains true" (p. 93). The LSD does not control α for partial null hypotheses, much less for multiple null hypotheses. For example, for $J = 4$, if the first three means were equal, but the fourth larger than the first three, there would be a partial null hypothesis in the three equal means. If the LSD made it past the first step (the *F* would be significant), then the three equal means would be tested with the very powerful *t* at the α level. The resulting *p*(at least one Type I error) could be as high as .15 if $\alpha = .05$ had been used for each *t* test. Poor α-control leads to the recommendation that the LSD method should not be used. It has been discussed here as background for the Fisher-Hayter, and to point out its problems in an attempt to convince researchers not to use it.

Shaffer-Ryan

Actually, the method introduced by Shaffer (1979) is not a stand-alone method per se, but a modification to any existing step-down MCP that does not already require a significant overall *F* test. It will be given here as a modification to the Ryan *q* method.

The decision rule for the Shaffer-Ryan has two steps: First, compute the overall ANOVA *F* test. If *F* is significant, proceed to the second step. If F is not significant, then fail to reject H_0 for all comparisons. The second step starts with the decision to reject H_0 for the comparison at stretch size $p = J$ if

$$| t_{\hat{\psi}} | \geq \frac{q_{J-1, df_w}^{\alpha}}{\sqrt{2}} \qquad (2.22)$$

and fail to reject otherwise. Note that the critical value for this comparison at the largest stretch size is the same as the critical value for stretch size $p = J - 1$. From this point on, the Shaffer-Ryan MCP proceeds exactly as the Ryan, that is, to reject H_0 if the means in the comparison are not contained in the stretch of a previously retained hypothesis and if

$$| t_{\hat{\psi}} | \geq \frac{q_{p, df_w}^{\alpha_p}}{\sqrt{2}} \qquad (2.23)$$

where

$$\alpha_p = \alpha \qquad \text{for } p = J - 1$$

$$\alpha_p = 1 - (1 - \alpha)^{p/J} \qquad \text{for } p \leq J - 2$$

otherwise fail to reject H_0. Confidence intervals cannot be computed using the Shaffer-Ryan method, and it is not available on major statistical packages. Also, like the LSD, it is not amenable to comparison of critical values to determine relative power due to the first step requiring F to be significant. Results for the depression data using Shaffer-Ryan are given in Figure 2.9, using the same format as typical SAS output. More information on the performance of the Shaffer-Ryan method will be given in Chapter 3.

Other MCPs

The methods discussed in this section are the last five MCPs to be covered in this chapter. These MCPs are either specialized for a restricted type of comparison (Dunnett) or newly introduced (Peritz, Holm-Shaffer, and Fisher-Hayter). Only Dunnett is currently available in SAS.

```
              ALPHA=0.1   DF=236   MSE=61.0362

        NUMBER OF MEANS        2        3        4
        CRITICAL RANGE     2.79394  2.94151  2.94151

MEANS WITH THE SAME LETTER ARE NOT SIGNIFICANTLY DIFFERENT.

    Shaffer-Ryan  GROUPING              MEAN      N   GROUP

                     A                 13.233    60   4_PLA
                     A
              B      A                 10.700    60   1_CBT
              B
              B                         9.800    60   2_IPT
              B
              B                         9.800    60   3_IMI
```

Figure 2.9. Results for Shaffer-Ryan, Depression Data

Dunnett

When a researcher is interested in comparing all treatment groups with a control group, the MCP due to Dunnett (1955) should be used. If J is the total number of groups, treatment and control, then there are $J - 1$ tests of treatment versus control. Without loss of generality, let the last group be the control group. Then the first $J - 1$ means will be compared with the Jth mean.

Since these comparisons all include the Jth (control) mean, they will not be orthogonal. The correlation coefficients of the comparisons of the jth mean versus control and the kth mean versus control are given by

$$\rho_{jk} = \sqrt{\frac{n_j\, n_k}{(n_j + n_J)(n_k + n_J)}} \quad \text{for } 1 \le j \ne k \le J - 1 \qquad (2.24)$$

Here the sample sizes could be unequal, but if they are equal, then the correlation coefficients of the comparisons are constant and equal to 0.5. For example, if the common sample size is $n = 20$, then the correlation coefficient between the pairwise comparisons of treatments 1 and 2 with the control is given as

$$\rho_{12} = \sqrt{\frac{(20)(20)}{(20+20)(20+20)}} = \sqrt{\frac{400}{1600}} = \sqrt{.25} = 0.5 . \quad (2.25)$$

If the sample sizes are all equal, then the correlation coefficients for all of the treatment-control comparisons will be equal to 0.5.

In the situation where the researcher is comparing all treatment means to a control mean, the desired inference often is directional, or one-sided. The question often is whether or not the treatment is better than the control. When this is the case, one-tailed critical values will be used. Sometimes the researcher wants to detect if the treatment means are simply different from the control mean, either larger or smaller. For such a nondirectional hypothesis, two-tailed critical values will be used. Critical values for Dunnett will be designated as a D and will be selected using a given level of α, J as the total number of means including the control, and df_W. Both one- and two-tailed critical values when sample sizes are equal are given in Table A.6 of Appendix A.

With equal sample sizes and the control mean as the Jth mean, the decision rule for the Dunnett MCP is to reject H_0 for a comparison

$$\psi = \mu_j - \mu_J \quad (2.26)$$

if

$$t_{\hat{\psi}} \geq D^{\alpha}_{J, \, df_w} \quad (2.27)$$

for directional inferences. Nondirectional inferences can be made by using the absolute value of the t statistic and a two-tailed critical value, $D^{(\alpha/2)}$, from Table A.6. Researchers interested in confidence intervals can combine Dunnett critical values and Equation 1.32 (Chapter 1) to compute interval estimates of ψ. SAS allows the researcher to compute Dunnett for nondirectional inferences with the statement

MEANS effect/DUNNETT ('label')

where *label* is the name the researcher gives to the control group in the SAS data. Directional inferences use

MEANS effect/DUNNETTL ('label')

if all treatments are expected to be less than control, and

MEANS effect/DUNNETTU ('label')

if all treatments are expected to be greater than control. Output for Dunnett is given in Figure 2.10.

Another situation that could occur is for the sample sizes for the $J - 1$ treatment groups to be equal, and the sample size for the control to have a different value. If this is the case, the correlations between comparisons would be constant, but not equal to 0.5, so Table A.6 cannot be used since a common correlation of 0.5 is assumed for those critical values. In this case, or if other inequalities occur in the sample sizes, the researcher should refer to Hochberg and Tamhane (1987) for the correct tables.

Peritz

When the Newman-Keuls q was discussed earlier, considerable attention was given to the fact that it does not control p(at least one Type I error) at α using ERFW for the situation in which there are multiple null hypotheses. Ryan's method corrects for this problem by altering the α for each stretch to α_p. Peritz (1970) developed a modification of the Ryan method that controls p(at least one Type I error) at α using ERFW and gives higher power than Ryan, even when there are multiple null hypotheses.

The Newman-Keuls method does not control α when there are multiple null hypotheses because the smaller stretch sizes, $p \leq J - 2$, have critical values that are too small if multiple null hypotheses exist. If $J = 4$ and the 1-2 comparison is being considered, then the 3-4 comparison represents the complement to 1-2 and it is possible that 1-2 and 3-4 could represent null hypotheses. The logic of Peritz is based on this idea: If the complement 3-4 comparison is not null, then the 1-2 comparison could be compared to a Newman-Keuls critical value and not inflate α. However, if the complement 3-4 comparison is null, then the 1-2 comparison should be compared to a Ryan critical value to give control of α.

The Peritz method essentially tests for the comparisons in the complement and, if all of them are declared significant using Ryan critical values, then it allows testing of the comparison of interest using Newman-Keuls critical values. Thus if the 3-4 comparison is declared significant using a Ryan critical value, this is a good indication that

```
                        The SAS System
                  Analysis of Variance Procedure
                  Dunnett's T tests for variable: Y

NOTE: This test controls the Type I experimentwise error for
      comparisons of all treatments against a control.

      Alpha= 0.1  Confidence= 0.9  df= 236  MSE= 61.03616
              Critical Value of Dunnett's T=2.073
              Minimum Significant Difference= 2.9562

Comparisons significant at the 0.1 level are indicated by '***'.

                    Simultaneous              Simultaneous
                      Lower     Difference      Upper
         GROUP       Confidence   Between     Confidence
       Comparison      Limit       Means        Limit

    1_CBT - 4_PLA      -5.490      -2.533       0.423
    3_IMI - 4_PLA      -6.390      -3.433      -0.477    ***
    2_IPT - 4_PLA      -6.390      -3.433      -0.477    ***

                        The SAS System
                  Analysis of Variance Procedure
              Dunnett's One-tailed T tests for variable: Y

NOTE: This test controls the Type I experimentwise error for
      comparisons of all treatments against a control.

      Alpha= 0.1  Confidence= 0.9  df= 236  MSE= 61.03616
              Critical Value of Dunnett's T=1.740
              Minimum Significant Difference= 2.4818

Comparisons significant at the 0.1 level are indicated by '***'.

                    Simultaneous              Simultaneous
                      Lower     Difference      Upper
         GROUP       Confidence   Between     Confidence
       Comparison      Limit       Means        Limit

    1_CBT - 4_PLA      -5.015      -2.533      -0.051    ***
    3_IMI - 4_PLA      -5.915      -3.433      -0.951    ***
    2_IPT - 4_PLA      -5.915      -3.433      -0.951    ***
```

Figure 2.10. SAS Output for Dunnett, Depression Data

the 3-4 comparison is not null. Then the Peritz method will do the 1-2 comparison at the α level of Newman-Keuls.

From Figures 2.5 for Newman-Keuls and 2.6 for Ryan, the significant (S) and contentious comparisons are:

Newman-Keuls (S)	Ryan (S)	Contentious	Peritz (S)
4_PLA vs 2_IPT	4_PLA vs 2_IPT		4_PLA vs 2_IPT
4_PLA vs 3_IMI	4_PLA vs 3_IMI		4_PLA vs 3_IMI
4_PLA vs 1_CBT		4_PLA vs 1_CBT	

Figure 2.11. Results for Peritz, Depression Data

The decision rule for Peritz is to follow a step-down logic that (a) retains H_0 for any comparison that Newman-Keuls retains, (b) rejects H_0 for any comparison that Ryan rejects, and (c) declares any comparison not in a or b as contentious. Contentious comparisons are declared significant if all comparisons in the complement are significant using Ryan critical values and step-down logic. For the depression data, Figure 2.11 contains the Peritz results.

Consider the compliment of 4_PLA versus 1_CBT, which is simply 2_IPT versus 3_IMI: Since the compliment is not significant using Ryan, then 4_PLA versus 1_CBT is declared nonsignificant using Peritz, and the results are identical to those for Ryan.

Computer programs are used to compute the Peritz MCP because all the complicated testing of comparisons in complements to all comparisons makes hand computation potentially tedious. A program is available for the Peritz q (Martin & Toothaker, 1989) in Appendix B. Confidence intervals cannot be computed using the Peritz method. Multiple F statistics can be used for the Peritz, but the Peritz F MCP suffers the same disadvantages as the Ryan F.

Holm-Shaffer

Holm (1979) presented a modified Dunn procedure in which the comparisons must first be placed in order from largest to smallest. With equal n, this ordering can be done with the difference in means, or the t statistic. With unequal n, the ordering must be done with the p value of the t statistic. First, the largest of the $C = J(J-1)/2$ pairwise comparisons is tested using the Dunn critical value, where $\alpha' = \alpha/C$. If the largest comparison is significant, then the second largest

```
Overall F is significant using α = .10,

                                        Dunn critical
Comparison            t     k    Cₖ       value      Significance
───────────────────────────────────────────────────────────────
4_PLA vs 3_IMI     2.4068   1    3        2.141      S
4_PLA vs 2_IPT     2.4068   2    3        2.141      S
4_PLA vs 1_CBT     1.7758   3    3        2.141      NS
1_CBT vs 3_IMI      .6310   4    3      NA (2.141)   NS by implication
1_CBT vs 2_IPT      .6310   5    2      NA (1.971)   NS by implication
2_IPT vs 3_IMI     0.0      6    1      NA (1.651)   NS by implication

NA=Not Applicable since this comparison is declared
non-significant by implication; critical values are
obtained by linear interpolation on 1/df.
```

Figure 2.12. Results for Holm-Shaffer, Depression Data

comparison is tested using a Dunn critical value with the number of comparisons equal to $C - 1$, that is, with $\alpha' = \alpha/(C - 1)$. For the kth largest comparison in order, $k = 1, \ldots, C$, test the hypothesis using a Dunn critical value with the number of comparisons equal to $C - k + 1$, that is, with $\alpha' = \alpha/(C - k + 1)$. If any comparison is not significant, then stop testing; that is, all remaining smaller comparisons are declared nonsignificant.

Shaffer (1986) modified the Holm test by dividing α by C_k, where C_k is defined as the maximum number of pairwise hypotheses that could be true, given that at least $k - 1$ hypotheses are false. For all possible pairwise comparisons, note that C_k also will be equal to the number of pairs of means that could be equal, given the previous $k - 1$ rejections. For example, if $J = 4$, for the largest comparison, all $J(J - 1)/2 = 6$ comparisons (pairwise hypotheses) could be true, so $C_k = 6$ for the Dunn critical value. If the largest comparison is significant, the second largest comparison is tested using a Dunn critical value with $C_k = 3$, because if $\mu_1 - \mu_4 = 0$ is rejected, then at most three pairwise hypotheses could be true: the set of $\mu_1 - \mu_2 = 0$, $\mu_1 - \mu_3 = 0$, and $\mu_2 - \mu_3 = 0$, or the set of $\mu_2 - \mu_4 = 0$, $\mu_3 - \mu_4 = 0$, and $\mu_2 - \mu_3 = 0$. The third and fourth largest comparisons also have $C_k = 3$, the fifth largest has $C_k = 2$, and the smallest ($k = 6$) has $C_k = 1$. Shaffer (1986) gives values of C_k for $J = 3$ to 10.

```
Overall F is significant using α = .10; using output in
Figure 2.6 to obtain q critical value for J - 1 = 3,
Fisher-Hayter critical value = 2.94151/√2 =
2.0799617 = 2.08.

     Comparison              t         Significance

     4_PLA vs 3_IMI        2.4068           S
     4_PLA vs 2_IPT        2.4068           S
     4_PLA vs 1_CBT        1.7758          NS
     1_CBT vs 3_IMI         .6310          NS
     1_CBT vs 2_IPT         .6310          NS
     2_IPT VS 3_IMI        0               NS
```

Figure 2.13. Results for Fisher-Hayter, Depression Data

One final improvement can be made in this test by using an overall ANOVA F test as the first stage. If it is significant, then test the largest comparison with the same critical value as for the usual second largest comparison. The remaining comparisons are tested as above. If $J = 4$, and the overall ANOVA is significant, test the largest comparison with a Dunn critical value with $C_k = 3$. Figure 2.12 contains the results of the Holm-Shaffer MCP for the depression data. The Holm-Shaffer MCP cannot be used to compute confidence intervals.

Fisher-Hayter

Hayter (1986) proposed a modification of the LSD to control the liberal α of that procedure. Instead of using a t critical value for the comparisons after a significant overall ANOVA F, Hayter suggested using a q critical value with $J - 1$ as the number-of-means parameter. That is, perform the overall F test and, if it is significant at level α, then reject H_0 if

$$| t_{\hat{\psi}} | \geq \frac{q_{J-1, df_w}^{\alpha}}{\sqrt{2}} \qquad (2.28)$$

and otherwise fail to reject H_0 for the pairwise comparisons. Figure 2.13 contains results for the Fisher-Hayter MCP on the depression data.

Summary

The 15 MCPs discussed in this chapter have included some methods that control α using ERPC, and some that control p(at least one Type I error) at α using ERFW (or ERPF). Some other procedures control α somewhere between ERPC and ERFW. Some traditional MCPs, such as Duncan's, have not been discussed, because they either do not control α using one of these two error rates or do not form the basis for one of the MCPs presented in this chapter. Some of the methods presented here are not recommended for use, but have been presented because they form foundations for "good" methods. Newman-Keuls methods serve as the starting point for Ryan and Peritz MCPs, and thus are discussed even though not recommended. The LSD serves as a starting point for Fisher-Hayter, and thus is discussed although it is not recommended, either. Further comparisons among the various MCPs will be given in the next chapter, including recommendations on which MCPs to use and when.

Notes

1. The probability of all decisions being correct is greater than or equal to the product of the probabilities of each separate decision being correct. Thus, for two comparisons, if we use α as the probability of an error on one decision, then p(all correct) $\geq (1 - \alpha)(1 - \alpha)$. For C comparisons, p(all correct) $\geq (1 - \alpha)^C$. Thus p(at least one Type I error) $\leq 1 - p$(all correct) $= 1 - (1 - \alpha)^C$.

2. Tukey's test is often referred to as the *honestly significant difference* (HSD) test or the *wholly significant difference* (WSD) test. Another name sometimes given to the Tukey test is *Tukey (a)*, because he developed a second test that has come to be called Tukey (b). The Tukey (b) will be discussed later.

3. Some authors refer to stepwise procedures as *layered* procedures.

4. For J=3, Newman-Keuls does control α using ERFW, but in general, it does not.

5. The critical value for Newman-Keuls for the largest stretch, $p = 4$, should equal the critical value for Tukey. For this example, the Newman-Keuls critical value is 2.3040 and the Tukey critical value is 2.3038. The difference is slight and is due to rounding in the q critical value given by SAS.

6. In addition to the modification that improved the Ryan (REGWQ) method, Welsch (1977a, 1977b) presented a method that has the distinction of being the only known step-up MCP. Step-up logic starts with statistics for the $p = 2$ comparisons and compares them with a critical value. If a comparison is significant, then all comparisons containing the significant comparison are declared significant by implication. Nonsignificant lower stretch comparisons simply lead to direct testing of the higher stretch comparisons not already declared significant by implication to see if they are

significant when compared with appropriate critical values. Comparisons at stretch size $p > 2$ proceed in a similar fashion of comparing a statistic with a critical value and, if the comparison is significant, declaring all comparisons containing the significant comparison as significant by implication.

Note that the Welsch method and step-up logic declare significance by implication in contrast to declaration of nonsignificance by implication for step-down logic. Since the Welsch step-up method requires special tables of critical values, it will not be presented in this book.

3 Comparison of MCPs

When a researcher is confronted with 15 or more MCPs from which to choose, there may be a tendency toward despair over the selection task. A legitimate question may be asked: How do I choose from among all of these MCPs? This chapter should help to answer that question. First, most of the MCPs presented in Chapter 2 will be compared with respect to their critical values and thus their power. Second, these MCPs will be computed on a common data set called the *Miller data*. Finally, results of research will be presented, showing error rates and powers from simulation studies. These three approaches to comparing the MCPs should help the researcher in the selection process.

Critical Values and Power

For many of the MCPs presented in Chapter 2, critical values were contrasted to those of other comparable methods. As long as the methods use the same statistic, such as t, the critical values can be compared because the common statistic's sampling distribution is the same for the different MCPs. That is, there is only one sampling distribution of the common statistic. Within that sampling distribution of the statistic, different MCPs will have different critical values. In that sampling distribution, the only difference in the MCPs will be the different critical values. The connection from the critical values to the power of these MCPs is then straightforward. For nondirectional hypotheses for most statistics and MCPs, a general rule is as follows:

The smaller the critical value, the higher the power. For directional hypotheses, the absolute value of the critical value must be considered.

In practice, the researcher makes decisions about error rate control, what type of comparisons, and how many, and then selects an MCP consistent with these decisions. Suppose that a researcher wants to control p(at least one Type I error) at α using ERFW for all possible pairwise comparisons. Then from among those MCPs that accomplish such control for these comparisons, the researcher can select the method with the highest power by finding the one with the smallest critical value. Of course, evaluating critical values can include even the critical value from a method that does not control p(at least one Type I error) at α using ERFW, such as that from the *usual t*. The *usual t* will have the smallest critical value and thus the highest power, but at the expense of excessive Type I errors and an inflated α using ERFW. Even though a comparison of critical values gives a comparison of powers for any methods using the same statistic, the MCPs to be contrasted are usually restricted to those that give the same error rate control. Another issue is that the researcher should do the comparison of critical values before the start of the data analysis, and not simply run many MCPs and see which one gives the most rejections.

Table 3.1 gives critical values for some of the MCPs that can use the *t* statistic when $J = 5$, $df_W = 20$, and $\alpha = .05$ for all possible pairwise comparisons ($C = 10$). Those MCPs that use a step-down logic are noted with an *s*. The Shaffer-Ryan and Holm-Shaffer critical values for $p = 5$ have asterisks because these MCPs require the overall F to be significant before doing the largest pairwise comparison. The values in parentheses beside the Peritz critical values for $p = 3$ and $p = 2$ are the Newman-Keuls critical values that are used if all of the comparisons in the compliment are Ryan significant. Newman-Keuls and LSD are not included because of lack of control of p(at least one Type I error) at α using ERFW, and because their critical values are already represented in the table (LSD as *t* except for the requirement that overall F is significant, and Newman-Keuls as the optional values for Peritz). The *usual t* is included as a benchmark to show the smallest critical value, and highest power, without regard to control of α. Also, Scheffé is included, in spite of its well-known conservatism for all possible pairwise comparisons, because it does control p(at least one Type I error) at α or less using ERFW. All critical values are given as t, $q/\sqrt{2}$, or $\sqrt{(J-1)F}$.

TABLE 3.1   Critical Values When J = 5, df$_W$ = 20, and α = .05 with C = 10
Pairwise Comparisons

p	Ryan^S	Shaffer^S	Peritz^S	Fisher-Hayter^S	C_k	Holm-Shaffer^S
5	2.991	2.800*	2.991	2.800*	6*	2.927*
4	2.800	2.800	2.800	2.800	6	2.927
3	2.765	2.765	2.765 (2.531)	2.800	3, 4, 6	2.613, 2.744, 2.927
2	2.510	2.510	2.510 (2.086)	2.800	2, 3, 4, 6	2.423, 2.613, 2.744, 2.927

NOTE: For simultaneous MCPs, there is a constant critical value: t, 2.086; Dunn, 3.160; Dunn-Šidák, 3.143; Tukey, 2.991; and Scheffé, 3.388. Note that C_k and Holm-Shaffer critical values depend on the pattern of significance in the actual data.

From Table 3.1 it is apparent that most of the MCPs can be ordered in terms of power from lowest to highest for those MCPs that control p(at least one Type I error) at α or less using ERFW. Except for Holm-Shaffer, the power ranking would be Scheffé (lowest), Dunn, Dunn-Šidák, Tukey, Ryan, Fisher-Hayter, and then the methods due to Shaffer-Ryan and Peritz. Note that the order among the pairs (Ryan, Fisher-Hayter) and (Shaffer-Ryan, Peritz) is not clear. The data-dependent nature of Holm-Shaffer as well as the differences in the logic and the complexity of the various approaches make it difficult to use critical values to detect which of Shaffer-Ryan, Peritz, and Holm-Shaffer would be most powerful.

Since the differences in critical values are not large for the most powerful of these MCPs, the power values might not be very different. However, comparison of critical values does not show the magnitude of the power differences. Results from simulation studies presented below will help answer questions about the most powerful MCPs, about magnitude of power differences, and different types of power.

Next, reconsider Table 3.1 using the same MCPs for C = 6 pairwise comparisons that are planned. That is, the researcher did not simply choose the 6 largest comparisons out of the 10 that could be done on five means, but planned to do a particular set of 6 pairwise comparisons. Values of J, df$_W$, and α are the same. Only the critical values for Dunn and Dunn-Šidák are sensitive to C, so these are the only values that are different, 2.930 and 2.918, respectively. Even though both Dunn and Dunn-Šidák are more powerful than Tukey, the picture relative to Ryan, Shaffer-Ryan, and Peritz is not clear. Since Ryan is the simplest of these three MCPs, consider it compared with Dunn-Šidák.

TABLE 3.2 Critical Values When J = 5, dfw = 60, and α = .05 with C = 10 Pairwise Comparisons

p	Ryan[S]	Shaffer[S]	Peritz[S]	Fisher-Hayter[S]	C_k	Holm-Shaffer[S]
5	2.814	2.645*	2.814	2.645*	6*	2.729*
4	2.645	2.645	2.645	2.645	6	2.729
3	2.598	2.598	2.598(2.404)	2.645	3, 4, 6	2.463, 2.575, 2.729
2	2.369	2.369	2.369(2.001)	2.645	2, 3, 4, 6	2.299, 2.463, 2.575, 2.729

NOTE: For simultaneous MCPs, there is a constant critical value: t, 2.000; Dunn, 2.920; Dunn-Šidák, 2.906; Tukey, 2.814; and Scheffé, 3.175. Note that C_k and Holm-Shaffer critical values depend on the pattern of significance in the actual data.

Dunn-Šidák is more powerful for the largest comparison, 2.918 versus 2.991, but Ryan is more powerful for all of the remaining comparisons. If one of the six that was planned happens to be the largest comparison, then Dunn-Šidák will be best for it, but poorer for the remaining. The Ryan has better power for the smaller stretch sizes. However, if the researcher selects Ryan and the largest comparison has a t of, say, 2.95, then the better power for the other comparisons will not be realized because the nonsignificant largest comparison stops the testing.

In this situation, Peritz is very similar to Ryan, but is even more powerful for the smaller stretch sizes. Shaffer-Ryan, Fisher-Hayter, and Holm-Shaffer again offer a cloudy picture on their power. If the overall F is significant, then Shaffer-Ryan and Fisher-Hayter are more powerful than Dunn-Šidák, if not, then Shaffer-Ryan and Fisher-Hayter stop testing. The data-dependent nature of Holm-Shaffer complicates all power comparisons.

Finally, it should be apparent that if C were smaller than 6, Dunn-Šidák would be even more powerful. In fact, if only two planned comparisons are done, the Dunn-Šidák critical value is 2.417, which is smaller than even the stretch size two critical value for Ryan. However, it is possible for Peritz to be more powerful than the Dunn-Šidák for two planned comparisons if the complement comparisons are all Ryan significant, since the Peritz would use the Newman-Keuls critical value of 2.086.

Now consider critical values for MCPs that can use the t statistic for J = 5, dfw = 60, and α = .05 for all possible pairwise comparisons (C = 10), as given in Table 3.2.

For this situation, the ranking of the critical values, and thus power of the MCPs, is the same as for dfw = 20: Scheffé (lowest), Dunn,

TABLE 3.3 Miller Data with Group Means (Variances) and ANOVA

Group	Miller Data 1	2	3	4	5
	18.61	18.86	18.22	22.43	26.32
	13.54	19.17	19.42	17.22	27.01
	16.08	13.69	20.25	22.31	27.08
	18.96	14.47	25.25	19.58	22.32
	13.31	18.81	20.36	23.96	29.77
mean	16.1	17.0	20.7	21.1	26.5
variance	7.2044	7.2004	7.2023	7.1943	7.1985

		ANOVA Summary Table			
Source	df	SS	MS	F	p
Between groups	4	338.84	84.71	11.77	.0001
Within groups	20	144.00	7.20		

Dunn-Šidák, Tukey, Ryan and Fisher-Hayter, and Shaffer-Ryan and Peritz, with Holm-Shaffer not clearly placeable. The critical values are closer together, which might indicate that the power differences are smaller. Regardless of actual power values, the ranking in power is the same for both $df_W = 20$ and 60 for all possible pairwise comparisons when $J = 5$.

Many more examples could be offered to compare power by comparing critical values.[1] To be safe, researchers should always compare critical values to find the most powerful MCP for the current research project.

Miller Data

Miller (1981, p. 82) used an example consisting of five means and a value for the standard error of a mean to illustrate many of the MCPs that he presented. Since this example nicely shows the power differences in many of the MCPs by giving different results, it is a good example to use to compare methods appropriate for pairwise comparisons. The data presented in Table 3.3 were simulated to give the values of the means and MS_W computed from the standard error of the mean as given in Miller (1981). The data are called the *Miller data* and have $J = 5$ and $n = 5$. Means and variances are given for each group.

TABLE 3.4 Mean Differences and *t* Statistics for Miller Data

group	2	3	4	5
1	0.9 (0.53)	4.6 (2.71)	5.0 (2.95)	10.4 (6.13)
2		3.7 (2.18)	4.1 (2.42)	9.5 (5.60)
3			0.4 (0.24)	5.8 (3.42)
4				5.4 (3.18)

The overall analysis shows that the five group means are significantly different. Some MCP must be selected to show which means differ significantly from the others. Each of the methods covered in Chapter 2 will be computed on the Miller data. For those that can be computed on all possible pairwise comparisons and are available on SAS, output from that package will be given. Table 3.4 contains all possible pairwise mean differences and *t* statistics.

The Usual t

If the researcher chose to control error rate ERPC, then the *usual t* would be selected as the MCP. It would give the highest power of all MCPs, but at the expense of a large *p*(at least one Type I error). The SAS output for the Miller data is given in Figure 3.1 for the *usual t*.

From this output, the *usual t* shows that mean 5 is significantly different from all other means. Mean 4 is significantly different from 2 and 1, but not 3. Mean 3 is significantly different from 2 and 1, and means 2 and 1 are not significantly different. Another way to present the same results is to list the pairs of means that are significantly different: 5-4, 5-3, 5-2, 5-1, 4-2, 4-1, 3-2, and 3-1. No other MCP will have this many pairs of means significantly different for the Miller data, because the *usual t* is the most powerful, although it does not control *p*(at least one Type I error) at α. Thus the only question is, Which of these significantly different pairs represent Type I errors?

Dunn, Dunn-Šidák, and Tukey

Since the Dunn and Dunn-Šidák MCPs are best used when *C* is small, they will be conservative relative to some of the other methods for all pairwise comparisons. However, they will control *p*(at least one Type I error) at or below the selected α. The Tukey method will

```
                            SAS
               ANALYSIS OF VARIANCE PROCEDURE

 T TESTS (LSD) FOR VARIABLE: Y
 NOTE: THIS TEST CONTROLS THE TYPE I COMPARISONWISE ERROR RATE,
       NOT THE EXPERIMENTWISE ERROR RATE

           APLHA=0.05  DF=20  MSE=7.20002
           CRITICAL VALUE OF T=2.08596
           LEAST SIGNIFICANT DIFFERENCE=3.54

 MEANS WITH THE SAME LETTER ARE NOT SIGNIFICANTLY DIFFERENT.

      T        GROUPING           MEAN      N   GROUP

               A                 26.500     5   5_FIVE

               B                 21.100     5   4_FOUR
               B
               B                 20.700     5   3_THREE

               C                 17.000     5   2_TWO
               C
               C                 16.100     5   1_ONE
```

Figure 3.1. SAS Output for *Usual t*, Miller Data

also control p(at least one Type I error) at α using ERFW, but should be more powerful for all pairwise comparisons than the Dunn and Dunn-Šidák. The SAS output is given in Figure 3.2 for Dunn's method.

For the Dunn method, mean 5 is significantly different from all other means. Means 4 through 1 are not significantly different from each other. Thus the significant pairs are 5-4, 5-3, 5-2, and 5-1. The expected conservatism of Dunn shows radically different results than the *usual t*. The Dunn-Šidák gives identical results for these data, even though the "CRITICAL VALUE OF T=3.14330" and "MINIMUM SIGNIFICANT DIFFERENCE=5.3344" are slightly smaller than the same quantities for Dunn.

Even though the Tukey MCP is ideally suited for all possible pairwise comparisons and is generally more powerful in this case than Dunn and Dunn-Šidák, for these data they all give the same results. The theoretical power advantage is shown by the fact that the "MINI-

```
                          SAS
              ANALYSIS OF VARIANCE PROCEDURE

BONFERRONI (DUNN) T TESTS FOR VARIABLE: Y
NOTE: THIS TEST CONTROLS THE TYPE I EXPERIMENTWISE ERROR RATE
      BUT GENERALLY HAS A HIGHER TYPE II ERROR RATE THAN REGWQ

          ALPHA=0.05  DF=20  MSE=7.20002
          CRITICAL VALUE OF T=3.15340
          MINIMUM SIGNIFICANT DIFFERENCE=5.3515

MEANS WITH THE SAME LETTER ARE NOT SIGNIFICANTLY DIFFERENT.

      BON      GROUPING           MEAN     N   GROUP

               A                26.500     5   5_FIVE

               B                21.100     5   4_FOUR
               B
               B                20.700     5   3_THREE
               B
               B                17.000     5   2_TWO
               B
               B                16.100     5   1_ONE
```

Figure 3.2. SAS Output for Dunn, Miller Data

MUM SIGNIFICANT DIFFERENCE" is 5.0783 for Tukey and 5.3344 and 5.3515 for Dunn-Šidák and Dunn, respectively. Also note that the critical values from SAS cannot be compared directly because Dunn and Dunn-Šidák use t and Tukey uses q. Of course, simply dividing the q by $\sqrt{2}$ makes the critical values comparable.

Newman-Keuls

There is an inherent danger in any further coverage of the Newman-Keuls method. The danger is that some researcher might see the information about this method and decide to use it, not realizing that it does not control error rate using ERFW. For this reason, any presentation of material on this MCP should include notice of its faults and should compare it with acceptable methods. In spite of all of its bad publicity, however, this method is available on SAS and SPSS

```
                                SAS
                  ANALYSIS OF VARIANCE PROCEDURE

STUDENT-NEWMAN-KEULS TEST FOR VARIABLE: Y
NOTE: THIS TEST CONTROLS THE TYPE I EXPERIMENTWISE ERROR RATE
      UNDER THE COMPLETE NULL HYPOTHESIS BUT NOT UNDER PARTIAL
      NULL HYPOTHESES

              ALPHA=0.05   DF=20   MSE=7.20002

   NUMBER OF MEANS          2        3        4         5
   CRITICAL RANGE       3.54003  4.29353  4.74996  5.07825

  MEANS WITH THE SAME LETTER ARE NOT SIGNIFICANTLY DIFFERENT.

      SNK        GROUPING         MEAN     N   GROUP

                    A            26.500    5   5_FIVE

                    B            21.100    5   4_FOUR
                    B
                    B            20.700    5   3_THREE
                    B
           C        B            17.000    5   2_TWO
           C
           C                     16.100    5   1_ONE
```

Figure 3.3. SAS Output for Newman-Keuls, Miller Data

and is even popularly used in some applied journals. Thus the SAS output is given in Figure 3.3 for the Newman-Keuls method.

Newman-Keuls shows mean 5 as significantly different from all other means, mean 4 as significantly different from mean 1, and mean 3 as significantly different from mean 1. All other differences are not significant. The significantly different pairs of means are 5-4, 5-3, 5-2, 5-1, 4-1, and 3-1. Since Newman-Keuls F gives similar results, it will not be presented.

Ryan

The Ryan MCP should give better power than Tukey for all pairwise comparisons but better α control than Newman-Keuls. Of course, it is possible for a method to have better power theoretically, but for that elevated power not to be manifested in the analysis of a

```
                              SAS
                 ANALYSIS OF VARIANCE PROCEDURE

  RYAN-EINOT-GABRIEL-WELSCH MULTIPLE RANGE TEST FOR VARIABLE: Y
  NOTE: THIS TEST CONTROLS THE TYPE I EXPERIMENTWISE ERROR RATE

                 ALPHA=0.05   DF=20   MSE=7.20002

       NUMBER OF MEANS         2        3        4        5
       CRITICAL RANGE    4.27793  4.70315  4.74996  5.07825

     MEANS   WITH   THE   SAME   LETTER   ARE   NOT   SIGNIFICANTLY
  DIFFERENT.

           REGWQ       GROUPING           MEAN      N   GROUP

                          A              26.500     5   5_FIVE

                          B              21.100     5   4_FOUR
                          B
                 C        B              20.700     5   3_THREE
                 C        B
                 C        B              17.000     5   2_TWO
                 C
                 C                       16.100     5   1_ONE
```

Figure 3.4. SAS Output for Ryan, Miller Data

given set of data, as was observed for the Tukey method. The SAS output is given in Figure 3.4 for Ryan's method.

The Ryan method shows that mean 5 is significantly different from all other means, that mean 4 is significantly different from mean 1, and that all other differences are not significant. The pairs of means that are significantly different are 5-4, 5-3, 5-2, 5-1, and 4-1. For the 3-1 comparison, note that Ryan shows it to be nonsignificant, but Newman-Keuls shows it to be significant. If Ryan is taken to be "correct," then the Newman-Keuls detection of 3-1 to be significant is potentially a Type I error.

Scheffé

The Scheffé MCP is noted for its conservatism with regard to both α and power, especially for all pairwise comparisons. The SAS results are given in Figure 3.5 for the Scheffé method.

```
                              SAS
                ANALYSIS OF VARIANCE PROCEDURE

SCHEFFE'S TEST FOR VARIABLE: Y
NOTE: THIS TEST CONTROLS THE TYPE I EXPERIMENTWISE ERROR RATE
      BUT GENERALLY HAS A HIGHER TYPE II ERROR RATE THAN REGWF
      FOR ALL PAIRWISE COMPARISONS

            ALPHA=0.05  DF=20  MSE=7.20002
            CRITICAL VALUE OF F=2.86608
            MINIMUM SIGNIFICANT DIFFERENCE=5.7461

MEANS WITH THE SAME LETTER ARE NOT SIGNIFICANTLY DIFFERENT.

      SCHEFFE  GROUPING            MEAN    N  GROUP

                      A           26.500   5  5_FIVE
                      A
              B       A           21.100   5  4_FOUR
              B
              B                   20.700   5  3_THREE
              B
              B                   17.000   5  2_TWO
              B
              B                   16.100   5  1_ONE
```

Figure 3.5. SAS Output for Scheffé, Miller Data

Scheffé detects mean 5 as significantly different from means 3, 2, and 1, and all other differences as nonsignificant. The significantly different pairs of means are 5-3, 5-2, and 5-1. Note for the 5-4 and 4-1 comparisons that Scheffé did not detect them as significant, but that Ryan showed them to be significant. If Ryan is taken to be "correct," then these omissions by Scheffé are likely to be Type II errors.

Ryan F

Even though the Ryan F lacks intuitive appeal and simplicity, at least the simplicity issue is handled with use of a computer program. The SAS output is given in Figure 3.6 for the Ryan F method.

The results for the Ryan F are identical to those for the Ryan using the q statistic, but are presented here to include the critical F values. Significantly different pairs of means are 5-4, 5-3, 5-2, 5-1, and 4-1.

```
                              SAS
                ANALYSIS OF VARIANCE PROCEDURE

RYAN-EINOT-GABRIEL-WELSCH MULTIPLE F TEST FOR VARIABLE: Y
NOTE: THIS TEST CONTROLS THE TYPE I EXPERIMENTWISE ERROR RATE

              ALPHA=0.05  DF=20  MSE=7.20002

    NUMBER OF MEANS        2        3        4        5
    CRITICAL  F      6.35462  4.18552  3.09839  2.86608

 MEANS WITH THE SAME LETTER ARE NOT SIGNIFICANTLY DIFFERENT.

        REGWF     GROUPING        MEAN     N    GROUP

                     A           26.500    5    5_FIVE

                     B           21.100    5    4_FOUR
                     B
              C      B           20.700    5    3_THREE
              C      B
              C      B           17.000    5    2_TWO
              C
              C                  16.100    5    1_ONE
```

Figure 3.6. SAS Output for Ryan F, Miller Data

Shaffer-Ryan

Because the overall F is significant for the Miller data, proceed to the largest comparison, 5-1, and compare it to the critical value for stretch size $p = J - 1 = 5 - 1 = 4$. Because the t statistic for the 5-1 comparison is $t = (26.5 - 16.1)/[2(7.20002/5)] = 6.13$, and the critical value for $p = 4$ is $q/\sqrt{2} = 3.96/\sqrt{2} = 2.80$, the 5-1 comparison is significant. The remainder of the comparisons are done exactly as for Ryan, so 5-4, 5-3, 5-2, 5-1, and 4-1 are significant differences.

Dunnett

Arbitrarily selecting group 1 as the control, Dunnett's two-tailed tests showed groups 3, 4, and 5 as significantly different from group 1

```
                          The SAS System
                   Analysis of Variance Procedure

              Dunnett's T tests for variable: Y

NOTE: This tests controls the Type I experimentwise error for
      comparisons of all treatments against a control.

      Alpha= 0.05  Confidence= 0.95  df= 20  MSE= 7.20002
               Critical Value of Dunnett's T= 2.651
               Minimum Significant Difference= 4.499

Comparisons significant at the 0.05 level are indicated by '***'.

                          Simultaneous              Simultaneous
                             Lower    Difference       Upper
                GROUP      Confidence   Between      Confidence
              Comparison     Limit      Means          Limit

5_FIVE   - 1_ONE             5.901      10.400         14.899    ***
4_FOUR   - 1_ONE             0.501       5.000          9.499    ***
3_THREE  - 1_ONE             0.101       4.600          9.099    ***
2_TWO    - 1_ONE            -3.599       0.900          5.399


         Dunnett's One-tailed T tests for variable: Y

NOTE: This tests controls the Type I experimentwise error for
      comparisons of all treatments against a control.

      Alpha= 0.05  Confidence= 0.95  df= 20  MSE= 7.20002
               Critical Value of Dunnett's T= 2.304
               Minimum Significant Difference= 3.9107

Comparisons significant at the 0.05 level are indicated by '***'.

                          Simultaneous              Simultaneous
                             Lower    Difference       Upper
                GROUP      Confidence   Between      Confidence
              Comparison     Limit      Means          Limit

5_FIVE   - 1_ONE             6.489      10.400         14.311    ***
4_FOUR   - 1_ONE             1.089       5.000          8.911    ***
3_THREE  - 1_ONE             0.689       4.600          8.511    ***
2_TWO    - 1_ONE            -3.011       0.900          4.811
```

Figure 3.7. SAS Output for Dunnett, Miller Data

(see Figure 3.7). Dunnett's one-tailed tests showed the same groups—
3, 4, and 5—as significantly different from the control group (1).

Peritz q

Even though the Peritz should be done using a computer program, it can be done by hand. It involves declaring as significant any comparison declared significant by Ryan, and declaring as nonsignificant any comparison declared nonsignificant by Newman-Keuls. Any comparison declared significant by Newman-Keuls and nonsignificant by Ryan is called *contentious*, and all of the comparisons in the complement must be examined. For the Miller data, the 5-4, 5-3, 5-2, 5-1, and 4-1 are Ryan and thus Peritz significant. Only the 3-1 is contentious; all others are nonsignificant. Since the Peritz *q* uses the range concept, the 3-1 is a range that contains three means (3, 2, 1), and its complement is the 5-4 range. Thus the 5-4 range must be examined to see if it is Ryan significant in order to decide if the 3-1 comparison is significant. Since the 5-4 is Ryan significant, then 3-1 is declared Peritz significant. Thus, for the Miller data, Peritz agrees with Newman-Keuls and declares 3-1 to be a significant difference.

Holm-Shaffer

Since the overall F is significant, the t for the largest comparison, 5-1, is compared with the Dunn critical value for $C = 6$ and $df_W = 20$. The observed t is 6.13 from Table 3.4 and the critical value is 2.927 from Table A.4 in Appendix A. Since the 5-1 comparison is significant, there are $C = 6$ pairwise null hypotheses that could be true in the means 1-4. So $t = 5.60$ for the next largest comparison, 5-2, is compared with the same critical value, 2.927, and is significant. The means 1-4 still could contain six pairwise null hypotheses, so the critical value is still 2.927 for the third largest comparison, 5-3. The $t = 3.42$ is significant. The fourth largest comparison, 5-1, uses the same critical value 2.927 and is significant, $t = 3.18$. Since the four means in 1-4 could still contain six pairwise null hypotheses, the fifth largest comparison, 4-1, uses the same critical value, 2.927. The $t = 2.95$ is significant. Now only the three means in 1-3 could be equal, yielding $C = 3$ pairwise potential null hypotheses, and a critical value of 2.613. The sixth largest comparison, 3-1, has $t = 2.71$ and is significant. At this point, the only potential null pairwise hypotheses would be 1-2 and 3-4, thus $C = 2$. The critical value is 2.423 and the seventh largest comparison, 4-2, has $t = 2.42$ and is not significant. Thus the significant differences using Holm-Shaffer are 5-4, 5-3, 5-2, 5-1, 4-1, and 3-1, in agreement with Peritz.

Fisher-Hayter

Since the overall F is significant, the Fisher-Hayter MCP proceeds to compare all t statistics to the $q/\sqrt{2}$ critical value with parameters $J - 1 = 4$ and $df_W = 20$ for the Miller data. Thus the critical value from Table A.3 in Appendix A is $3.96/\sqrt{2} = 2.80$. From Table 3.4, the significant differences using Fisher-Hayter are 5-4, 5-3, 5-2, 5-1, and 4-1. Thus, for the Miller data, the Peritz q and the Holm-Shaffer give the same results and the highest power of the MCPs considered.

Results of Research

While comparison of critical values gives the relative power of different methods, there are limitations on the information to be gained from this approach. First, some of the MCPs do not lend themselves to critical values comparisons. Notably, the Peritz, with its complex complement-checking logic, the Shaffer-Ryan, with its contingency on the significance of the overall ANOVA F test, and the Holm-Shaffer, with its data-dependent nature, are not easily compared. Also, any stepwise procedure is difficult to compare with methods that are not stepwise. Finally, comparison of critical values tells only the rank of the MCPs with respect to power; it does not give absolute power values or differences in power.

Use of the Miller data facilitates comparison of MCPs, but only for that data set. That is, the generalizations are limited to the Miller data or very similar data sets. Both comparison of critical values and use of specific data sets have limitations with respect to the information that can be gained from them. However, research on MCPs provides the needed information.

Research on statistics can be one of two types: analytical derivations or Monte Carlo simulations. In the area of multiple comparisons, simulations have prevailed. To compare the many MCPs in one analytical study would present mathematical nightmares, so the computer is used to simulate the behavior of MCPs. Most simulation studies use the one-way ANOVA design with varying number of groups, J, and varying number of observations per group, n, but with equal n.

Most simulation studies have all ANOVA assumptions met, and those that do not will be discussed in Chapter 4. The MCPs are compared with respect to control of α and power for varying degrees and types of differences in the population means. The actual MCPs that are re-searched usually differ, although almost all simulation studies are done for all possible pairwise comparisons. Since most authors do not agree on the names for some of the MCPs, the names that have been used in this text will continue to be used in the discussion of the fol-lowing articles. Anyone referencing an original article will need to get acquainted with the labeling for MCPs used in that article. Some MCPs discussed in the articles were not discussed in Chapter 2, but are included here to give an overall picture of the research. Finally, readers who are searching for the best MCP to use in a given situation may want to see the "bottom line" in this chapter's summary.

Petrinovich and Hardyck

Petrinovich and Hardyck (1969) compared MCPs due to Duncan,[2] Scheffé, Tukey, Tukey (b),[3] Newman-Keuls, two-independent sample *t* test, and the *usual t*. The number of groups varied from $J = 2$ to 10 and sample size varied from $n = 5$ to 50. Three types of mean config-urations were examined: equal means (overall null hypothesis), equally spaced, and multiple null hypotheses. The multiple null hypotheses were configured for $J = 5$ and 6. For five groups, the first two population means were equal, the third and fourth means were equal but 2.67σ above means 1 and 2, and the fifth mean was 2.67σ above means 3 and 4. For six groups, means 1 through 4 were equal, and means 5 and 6 were equal but 2.67σ above means 1 through 4. Type I and Type II error rates examined were ERPC, ERPF, and ERFW. One minus the Type II ERFW would give the rough equiva-lent of all-pairs power. One minus the Type II ERPC would give the rough equivalent of per-comparison power. In each condition, 1,000 replications were done.

Results for the equal means showed adequate control of ERPC at .05 for the two-independent sample *t* test, *usual t*, and Duncan, and conservative control for the other MCPs. Results for ERPF and ERFW showed Scheffé to have increasing conservatism as J in-creased; Tukey, Tukey (b), and Newman-Keuls to control α ade-quately; and the two *t* tests and Duncan to be liberal. The liberal nature of these last three tests increased as a function of J to the point of .731 (two-independent sample t test), .313 (*usual t*), and .353 (Duncan) for $J = 10$, $n = 5$, and $\alpha = .05$.

Converting Type II error rates into power, the results showed that Tukey had power of .26 for mean differences of .6 when $J = 3$ and $n = 30$. For larger mean differences, power increased, and for smaller sample sizes, very large mean differences were required to get adequate power for Tukey and the other MCPs. Petrinovich and Hardyck (1969) concluded that for n less than 10 "it scarcely seems worthwhile to carry out the computations for multiple comparisons" because of the low power to detect differences (p. 53). Of course, this conclusion is limited to the specific values of df, and is based on the power to detect all true differences, not any-pair power. Keselman and Toothaker (1973) pointed out that comparisons among means differ in value and that the power of Tukey and Scheffé for the largest comparison would be about the same as the power of the ANOVA. The power for the smallest comparison agreed closely with the power from Petrinovich and Hardyck.

Results for the mean configurations with multiple null hypotheses showed Newman-Keuls to have Type I error rates using ERFW that were very similar to those of Duncan and approximately the number of null hypotheses times α, or 2α. Petrinovich and Hardyck declared as unsuitable Duncan, both types of t tests, and Newman-Keuls because of excessive Type I error rates using ERFW, and recommended Tukey and Scheffé.

Carmer and Swanson

Carmer and Swanson (1973) presented an evaluation of 10 MCPs for pairwise comparisons: *usual t*, Tukey, Newman-Keuls, Duncan, Scheffé, three versions of the Fisher's LSD that differed with respect to the α for the overall F test (.01, .05, and .10), a Bayesian test due to Duncan, and a second Bayesian test due to Duncan and Waller. The number of groups ranged from $J = 5$ to 20, and the sample size was $n = 3$, 4, 6, or 8. A large number of mean configurations were examined, including equal means (overall null hypothesis), multiple null hypotheses, partial null hypotheses, and equally spaced means. Type I errors were examined using ERPC and ERFW. Power was examined using per-comparison power. For each condition, 1,000 replications were run.

Results for the equal means using ERPC showed the *usual t* giving α of about .05 with all other MCPs giving conservative α. Using

ERFW showed α of .256 ($J = 5$), .584 ($J = 10$), and .895 ($J = 20$) for *usual t*; .182 ($J = 5$), .373 ($J = 10$), and .626 ($J = 20$) for Duncan; with the Bayesian methods giving .150 to .187 (relatively constant with respect to J). The LSD methods controlled α at the level of the overall F, .01, .05, or .10, and Tukey and Newman-Keuls controlled α close to .05. Only Scheffé was conservative, and this conservatism increased as J increased. This result would be expected for pairwise comparisons for Scheffé since all possible pairwise comparisons represent an increasingly smaller proportion of the total possible comparisons as J increases.

When the mean configurations that had multiple null hypotheses or a partial null hypothesis were examined using ERFW, only Tukey and Scheffé gave values not exceeding .05. Newman-Keuls yielded values that were as high as .11. The other methods gave values that were as high as .585, and varied largely as a function of the number of multiple null hypotheses and the number of comparisons that had true differences of zero.

Given the wide differences in control of α, the power results are neither surprising nor interesting. Any method that controls α using ERPC but not using ERFW will automatically be more powerful than another method that controls α using ERFW if they both use .05 as the nominal value. When MCPs differ widely in α control, comparison of power is generally not recommended. Carmer and Swanson recommended use of the LSD with α = .05 or one of the Bayesian methods, but they based that recommendation on power with only coarse consideration of control of α. The major problem with either of their recommended methods is that the ERFW is not known and can be very high. If a researcher wants high power at the expense of high α, then a better recommendation would be to use one of the methods that controls α using ERFW, but choose α to be, say, .25, or some other high value. Then the researcher gets high power with *known* high α.

Einot and Gabriel

Einot and Gabriel (1975) examined MCPs using the statistics q and an augmented F ratio (SS_B/MS_W) for methods due to Newman-Keuls, a modified Duncan method, simultaneous test procedures (STPs) based on Tukey and Scheffé, an early version of Ryan without the modification due to Welsch, and the Peritz. The modification to

Duncan gives it control of α using ERFW, making it comparable to Ryan in this regard. However, this modified Duncan always gave less power than Ryan when both are used in a similar manner with respect to α control. The number of groups was $J = 3$, 4, and 5, and the sample size was $n = 9$. A large number of mean configurations were used, including equal means (overall null hypothesis), partial null hypotheses, multiple null hypotheses, and equally spaced means. Power was examined using per-pair power for different subset of the means. For each condition, 1,000 replications were run.

Results for the Newman-Keuls showed an α of about .05 for each set of equal means, and thus too large an overall α for the experiment. All other MCPs controlled α.

Power differences were slight (.04 to .06) for the MCPs using the q statistic, but more substantial (.15 to .22) for the MCPs using the (augmented) F. Some of these latter differences may have been due to the conservative nature of the F STP, which is essentially Scheffé. Einot and Gabriel recommended the range STP (Tukey) over the Ryan because of simplicity. If the researcher desires to use an F statistic, then the Ryan is recommended. In the case that confidence intervals are required, then the Tukey or Scheffé are recommended. Finally, the modified Duncan showed adequate α control, but lower power than Ryan. Previous research has shown that the Duncan MCP (without the modification) does not control α and thus has high power at the expense of high Type I error rate.

Ramsey

Ramsey (1978a, 1981) did two studies on the power of MCPs in which he also defined any-pair and all-pairs power. In the first, Ramsey (1978a) studied the MCPs in two groups. The first group used the q statistic: Newman-Keuls, Tukey, Ryan (plus an earlier version of Ryan without the modification due to Einot and Gabriel), and Peritz. The second group used the F statistic: Ryan (plus the earlier version without the Einot and Gabriel modification) and Peritz. Number of groups was $J = 3$, 4, 5, and 6, with respective equal sample sizes of $n = 21$, 16, 13, and 11, so as to give $df_W = 60$ for all conditions. Means were configured in three ways: equally spaced means, maximum range means, and minimum range means (see Chapter 1). Each mean configuration was examined for several different effect sizes.[4] In each condition, 1,000 replications were done. Type I error rate was examined using ERFW for the minimum range configuration that would give the multiple null hypothesis situation with two groups of equal means. Power was examined using any-pair and all-pairs power as defined in Chapter 1.

The Newman-Keuls method had empirical α values as large as .117 when α ERFW was set at .05, with the empirical α generally increasing as a function of effect size. That is, as the difference between the two sets of means increased, the chance of false rejections within the sets increased. Newman-Keuls was expected to give α values of about twice .05 since there were two null hypotheses within the minimum range configuration. All of the other MCPs gave good control of α, even though Tukey was slightly conservative, with values from .016 to .029.

Any-pair power results revealed that there were only slight differences in power for the MCPs in this study. Methods based on the F statistic (Ryan and Peritz) were more powerful in the minimum range conditions, and those based on the q statistic were more powerful in the maximum range conditions.

All-pairs power results showed that the Peritz methods and the Ryan F gave superior power, especially compared with Tukey. The most dramatic differences (up to .52) were for equally spaced means, but were substantial in all mean configurations. Effect sizes for large power (about .90) ranged from .6 for minimum range means with $J = 3$ ($n = 21$), up to 3.3 for equally spaced means with $J = 6$ ($n = 11$). To obtain large all-pairs power, the researcher would need large n or large effect size (large true differences in the population means).

In the second study by Ramsey (1981), the MCPs studied were also in two groups. The first group used the q statistic: Tukey, Ryan, Welsch step-up (see note 6 in Chapter 2), Peritz, Newman-Keuls, and Shaffer-Ryan. The second group used the F statistic: Ryan, Peritz, Newman-Keuls, and a model-testing approach introduced by Ramsey. The number of groups was $J = 4$ and $J = 6$, with equal sample sizes of $n = 5, 6,$ or 7. Means were configured four ways: equally spaced means, equally spaced null pairs ($\mu_1 = \mu_2$, $\mu_3 = \mu_4$, and so on), maximum range means, and minimum range means. Each mean configuration was examined for several different effect sizes. In each condition, 1,000 replications were done. Type I error rate was examined using ERFW for the equally spaced null pairs of means. Power was examined using any-pair and all-pairs power as in Ramsey (1978a).

Only the two Newman-Keuls methods exceeded $\alpha = .05$ using ERFW. For $J = 6$, $n = 5$, the empirical Type I error rate for both Newman-Keuls methods ranged from .132 to .153. All of the other MCPs in the study gave adequate control of α, although Tukey was somewhat conservative, with values from .015 to .022. Since this is a multiple null case with three sets of equal pairs of means, the Newman-Keuls would be expected to give values of α up to .15. Note that the differences between the equal pairs of means was quite large, with effect sizes ranging from 2.2 to 3.0.

For any-pair power, effect sizes of up to .7 gave power for the overall ANOVA F of up to .83, depending upon J and n. Only the Shaffer-Ryan MCP gave any-pair power that was always comparable to that of the ANOVA. For the MCPs using the q statistic, the Tukey, Ryan, and Peritz were always close in power, never differing by more than .002. These three were usually fairly close to the Welsch (largest difference was .018) and had an advantage over Shaffer-Ryan for the maximum range means of up to .032, but a disadvantage relative to Shaffer-Ryan for the minimum range means of up to .107. The MCPs using the F statistic only rarely gave any-pair power higher than all the other procedures.

For all-pairs power, effect sizes of up to 2.4 were required to give power values up to .723, with the largest effect sizes needed for equally spaced means. Tukey had the lowest power of all the methods, with differences up to about .35 compared with the most powerful of the other MCPs. Ryan (q and F statistics), Welsch, and Shaffer-Ryan gave similar intermediate all-pairs power values. The Peritz (q and F statistics) and the model-testing approach gave the best power, with differences up to about .18 over the intermediate group.

A desire to have good all-pairs power and use of computer analysis would lead to selection of one of the Peritz procedures or Ramsey's model-testing procedure. One final note for the researcher to remember is that either large effect size or large sample size is necessary before all-pairs power is appreciable.

For researchers who do not know the population mean configuration and are selecting a good general procedure based on any-pair power, Ramsey's recommendation after the second study is the Shaffer-Ryan MCP. However, the MCPs in these studies did not differ much with regard to any-pair power. The researcher should remember that any-pair power is very similar to the power of the overall ANOVA.

Martin, Toothaker, and Nixon

Martin, Toothaker, and Nixon (1989) examined the two-independent sample *t* test, LSD, Tukey, Scheffé, Dunn, Dunn-Šidák, a test due to Hochberg called GT2 (see the section on unequal sample sizes in Chapter 4; also see Hochberg, 1974), Newman-Keuls *q*, Duncan *q* and *F*, modified Duncan *q* and *F* (see coverage in the section on Einot and Gabriel, above), Ryan *q*, Peritz *q*, Shaffer-Ryan, a version of Peritz using the Shaffer modification and called Shaffer-Peritz, Welsch step-up, Newman-Keuls *F*, Ryan *F*, and Peritz *F*. The number of groups was $J = 6$, with sample size of $n = 11$. Mean configurations were equal means (overall null hypothesis), minimum range means, maximum range means, and equally spaced means. For each condition, 10,000 replications were run. Type I error rate was examined using ERFW. Power was examined using any-pair power, all-pairs power, and per-pair power for mean differences that would give power of about .85 for the overall ANOVA *F* test.

Results for the Type I error rates showed large empirical estimates of α for the *t* test, Duncan *q* and *F*, Newman-Keuls *q* and *F*, and LSD, consistent with prior research. Also, Scheffé showed the conservatism found in previous research. The remaining methods gave empirical values of α that were either very close to .05 or slightly conservative depending upon mean configuration. For example, Ryan *q* gave values of .0508, .0491, and .0329 for equal means, minimum range means, and maximum range means, respectively. Shaffer-Ryan gave values of .0428, .0491, and .0331, and Peritz *F* gave .0370, .0505, and .0342, for equal means, minimum range means, and maximum range means, respectively.

Results for power for those methods that did not yield excessive α showed no method having all-pairs power larger than .04. The mean differences that gave power of .85 for the overall ANOVA were not sufficiently large to give adequate all-pairs power. Per-pair power, which is an average power across all comparisons, showed nine MCPs in a cluster separate from Tukey in tenth place, and a cluster of four with lower power. Shaffer-Peritz with .3219 had the highest power for the minimum range means. The next eight MCPs in order are Peritz *q* and *F*, Shaffer-Ryan, Welsch, Ryan *q* and *F*, and modified Duncan *q* and *F*; power for the last method was .2844. Tukey gave .2653 and Dunn, Dunn-Šidák, and Hochberg were from .2306 to .2359, with Scheffé at .1375. The maximum range means showed the same nine MCPs with power of .2673 or better, Tukey at .2541, and the remaining four even lower. The largest difference between the best MCP and Tukey is .0566. Equally spaced means gave the highest power of .1862 for Shaffer-Peritz down to .1554 for Tukey, a difference of .0308.

Any-pair power also showed similar results for many of the MCPs. For minimum range means, Shaffer-Ryan and Shaffer-Peritz had a value of .7865, then a middle group of eight methods including Tukey with .7512 (low of .7437 in this group). Hochberg, Dunn-Šidák, and Dunn form the next cluster from .7110 to .7023, and Scheffé had .5193. Here the difference between Tukey and the best method is .0353, and Tukey is tied with the q statistics of Ryan, Peritz, and modified Duncan. For maximum range means, the order of MCPs changed somewhat: The lowest in terms of power was still Scheffé (.7181), but the next cluster of low-power MCPs included the F statistics for modified Duncan, Ryan, and Peritz (.8192 to .8300). The remaining top ten ranged from .8386 for Dunn to .8684 for the q statistics of modified Duncan, Ryan, and Peritz, with Tukey at .8683. Here the Tukey has only negligibly the second highest power, and less than .03 separates the best and tenth best. Any-pair power results for equally spaced means return to the more familiar pattern of a top cluster of nine MCPs ranging down from .8202 for Shaffer-Ryan and Shaffer-Peritz to .7982 for Ryan F. Tukey had .8075, only .0127 from the best method. Modified Duncan F joins Dunn, Dunn-Šidák, and Hochberg (.7778 to .7684) in a cluster with lower power, and Scheffé has .6101.

Summary

Considerable detail has been given in each of the preceding reviews to show that many of the MCPs considered in this book are very similar with respect to some types of power for all possible pairwise comparisons. Large differences show up only when all-pairs power is considered. A choice from MCPs in this text based completely on good showing across all types of power would lean toward Shaffer-Ryan and Peritz q, not in any particular order. The Holm-Shaffer and Fisher-Hayter MCPs have not been evaluated in comparative power studies, but might be competitive with this top group.

If the researcher is convinced that all-pairs power is important and the research project has the sample sizes or mean differences necessary to give high all-pairs power, then Peritz F would be the best choice. Other alternatives would be Peritz q, Ryan F, and Shaffer-Ryan.

Minimum range configurations in the means would favor Shaffer-Ryan and Peritz F, maximum range mean patterns favor Ryan q and Peritz q, and equally spaced means show highest any-pair power for Shaffer-Ryan.

If availability in commercial statistical packages is important, Ryan q would be the best choice and would lose at most .11 for any-pair power and slightly more than .01 for per-pair power compared with the best of the most powerful MCPs. In some cases, Ryan q would have better power. If use of an F statistic is important in addition to commercial statistical package availability, then select Ryan F. Peritz F is not currently available in commercial computer packages.

If importance is placed on simplicity, confidence interval computation, or using widely available tables to do the MCP by hand computation, then Tukey would be recommended. Loss of power would be at most .11 for any-pair power and at most .06 for per-pair power compared with the best of the most powerful MCPs. Some classroom applications would dictate use of Tukey due to time constraints. The Fisher-Hayter MCP has all of these characteristics except confidence interval computation, and should be more powerful than the Tukey.

Of course, if the research does not demand all possible pairwise comparisons, or does demand some comparisons that are not pairwise but the more general type of comparison, then the researcher must compare critical values to decide which MCP is most powerful for his or her particular situation. It is very likely that Dunn or Dunn-Šidák has applicability in situations where comparisons are planned but are not all possible pairwise comparisons. For the more general comparisons, Scheffé also can be useful to the researcher.

The "bottom line" choice of MCP for the "average" researcher who does all possible pairwise comparisons, who has equal sample sizes, who has access to computer packages, and who wants good power would be the Ryan q.

Finally, all of the above results have been obtained with equal sample sizes and all of the ANOVA assumptions met. If any of the assumptions of normality, equal variances, or independence have been violated, or if unequal sample sizes are present, then these recommendations may not hold. Chapter 4 deals with these issues.

Notes

1. For example, C could be chosen to be a large value and type of comparison could be the more general comparisons. Then only Dunn, Dunn-Šidák, and Scheffé would be appropriate to compare because the other MCPs are used only for pairwise comparisons. Such comparing of critical values was done in Chapter 2 at the time these methods were introduced.

2. The MCP due to Duncan (1955) is not included in this book because, in its unmodified form, it does not control α using ERFW, nor has it been used to develop another, acceptable, MCP.

3. Tukey (b) is an MCP that uses the average of the critical values from the Tukey and Newman-Keuls MCPs.

4. *Effect size* is generally used to indicate some function of differences in means divided by a standard deviation. Here it is used as a function of the noncentrality parameter for the ANOVA and is symbolized as f where

$$f = \frac{\varphi}{\sqrt{n}} = \frac{\sqrt{(n \sum_{j=1}^{J} \alpha_j^2)/J\sigma^2}}{\sqrt{n}}$$

Cohen (1969) gives effect sizes of 0.1, 0.5, and 0.8 as small, medium, and large, respectively.

4 Violations of Assumptions and Robustness

When multiple comparisons are first introduced, it is natural to consider them as extensions of the ANOVA. As such, it is also natural to base that consideration on the same assumptions as are made for the ANOVA. Of course, the real-world applications of both ANOVA and MCPs do not exactly meet all of these assumptions. That is, it is a very rare case when the actual data from a research project come from normal populations with equal variances and independent observations.[1]

When an assumption of a statistic is not met, that assumption is said to be violated. Statisticians are concerned with the performance of the statistic in the presence of violations of the assumptions. The quality of the statistic when an assumption is violated is called the *robustness* of the test. Generally, a statistic is said to be robust to violation of one of its assumptions if the sampling distribution of the statistic is well fit by the theoretical distribution when the assumption is not met. More specifically, for any assumption violation, robustness can be investigated by examining the fit of the theoretical distribution to the sampling distribution given either H_0 or H_1. Certain areas, or probabilities, of the sampling distribution are examined to check for robustness. When an assumption is violated under H_0, the statistic is considered robust to violation of that assumption if α_{true} is approximately equal to α_{set}. A statistic is considered robust with respect to power when an assumption is violated and power is still comparable to power if the assumption is met. Power robustness can also

93

take the form of seeing which of two competitive methods is more powerful when the assumption is violated. Each statistic must be examined for each assumption to answer the question of robustness of the statistic.

Of the three ANOVA assumptions, the least likely to be met is normality. Very few of the dependent variables used by applied researchers have normal distributions in the population. In fact, most researchers are not sure of the shape of the distribution, or have not actually given the idea much thought. But if they are asked, most will admit that they do not think the population distribution will be normal in shape. Also, the shape of the distribution of the sample data is not much help. Except for extremely large sample sizes, the distribution of the sample data is not a good indicator of the shape of the population. Very nonnormal distributions of sample data can be obtained from normal populations with small to moderate sample sizes. Because of this, a natural next question to ask is, How do MCPs perform if the normality assumption is not met? This question, and one like it for each of the other assumptions, is at the heart of the issue of violations of assumptions and the robustness of MCPs.

The next least likely of the three assumptions to be met is equal population variances. Most treatments that are designed to accomplish change in some measure of central tendency also change variability, and they likely do not change variability in the same way or to the same degree. Even though the sample variances give some picture of the population variances, they are statistics and contain sampling variability as well as true variance differences. So the differences that are present in the sample variances may or may not indicate assumption violation. Then the question is, How do MCPs perform if the equal variance assumption is not met? In the presence of unequal variances, can the MCPs presented in this text still be used?

The most likely assumption to be met is independence. Careful experimental procedures, including randomization of subjects to groups, will likely assure independence of observations. If independence is not met, two points need to be made. First, violations of the independence assumption are usually obvious. For example, subjects worked together in groups, but the dependent variable was an individual score for each subject. Or a study was made of cheating behavior. Or each subject was measured twice. Any process that results in dependent or related scores will give data that violate the independence assumption. Second, if independence is violated for the one-way ANOVA, the effect on α_{true} is dramatic. Research has shown that either the true α is very much larger than the set α, such as $\alpha_{set} = .05$ and $\alpha_{true} = .45$, or it is very much smaller, such as $\alpha_{true} = .001$. The ANOVA F test is not robust to violation of the independence assumption, and MCPs will fit the same pattern. Thus, if the researcher is careful to include randomization of subjects to groups and to avoid obvious dependence in the data, the independence assumption of the MCPs will be met.

In the following sections MCPs will be considered for the one-way ANOVA situation with unequal sample sizes, with unequal variances, and with nonnormal distributions.

Unequal Sample Sizes

When a researcher has unequal sample sizes in a one-way design, it is often referred to as an *unbalanced* design. Exact MCPs for this case are difficult to use because of numerical computation problems except when the number of groups is small (see Hochberg & Tamhane, 1987, p. 91). Because of these computational difficulties, modifications to existing procedures have been proposed and investigated. The first of these is called the *Tukey-Kramer* procedure.

Tukey-Kramer

Originally proposed by Tukey (1953) and later proposed independently by Kramer (1956, 1957), this procedure is a modification to the Tukey method. Since the Tukey method uses the t statistic with a common sample size, n, the t statistic must be modified if it is to be used when sample sizes are not equal. The Tukey-Kramer formula for t is given as

$$t_{\hat{\psi}} = \frac{\hat{\psi} - \psi}{\sqrt{MS_W\left(\frac{1}{n_j} + \frac{1}{n_k}\right)}} \tag{4.1}$$

where MS_W is the mean square within from the whole design, but the n_j and n_k are the sample sizes for only the two groups whose means are in the comparison. The Tukey-Kramer procedure follows a decision rule, using the above modified statistic, which is exactly like that for the Tukey: Reject H_0 if

$$|t_{\hat{\psi}}| \geq \frac{q^{\alpha}_{J, \, df_w}}{\sqrt{2}} \qquad (4.2)$$

and otherwise fail to reject H_0. Critical values of q are obtained from Table A.3 in Appendix A in the same manner as for Tukey. The Tukey-Kramer is simple and maintains control of α using ERFW, and is generally recommended when sample sizes are unequal. However, Tukey-Kramer is not robust to unequal variances (Keselman & Rogan, 1978), yielding liberal α when sample sizes and population variances are inversely paired. Thus it can be recommended only for the unlikely situation in which the researcher is absolutely sure that the population variances are equal.

Miller-Winer

A second modification to the Tukey procedure when sample sizes are unequal was suggested by Miller (1981, p. 43, and in the original 1966 source) and Winer (1971, p. 216, and in the original 1962 source). Miller suggested using the usual equation for Tukey "with an average or median value of n" substituted for n as "preferable to chucking out observations to bring all samples down to the same common size." Winer said that if the sample sizes are not markedly different, then "the harmonic mean of the ns may be used instead of n" in the usual equation for Tukey. That is, compute the harmonic mean of the unequal ns as

$$\tilde{n} = \frac{J}{1/n_1 + 1/n_2 + \ldots + 1/n_J} = \frac{J}{\displaystyle\sum_{j=1}^{J} 1/n_j} \qquad (4.3)$$

and substitute it for n in Equation 1.19 (Chapter 1), then follow the decision rule as given for the Tukey in Chapter 2. Even though the Miller-Winer has intuitive appeal, it has been shown to be liberal with respect to α (see Hochberg & Tamhane, 1987, p. 94; see also Dunnett, 1980a). Also, Miller-Winer is not robust to unequal variances (see Howell & Games, 1973; Keselman, Toothaker, & Shooter, 1975). Thus it is recommended that it not be used; it is presented here only because it has been popular among applied researchers.

Hochberg GT2

Hochberg (1974) proposed a method that would refer the t statistic with the unequal ns (Equation 4.1) to a critical value from the distribution of the Studentized maximum modulus.[2] The decision rule is to reject H_0 if

$$| t_{\hat{\psi}} | \geq | M |_{J^*, df_w}^{\alpha} \qquad (4.4)$$

and otherwise fail to reject. $|M|$ is the α-level critical value from the distribution of the Studentized maximum modulus that has parameters $J^* = J(J - 1)/2$ and df_w. Table A.7 in Appendix A gives critical values for the distribution of the Studentized maximum modulus. Dunnett (1980a) has shown that the Hochberg GT2 is conservative with respect to α when variances are equal. This conservatism would make the Tukey-Kramer the more preferred statistic of the two if sample sizes are unequal in the presence of equal variances. Finally, Tamhane (1979) showed that GT2 is not robust to unequal variances when combined with unequal sample sizes.

When sample sizes are unequal, most of the MCPs presented in Chapter 2 cannot be used without modification. The three methods introduced in this section were designed to be used with unequal sample sizes, but are appropriate only if the population variances are equal. Most researchers do not know if the population variances are equal or unequal for the groups in their studies. Thus the typical state of affairs for most applied researchers is that they would have to allow for the possibility of unequal variances. This means that they should consider only statistics that also make this allowance. Simply restated, they should select statistics that are robust to unequal variances.

Given that none of the methods in this section is robust to unequal variances, none can be recommended for use unless the researcher strongly believes that the population variances are equal. Evidence for such belief should include approximately equal sample variances and evidence that the sample variances have been similar in previous studies in the research area. Otherwise, when sample sizes are unequal, applied researchers should use one of the MCPs in the next section.

Unequal Population Variances

Since violation of the equal variance assumption is likely to occur in many applied research settings, researchers need MCPs that are robust to unequal population variances. Two approaches have been taken to this problem: The first is to develop new MCPs that do not depend upon equal variances, and the second is to examine the existing MCPs to see if they are robust to unequal variances. These two approaches have to be considered in the context of the equality or inequality of the sample sizes of the groups.

Most of the special MCPs that have been proposed for the unequal variance case (see Keselman, Games, & Rogan, 1979; Tamhane, 1979) also contain unequal sample sizes in the formulas. Research on these MCPs for all possible pairwise comparisons has narrowed the field to three acceptable procedures: the GH procedure, the C procedure, and the T3 procedure.

The GH Procedure

Games and Howell (1976) proposed a solution similar to the Welch (1949) approximate solution to the Behrens-Fisher problem. Named GH by researchers since Games and Howell, this MCP uses the statistic

$$t_{jk} = \frac{\overline{Y}_j - \overline{Y}_k}{\sqrt{s_j^2/n_j + s_k^2/n_k}} \tag{4.5}$$

for each pair of means $j \neq k$. The decision is to reject H_0 if

$$|t_{jk}| \geq \frac{q_{J, df_{jk}}^{\alpha}}{\sqrt{2}} \tag{4.6}$$

and otherwise fail to reject, where

$$df_{jk} = \frac{(s_j^2/n_j + s_k^2/n_k)^2}{[(s_j^2/n_j)^2/(n_j - 1)] + [(s_k^2/n_k)^2/(n_k - 1)]} \tag{4.7}$$

Thus the researcher uses an α-level critical value from the Studentized range in Table A.3 in Appendix A with parameters J and df_{jk} as given in Equation 4.7. A practical suggestion is to round df_{jk} to the nearest whole number to use as the df for the q critical value of the Studentized range in Table A.3.

The C Procedure

Dunnett (1980b) suggested the use of an alternative critical value with the same t statistic as given in Equation 4.5. The decision is to reject H_0 if

$$
|t_{jk}| \geq \frac{q_{J,n_j-1}^{\alpha}(s_j^2/n_j) + q_{K,n_k-1}^{\alpha}(s_k^2/n_k)}{\sqrt{2}\,(s_j^2/n_j + s_k^2/n_k)} \tag{4.8}
$$

and otherwise fail to reject. Basically, for each comparison of the means of two samples, the researcher finds two q critical values, each based on df from each sample, and uses these and the two sample variances and sample sizes to compute the critical value. Note that the critical value corresponds to Cochran's (1964) approximate solution to the Behrens-Fisher problem, and thus the C procedure would be predicted to be conservative.

The T3 Procedure

Dunnett (1980b) proposed a modification to a procedure called T2 by Tamhane (1979), and called it the T3 procedure. It uses the same t statistic as given in Equation 4.5, and gives a decision to reject H_0 if

$$
|t_{jk}| \geq |M|_{J^*,\mathrm{df}_{jk}}^{\alpha} \tag{4.9}
$$

and otherwise fail to reject. $|M|$ is the α-level critical value from the distribution of the Studentized maximum modulus (Table A.7, Appendix A) with parameters $J^* = J(J-1)/2$ and df_{jk} as given in Equation 4.7.

Tamhane (1979) and Dunnett (1980b) presented comprehensive simulation studies of MCPs for the unequal variance case, for both equal and unequal sample sizes. Tamhane showed that the GH procedure occasionally gave liberal α values, as high as .084 for $J = 8$ when sample sizes were unequal (7, 7, 9, 9, 11, 11, 13, 13) and variances were equal. Otherwise, the largest empirical α was .065. Dunnett noted this same phenomenon of liberal α for large J with equal variances, but also noted that GH became slightly conservative as variances became increasingly divergent.

For the C procedure, Dunnett (1980b) found that it is basically conservative and tended toward GH as df approached infinity. It will give tighter α control but lower power compared with GH.

Dunnett (1980b) found that the T3 procedure too is basically conservative. When df are large or moderately large, the C procedure is preferred over the T3 procedure on the basis of better power. For small df, T3 will be more powerful than the C procedure. The breaking point between small and large df for the purpose of choosing between C and T3 depends somewhat on the ratio of variances: For equal or close-to-equal variances, large is defined as df $\geq$ 220 for $J = 4$ and df $\geq$ 440 for $J = 8$. For a variance ratio of 10, large is defined as df $\geq$ 52 for $J = 4$ and df $\geq$ 56 for $J = 8$.

Given that GH is only rarely liberal when variances are unequal, and then by only a small amount, and that GH is always more powerful than the C and T3 procedures, GH would be recommended for most applied researchers. Only if it were crucial to maintain strict α control would a researcher choose C or T3, and then the choice between these two depends upon the df and severity of the inequality of the variances.

Example

As an example, consider the depression research with the completer sample of 155 patients with scores on the Hamilton Rating Scale for Depression (HRSD). This is the same outcome measure as used for the end-point 239 sample in the equal sample size example in Chapter 1. The completer sample ended up with 37 patients in CBT, 47 in IPT, 37 in IMI, and 34 in PLA with scores on HRSD. Simulated data are given in Table 4.1, along with the means and variances for each of the four groups.

All of the procedures, GH, C, and T3, use the t_{jk} statistic as given in Equation 4.5. The values of t_{jk} and df_{jk} for the HRSD data are given in Table 4.2. Critical values for GH, C, and T3 are computed for the HRSD data in Table 4.3. There are no significant differences among the means of the four groups with any of the methods, but note that for this data set, GH would be the most powerful, C the next most powerful, and T3 the least powerful. Also note that the critical values of the three methods are very close.

TABLE 4.1 Depression Data, HRSD, Completer Sample

CBT (n = 37)					IPT (n = 47)					IMI (n = 37)					PLA (n = 34)				
3	2	5	3	13	4	4	3	13	2	9	9	3	4	2	8	2	7	17	8
3	11	7	5	19	6	3	13	5	3	4	3	2	1	8	4	15	6	8	7
3	4	2	19	9	9	2	6	3	2	3	2	8	20	3	4	7	2	8	19
3	5	1	2	6	1	5	19	16	4	1	5	2	2	8	4	19	2	1	9
5	5	16	4	9	15	2	13	3	13	2	6	3	8	9	12	1	16	11	17
6	15	18	5	2	13	4	1	17	9	4	9	3	2	20	18	2	9	7	8
13	11	7	1	3	5	2	6	1	23	5	9	13	17	15	6	8	20	7	
16	20				5	18	5	2	3	20	15								
					1	4	4	14	2										
					3	13													

| 7.59 (5.81) | | | | | 6.89 (5.80) | | | | | 7.00 (5.71) | | | | | 8.79 (5.69) | | | | |

TABLE 4.2   Values of t_{jk} (and df_{jk}) for HRSD Completer Sample Data

Mean	IPT	IMI	PLA
CBT	0.5486	0.4406	0.8788
	(77.37)	(71.98)	(68.71)
IPT		0.0870	1.4712
		(77.97)	(72.05)
IMI			1.3220
			(68.54)

Research on Other MCPs

The second approach to unequal variances is to examine the performance of the MCPs presented in Chapter 2 when variances are unequal. Most of those methods use equal sample sizes, so primary attention will be given to their robustness to unequal variances when sample sizes are equal. However, when information is available concerning robustness to unequal variances when sample sizes are unequal, it will be discussed.

Petrinovich and Hardyck (1969) combined unequal sample sizes and unequal variances in a simulation study on MCPs that included Tukey and Scheffé. Although they did not indicate what modification was made on Tukey for the unequal ns, they did report findings consistent with the effect of unequal variances on the overall ANOVA F test (Box, 1954). If the sample sizes and variances are directly paired (or positively related, with the smallest variance paired with the smallest sample size, and so on), then the tests are conservative, giving $\alpha_{true} \leq \alpha_{set}$. If the sample sizes and variances are inversely paired (or negatively related, with the smallest variance paired with the largest sample size and vice versa), then the tests are liberal, giving $\alpha_{true} \geq \alpha_{set}$.

Keselman and Toothaker (1974) found that unequal variances in a ratio of 1:4 had little effect on α if sample sizes were equal for Tukey (for all possible pairwise comparisons) and Scheffé (for all possible general and pairwise comparisons) procedures. They also observed the expected results of conservatism when unequal ns and variances were positively related, and of liberality when unequal ns and variances were negatively related. The Miller-Winer harmonic mean of the sample sizes was used for Tukey when the ns were unequal.

TABLE 4.3 Critical Values for GH, C, and T3

Mean	IPT	IMI	PLA
CBT			
GH	2.626	2.630	2.633
C	2.682	2.694	2.701
TC3	2.694	2.700	2.704
IPT			
GH		2.625	2.630
C		2.682	2.689
TC3		2.692	2.700
IMI			
GH			2.633
C			2.701
TC3			2.704

Keselman et al. (1975) showed that for equal ns and unequal variances, Tukey had a slightly liberal α (.0615 compared with .05). Several variance patterns were used that had up to 1:4 ratios of smallest to largest variance for $J = 4$. These findings are also consistent with Box (1954).

Martin et al. (1989) investigated the effect of unequal variances on a large number of MCPs with equal sample sizes. Several variance patterns were examined, with the ratio of variances ranging from 1:2.5 to 1:47.8. Results were tabulated over 156 mean/variance/distribution configurations to give the average empirical α using ERFW, the maximum, the percentage less than .05, the percentage less than .06, and the percentage less than .075. These last two values were chosen because other authors had mentioned them as standards for determining robustness of statistics (see Bradley, 1978; Cochran, 1954; Ramsey, 1980). Table 4.4 shows these results for the MCPs covered in Chapter 2.

If a researcher is seeking a maximum α of .06, then the choice is limited to one of the procedures that is generally conservative (see the average Type I error rate). That is, Dunn, Dunn-Šidák, and Scheffé offer very strict control of α (about 100% of the cases had empirical α below .06) by being conservative procedures, not because they are robust. Since α is generally low, the effect of unequal variances on α is such that it is not elevated beyond .06. Of course, use of one of the more powerful MCPs, such as the Peritz q, with a more

TABLE 4.4 Type I Error Rates

MCP	Average	Maximum	% < .05	% < .06	% < .075
Dunn	.0311	.0609	85.26	99.36	100.00
Dunn-Šidák	.0319	.0620	83.33	99.36	100.00
Tukey	.0403	.0740	72.44	79.49	100.00
Ryan (q)	.0517	.0773	36.54	66.67	98.08
Scheffé	.0127	.0350	100.00	100.00	100.00
Ryan (F)	.0481	.0849	50.64	82.69	95.51
Shaffer	.0494	.0779	39.74	85.26	98.08
Peritz (q)	.0545	.0870	35.90	62.18	94.87
Peritz (F)	.0506	.0852	47.44	76.28	94.87

stringent α, say .01, will also give very strict control of α, due to conservatism. Selecting Dunn, Dunn-Šidák, or Scheffé and using $\alpha = .05$ will only rarely give a true α larger than .06, but at the expense of power.

If a researcher is willing to adopt .075 as a standard, then Tukey enters the picture with 100% below .075 (.074 maximum). Shaffer (98.08% and .0779 maximum) and Ryan q (98.08% and .0773 maximum) also have good performance at this standard. Ranking these three MCPs with respect to their percentage below .06 also is helpful: Shaffer (85.26%), Tukey (79.49%), and Ryan q (66.67%). Paradoxically, even though Shaffer has the highest maximum of these three, it has the greatest percentage below .06.

Finally, Ryan F and the Peritz methods all have maximums of .0849 to .0870, even though the percentage below .075 is no worse than 94.87%. These procedures would not be bad choices for a researcher willing to tolerate a .075 standard for α.

Overall, when ns are equal, the effect of unequal variances on the above list of MCPs is not severe. A researcher could choose any one of the methods and use it with little consequence of unequal variances if a .075 standard were adopted. A standard closer to .05 would lead to a narrowing of choices as discussed above. Two notes of caution: First, these results are for equal ns; second, these results are for all of the possible pairwise comparisons. Doing fewer than all possible pairwise comparisons might make one of the conservative procedures more attractive in terms of power. Also, the impact of unequal variances might be higher or lower on specific comparisons than what is shown here for the set of all possible comparisons.

Games and Howell (1976) investigated three MCPs when *n*s were equal and unequal and when variances were equal and unequal. The first of these procedures was the Tukey-Kramer, the second was the GH, and the third was a *t* test with sample variances of the two groups being compared but that used a $q/\sqrt{2}$ critical value with df = $n_j + n_k -$ 2. Only the GH procedure maintained α using ERFW close to .05 for all variance and sample size combinations. The other two procedures were liberal or conservative similar to results for the overall ANOVA *F*. GH had a maximum empirical α of .071 for the case of equal variances but unequal sample sizes (*J* = 4, and *n*s of 6, 10, 14, 16) and .065 or lower for all other conditions. For smaller sample sizes, GH gave empirical αs up to .092 for variances of 1, 3, 5, 7 when paired with *n*s of 11, 8, 4, 3. They also examined specific comparisons for the effect of unequal variances and/or sample sizes for the three procedures. Only the GH maintained α close to .05. Using the MS_W in the Tukey-Kramer gave very biased results for the specific comparisons even in the equal *n*s case (empirical αs of .010 to .118 even though the overall α was .056). The *t* with separate variance estimates had less bias for the specific comparisons, but was inferior to GH if both *n*s and variances were unequal. Because the GH method can be liberal with respect to α if sample sizes are small, Games and Howell recommended its use if *n*s are six or larger.

Robustness to Nonnormality

When the assumption of normality is violated, there are two basic approaches: Rely upon the robustness of the MCPs presented in Chapter 2 or turn to procedures that do not assume normality. Nonnormality can occur in a variety of ways, but the two basic ways are skewness (including outliers in one tail) and kurtosis (including outliers in both tails).[3] Another way to describe distributions is in terms of the length of the tails of the distribution: A distribution can be short tailed relative to the normal, such as the uniform distribution, or long tailed, such as the *t*.

Robustness of Classical MCPs

Several studies have considered the performance of MCPs when sampling from nonnormal distributions. Petrinovich and Hardyck

(1969) investigated several MCPs, including Tukey and Scheffé, for an exponential distribution that is positively skewed ($\gamma_1 = 2$, when for a normal distribution $\gamma_1 = 0$) and sharply peaked ($\gamma_2 = 6$, when for a normal distribution $\gamma_2 = 0$). They found little impact of sampling from an exponential distribution except that the power was higher for large differences in means. All MCPs in their study behaved similarly for the exponential distribution.

Keselman and Rogan (1978) studied Tukey modifications for unequal ns and unequal variances as well as the Scheffé procedure, and included sampling from a chi-square distribution with df = 3 ($\gamma_1 = 1.663$ and $\gamma_2 = 4$). They reported that distribution shape had negligible effect on α.

Dunnett (1982) reported that Tukey is conservative (with respect to both α and power) for long-tailed distributions and for distributions that might also be prone to outliers. Ringland (1983) found that Dunn and a procedure based on the Studentized maximum modulus were liberal for outlier-prone distributions but that Scheffé was conservative. He investigated several robust estimates of location in each of these MCPs and found Scheffé to be robust regardless of situation.[4]

Rank Tests

The rank tests for pairwise comparisons to be presented here fall into the category of tests that do not assume normality, as do the MCPs using robust estimates mentioned above. When rank-sum tests are contemplated for MCPs, two different types of ranking must be considered: separate rankings and joint rankings.

In doing separate rankings, the researcher examines two groups at a time and ranks the observations separately for each pair of groups. For example, for $J = 3$ with $n = 10$, the observations would be ranked from 1 to 20 for groups 1 and 2 without considering group 3. Then this would be repeated for groups 1 and 3 and for groups 2 and 3. A rank-sum statistic based on separate rankings for the case of equal ns is often called the Steel-Dwass test (Dwass, 1960; Steel, 1960).

Rank the $2n$ observations from groups j and j', where $1 \leq j < j' \leq J$, compute the rank sum for the jth group, and call this rank sum $RS_{jj'}$. Then the rank sum for the other group is called $RS_{j'j}$ and is equal to $n(2n + 1) - RS_{jj'}$. For the pairwise comparison to test the hypothesis of equal means for groups j and j', the test statistic is given as

$$t_{SR_{jj'}} = \frac{|\ RS_{jj'} - n\ (2n+1)/2\ |}{\sqrt{n^2\ (2n+1)/12}} \qquad (4.10)$$

and the decision rule is to reject H_0 if

$$t_{SR_{jj'}} \geq \frac{q_{j,\infty}^{\alpha}}{\sqrt{2}} \qquad (4.11)$$

where the q is the α-level critical value from the Studentized range, Table A.3, with J as the number-of-means parameter and df = ∞. Note that some authors prefer using the continuity correction of subtracting one half from the numerator of t_{SR} (see Hochberg & Tamhane, 1987, p. 244).

Joint rankings give another MCP rank test for pairwise comparisons that is attributed to Nemenyi (1963) and Dunn (1964). First, rank all observations from all groups and let the rank be R_{ij}. For n_j in the jth group, rank the observations from one to $N = \Sigma n_j$, obtain the rank sum for each group, and compute the mean of the ranks for each group:

$$\bar{R}_j = \frac{\displaystyle\sum_{i=1}^{n_j} R_{ij}}{n_j} \qquad (4.12)$$

The test statistic to test the hypothesis of equal means for groups j and j' is given as

$$t_{JR_{jj'}} = \frac{|\bar{R}_j - \bar{R}_{j'}|}{\sqrt{\dfrac{N\ (N+1)}{12}\left(\dfrac{1}{n_j} + \dfrac{1}{n_{j'}}\right)}} \qquad (4.13)$$

and the decision rule is to reject H_0 if

$$t_{JR_{jj'}} \geq h^{\alpha} \qquad (4.14)$$

where h^{α} is an α-level critical value that can be from any one of several distributions. Originally, the critical value was $z^{\alpha/2C}$, where $C = J(J-1)/2$ and z is the upper $\alpha/2C$ point of the standard normal distribution. Hochberg and Tamhane (1987, p. 245) give $z^{\alpha*}$

TABLE 4.5   Separate Rankings Illustrations and All t Tests: Miller Data, Observation (Rank in the Pair of Groups)

Group 1	Group 2		Group 1	Group 5
18.61 (6)	18.86 (8)		13.31 (1)	26.32 (7)
13.54 (2)	19.17 (10)	$5[2(5)+1]/2 = 27.5$	13.54 (2)	27.01 (8)
16.08 (5)	13.69 (3)		16.08 (3)	27.08 (9)
18.96 (9)	14.47 (4)	$\sqrt{5^2[2(5)+1]/12} =$	18.96 (5)	22.32 (6)
13.31 (1)	18.81 (7)	$\sqrt{22.9167} = 4.7871354$	13.31 (1)	29.77 (10)
Total 23	32		15	40

$$t = \frac{|23 - 27.5|}{4.7871354} \qquad\qquad t = \frac{|15 - 27.5|}{4.7871354}$$
$$t = 0.94 \qquad\qquad\qquad\qquad t = 2.61$$

Group	2	3	4	5	
1	0.94	2.19	2.19	2.61	$q/\sqrt{2} = 3.86/\sqrt{2}$
2		1.98	1.98	2.61	$= 2.7294322$
3			0.31	2.40	
4				2.19	

where $\alpha^* = \frac{1}{2}[1 - (1 - \alpha)^{1/C}]$ and z is the upper α^* point of the standard normal distribution. For large samples, the critical value can be $q^\alpha_{J, \infty}/\sqrt{2}$ or a more conservative $\sqrt{\chi^2}$ critical value at the α level with df $= J - 1$.

Tests using separate rankings can have lower power than tests using joint ranking, especially for extreme means with intermediate means present. However, the tests using joint ranking do not control α using ERFW for skewed distributions with one mean different from the others, due to the interrelations of the ranks. The problem is that the ranks for groups j and j' depend on the observations (and their ranks) from other groups, thus the distribution of the test statistic is not completely determined under the H_0 for groups j and j' (see Hochberg & Tamhane, 1987, p. 249). Tests based on separate rankings generally would be preferred, in spite of their conservatism.

The Miller data from Table 3.3 (Chapter 3) are used to compute these two rank methods. Separate rankings of the $2n = 10$ observations in each pair of the five groups gives the 10 different statistics in Table 4.5. The separate rankings and sums used in the computations are given for group 1 with 2 and group 1 with 5 for illustration.

TABLE 4.6 Joint Ranking Illustration, Miller Data: Observation (Joint Rank)

Group	1	2	3	4	5
	18.61 (8)	18.86 (10)	18.22 (7)	22.43 (19)	26.32 (24)
	13.54 (2)	19.17 (12)	19.42 (13)	17.22 (6)	27.01 (22)
	16.08 (5)	13.69 (3)	20.25 (15)	22.31 (17)	27.08 (23)
	18.96 (11)	14.47 (4)	25.25 (21)	19.58 (14)	22.32 (18)
	13.31 (1)	18.81 (9)	20.36 (16)	23.96 (20)	28.77 (25)
Sum	27	38	72	78	112
Mean	5.4	7.8	14.4	15.8	22.4

For Groups 1, 5

t denominator is

$$\sqrt{\frac{25\,(25+1)}{12}\left(\frac{1}{5}+\frac{1}{5}\right)} = 4.6547466$$

$$t = \frac{|5.4 - 22.4|}{4.6547466} = 3.65$$

Critical Values

$$z^{\alpha/2C} = z^{.05/20} = z^{.0025} = 2.81$$

$$z^{\alpha^{*}} = z^{.002558} = 2.80$$

$$q/\sqrt{2} = 3.86/\sqrt{2} = 2.73$$

for df = 4

$$\sqrt{\chi^2} = \sqrt{9.49} = 3.081$$

Since the critical value is 2.73, none of the differences are significant using the Steel-Dwass separate rankings rank-sum MCP. The joint rankings and sums used in the computations are given in Table 4.6: ts for comparisons 5-1 and 5-2 are 3.65 and 3.14, respectively.

The 5-2 and 5-1 comparisons are significant with all of the different critical values using the Nemenyi-Dunn joint ranking rank-sum MCP. That both rank MCPs are conservative is obvious when their results are compared with those of Scheffé, which is considered the standard of conservatism. From Chapter 3, comparisons 5-3, 5-2, and 5-1 are significant using Scheffé, which is one more significant comparison, 5-3, than found with the most powerful of these two rank methods.

Finally, a word of caution is offered with respect to a general group of rank tests called *rank transforms* (for example, see Conover & Iman, 1981). Concern over the accuracy of these tests has been raised by Sawilowsky, Blair, and Higgins (1989), and researchers should avoid using MCPs on rank transforms until more information is available.

Summary

If the researcher is assured that the assumption of equal variances has been met, then the Tukey-Kramer or the Hochberg GT2 could be used with unequal sample sizes. Otherwise, unequal ns should trigger the use of one of the MCPs called GH, C, and T3, with GH recommended unless it is crucial to maintain strict α control. With equal ns and unequal variances, several MCPs give adequate α control for the set of all pairwise comparisons, but not necessarily for specific comparisons by themselves. Only the GH procedure offers α control for the entire set of comparisons and for individual comparisons. Most MCPs seem to be robust to moderate departures from nonnormality, and the existing rank tests have been found to be conservative.

Notes

1. Of course, the ANOVA assumptions are on the error component of the linear model, but, since it is a fixed-effects model, the assumptions also apply to the observed score in the model. Thus it is accurate to say that the data have the same three assumptions of normality, equal variances, and independence.

2. The Studentized maximum modulus is the maximum absolute value of J independent unit normal variables, which is then Studentized by dividing by the standard deviation.

3. Technically, kurtosis is peakedness relative to the normal distribution, but a highly peaked distribution often has long tails. That is, it has outliers in both tails if it is symmetric. Of course, a distribution can be both peaked and skewed.

4. For a summary of robust estimation in MCPs, see Hochberg and Tamhane (1987, pp. 271-273).

5 Multiple Comparisons for the Two-Way ANOVA: Factorial, Randomized Blocks, and Repeated Measures Designs

When the topic of multiple comparisons is covered in most statistics or experimental design texts, considerable attention is placed upon MCPs for a one-way ANOVA, that is, a completely randomized design. Less attention is paid to multiple comparisons in higher-order designs using a two-way or higher ANOVA. One reason for this lesser coverage may be that less is known about MCPs as they are used in higher-order ANOVAs. Another reason may be that much of the information available from the one-way ANOVA may be extended into the higher-order designs. However, there are some unique problems for the researcher wanting to use MCPs in higher-order ANOVAs.

There is the overarching problem of complexity: Instead of one F ratio, in the two-way ANOVA with more than one observation per cell there are three F ratios. In even higher-order ANOVAs, there are more than three Fs. In these two-way and higher-order ANOVAs, there are not only main effect means, the means for the levels of the variables establishing the design, but additionally there are cell means. With the cell means and the means for two main effects in a two-way ANOVA, there are three sets of means and three families of comparisons. Multiple comparisons may be needed for each of these sets of means. Once a researcher acknowledges that any two-way design leads to greater complexity in the area of multiple comparisons, there are some other important issues that must be considered, each tied somewhat to the complexity of the design. First, there is the issue of α control: Should the researcher control α for each comparison, for each family of comparisons, or for the entire experiment? Also, there is the issue of cell means versus interaction effects: Which does the researcher want to test? Finally, special attention is given later in this chapter to MCPs for repeated measures designs.

Control of α

The issue of control of α for a two-way ANOVA has one more level of complexity than the control of α in a one-way design.[1] For a one-way ANOVA, the researcher was faced with choosing to control α for each comparison (ERPC) or for some group of comparisons. To control α for some group of comparisons meant to control error rate per family (ERPF) or to control error rate family-wise (ERFW). However, a two-way ANOVA has three families in the experiment. Thus a new way to control α would be to control error rate for the entire experiment, that is, per experiment or experimentwise.

Even though controlling α per experiment is relatively easy for a two-way ANOVA, it is rarely done by applied researchers. Merely dividing the total α into an α' for each family will control error rate per experiment, but applied researchers usually choose the middle road of controlling α for each family. Perhaps the reason for this choice is that there are originally three F tests, or perhaps the reason is simplicity. Whatever the reason, the most frequent choice by applied researchers is to control α for each family, that is, the two main effects and the cell means (or interaction effects). When this choice is made, the researcher must realize that the error rate for the whole experiment is approximately three times α.

Main Effect Means

MCPs on the main effect means in a two-way ANOVA are a simple extension of the same procedures for a one-way ANOVA. That is, to do Tukey tests on the means for one of the main effects from a two-way ANOVA requires very few adjustments to the formulas or concepts used for Tukey on means in a one-way ANOVA. First, we need to consider a few basics for the two-way ANOVA.

Linear Model

For $J \geq 2$ levels of the first main effect, A, $K \geq 2$ levels of the second main effect, B, and with n observations in each group, the total number of observations is $N = nJK$. A linear model for the N scores on the dependent variable, Y, is given by

$$Y_{ijk} = \mu + \alpha_j + \beta_k + \alpha\beta_{jk} + e_{ijk} \qquad (5.1)$$

where μ is the common grand mean, $\alpha_j = \mu_j - \mu$ is the fixed treatment effect for the jth level of A, $\beta_k = \mu_k - \mu$ is the fixed treatment effect for the kth level of B, $\alpha_{jk} = \mu_{jk} - \alpha_j - \beta_k - \mu = \mu_{jk} - \mu_j - \mu_k + \mu$ is the fixed interaction effect of A and B, and $e_{ijk} = Y_{ijk} - \mu_{jk}$ is the random error for the ith subject in the jth level of A and the kth level of B. Fixed treatment effects lead to the following restrictions:

$$\sum_{j=1}^{J} \alpha_j = 0$$

$$\sum_{k=1}^{K} \beta_k = 0 \qquad (5.2)$$

$$\sum_{j=1}^{J} \alpha\beta_{jk} = \sum_{k=1}^{K} \alpha\beta_{jk} = 0$$

The e_{ijk} are assumed to be normally distributed, to have equal variances in the populations, and to be independent. That is,

$$e_{ijk} \overset{d}{\sim} \text{NID}(0, \sigma_e^2) \qquad \text{for each cell} \qquad (5.3)$$

which shows that the population variances are assumed to be equal for the cells.

In the same way that the above linear model partitions the scores into the four parts due to A, B, the AB interaction, and error, the two-way ANOVA partitions the variability of the scores into four sums of squares. These are SS_A, SS_B, SS_{AB}, and SS_W, with degrees of freedom $df_A = J - 1$, $df_B = K - 1$, $df_{AB} = (J - 1)(K - 1) = JK - J - K + 1$, and $df_W = JK(n - 1) = N - JK$.

Overall F Tests

These tests are omnibus tests of the overall null hypotheses of equality of the J means for A, equality of the K means for B, and zero interaction. Zero treatment effects give equivalent null hypotheses for the two main effects. The F ratios are given by

$$
\begin{aligned}
F_A &= \frac{MS_A}{MS_W} = \frac{SS_A/df_A}{SS_W/df_W} \\[2ex]
F_B &= \frac{MS_B}{MS_W} = \frac{SS_B/df_B}{SS_W/df_W} \\[2ex]
F_{AB} &= \frac{MS_{AB}}{MS_W} = \frac{SS_{AB}/df_{AB}}{SS_W/df_W}
\end{aligned}
\qquad (5.4)
$$

Decision rules are the same as for the one-way ANOVA: Reject H_0 if the observed F equals or exceeds the critical F or, equivalently, reject H_0 if the observed p value is less than or equal to α. If any of the three F tests rejects the corresponding hypothesis, the location or type of the difference is not stipulated.

Example

Frank (1984) investigated the effect of note-taking study technique and field independent-dependent cognitive styles on learning from a lecture. Subjects were selected from 160 undergraduate female students. The field-independent group was made up of 52 students who scored high (≥ 14) on the Hidden Figures Test (French, Ekstrom, & Price, 1963); 52 students who scored low (≤ 9) on that test were the field-dependent group. Students in each cognitive style group listened to a taped lecture under one of the following study techniques:

(1) No notes were allowed (NONOTES).
(2) Students were told to take their own notes (STUNOTES).
(3) Students were given an outline framework with major headings and sub-headings and told to take additional notes on the framework pages (OUTFRAME).
(4) Students were given a complete outline with key terms, brief definitions, and important ideas given in addition to the major headings and subheadings and told to take additional notes on the outline pages (COMPOUT).

After a 10-minute review period, students took a 20-item multiple-choice test on the lecture material. Students had been randomly assigned to one of the four study techniques from within each of the cognitive styles, giving a 2 × 4 randomized block design with 13 observations per cell. Results include data,[2] cell means and standard deviations (in parentheses) on number of correct items, and the overall *F*s; all of these are given in Table 5.1.

MCPs on Main Effect Means

The *t* statistic for a comparison on main effect means is a simple extension of the *t* statistic used in the one-way ANOVA. For the A means, the statistic is

$$t_{\hat{\psi}A} = \frac{\hat{\psi} - \psi}{\sqrt{\dfrac{MS_W}{nK} \displaystyle\sum_{j=1}^{J} c_j^2}} \qquad (5.5)$$

which for pairwise comparisons simplifies to

$$t_{\hat{\psi}A} = \frac{\overline{Y}_j - \overline{Y}_{j'}}{\sqrt{\dfrac{MS_W}{nK}(2)}} \qquad (5.6)$$

where the MS_W from the two-way ANOVA is divided by *n* times *K*, which is the number of observations that are summed to compute one

TABLE 5.1 Data, Cell Means, Overall Fs, Study Technique and Cognitive Style

Data	NONOTES	STUNOTES	OUTFRAME	COMPOUT
FI	13 13 10 16 14	15 19 19 17 19	19 18 17 19 17	15 19 16 17 19
	11 13 13 11 16	17 20 17 18 17	19 17 19 17 15	15 20 16 19 16
	15 16 10	18 18 19	18 17 15	19 19 18
FD	11 14 11 10 15	12 16 16 17 16	18 15 15 15 15	18 19 15 16 19
	10 16 16 17 11	16 16 14 14 16	18 19 18 18 16	18 19 19 18 17
	16 11 10	15 15 15	16 18 16	16 17 15

Cell means

	NONOTES	STUNOTES	OUTFRAME	COMPOUT
FI	13.15 (2.19)	17.92 (1.32)	17.46 (1.39)	17.54 (1.76)
FD	12.92 (2.75)	15.23 (1.30)	16.62 (1.61)	17.38 (1.50)
	13.04	16.58	17.04	17.46

Overall Fs

Source	df	SS	MS	F	p
COGSTYLE	1	25.01	25.01	7.78	.0064
STUDYTEC	3	320.18	106.73	33.22	.0001
COG × STU	3	27.26	9.09	2.83	.0426
WITHIN	96	308.46	3.21		

of the A means. The use of nK instead of n in the formula for t is the only difference from the same formula for a one-way ANOVA. For the B means, the statistic is

$$t_{\hat{\psi}B} = \frac{\hat{\psi} - \psi}{\sqrt{\dfrac{MS_W}{nJ} \displaystyle\sum_{k=1}^{K} c_k^2}} \tag{5.7}$$

which for pairwise comparisons simplifies to

$$t_{\hat{\psi}B} = \frac{\bar{Y}_k - \bar{Y}_{k'}}{\sqrt{\dfrac{MS_W}{nJ}(2)}} \tag{5.8}$$

where the MS_W is divided by n times J, which is the number of observations that are summed to compute one of the B means. The only other difference in the process of doing any of the MCPs on main effect means is to remember that MS_W has $df_W = JK(n-1) = N - JK$, which is a different formula from that for a one-way ANOVA. Once the t statistic is computed, any of the MCPs covered in Chapter 2 (or Chapter 4) may be done simply by comparing the t to the critical value as given earlier, remembering that df_W has a different formula and that the number of means is J for A means and K for B means. The researcher must also make a choice with respect to how α should be controlled: for the entire experiment, for each of the three families of means, or per comparison.

Using the Tukey method to compare the means for the main effect of study technique in the example would yield six pairwise comparisons on the four means. Controlling α for the family of study technique means, the comparison of means for groups NONOTES and STUNOTES gives

$$t = \frac{16.5769 - 13.0385}{\sqrt{\dfrac{3.2131}{(13)(2)}(2)}} = 7.1173 \tag{5.9}$$

which is compared with

$$\frac{q_{4,60}^{\alpha}}{\sqrt{2}} = \frac{3.74}{\sqrt{2}} = 2.64 \tag{5.10}$$

Since 7.12 is larger than 2.64, the difference in the means for NONOTES and STUNOTES is significant. Similar pairwise comparisons using Tukey show that the means for OUTFRAME and COMPOUT also differ significantly from NONOTES, but no other significant differences exist in the main effect means for study technique.

SAS and SPSS

For main effect means, SAS is easy to use to get MCPs. Simply use the optional statement

MEANS *effects/mcp names*;

where effects is one or more of the variables used in the CLASS statement as main effects. If tests on main effect means are wanted for both main effects, simply put the names of both variables in the MEANS statement in place of *effects*, separated by a blank. Also, remember that the MCP names are separated by blanks.

An example is given below of the SAS code necessary to run a two-way ANOVA and compute the Tukey and Ryan MCPs for all possible pairwise comparisons on the means for both main effects. The main effects are called simply A and B.

```
(systems lines)
DATA EXAMPLE;
INPUT A$ B$;
DO I=1 TO 10;
INPUT Y @@;
OUTPUT;
END;
CARDS;
(data)
PROC PRINT;
PROC ANOVA;
CLASS A B;
MODEL Y=A B A*B;
MEANS A B/TUKEY REGWQ;
```

The SAS output for MCPs for two-way ANOVAs is the same as that for the one-way ANOVA.

For SPSS, MCPs cannot be done from the command that computes two-way and higher ANOVAs.

Interaction Tests Versus Cell Means Tests

At various times in the past, controversy has surfaced regarding the proper methodology to use in doing multiple comparisons in a two-way ANOVA. The typical location of this controversy has been a psychological journal specializing in methodology, and the typical content was filtered through the opinions of the authors.[3] Since there are no truly definitive answers to many of the questions, both sides of the arguments will be presented here, but the final opinions given will be mine.

One facet of the controversy has been focused on which tests should be done following the two-way ANOVA F test for interaction.[4] Should tests be done on interaction effects or on cell means? First, the arguments for tests on interaction effects.

Interaction Tests

The overall test F_{AB} has a hypothesis of no interaction effect, that is, that all $\alpha\beta_{jk}$ are equal to zero. If F_{AB} is significant, it is telling the researcher that not all of the $\alpha\beta_{jk}$ are zero. Tests on interaction effects merely detect which of these $\alpha\beta_{jk}$ are significantly different from each other. Those authors who advocate doing tests on interaction effects properly emphasize that tests on the $\alpha\beta_{jk}$ are the only tests that are directly related to the overall test F_{AB}. Thus tests on $\alpha\beta_{jk}$ have the advantage of direct association with the overall test: The F_{AB} tests to see if any of the interaction effects are different from zero, and the tests on $\alpha\beta_{jk}$ determine whether differences in cell interaction effects are significant. However, interaction effects are difficult to interpret since they are not the cell means per se, but the effects of the cell means after the main effects have been removed. That is, $\alpha\beta_{jk}$ is the effect of the jkth cell mean over and above the main effects, which is shown in the equation for interaction effect:

$$\alpha\beta_{jk} = (\mu_{jk} - \mu) - \alpha_j - \beta_k \qquad (5.11)$$

TABLE 5.2   Ralphing Example

	Means			Interaction Effects	
	Ralphing	Control	Average	Ralphing	Control
Experienced	7	3	5	.5	−.5
Inexperienced	5	3	4	−.5	.5
Average	6	3	4.5		

To illustrate the difficulty with interpretation, consider an example given in Rosnow and Rosenthal (1989). It seems the owners of a baseball team want to improve the players' ability to deal with the pressures of real competition and want to evaluate a technique designed to do this that is called *Ralphing*. Experienced and inexperienced players are used and, within each group, are randomly assigned to treatment: Ralphing or control. There are 18 of each type of player and thus 9 players per cell. Performance is number of hits in an experimental game. Table 5.2 gives cell and main effect means and interaction effects for the Ralphing example.

The interaction effect of 0.5 for the Ralphing and experienced cell is the amount of the effect of the cell mean (7 − 4.5 = 2.5) that is remaining after the main effect of Ralphing (6 − 4.5 = 1.5) and the main effect of experience (5 − 4.5 = 0.5) are removed from the cell mean effect (7 − 4.5 − 1.5 − 0.5 = 2.5 − 1.5 − 0.5 = 0.5). The −0.5 for the Ralphing and inexperienced cell is the amount of the effect of the cell mean (5 − 4.5 = 0.5) that is remaining after the main effects of Ralphing (1.5) and inexperience (4 − 4.5 = −0.5) are removed from the cell mean effect [5 − 4.5 − 1.5 − (−0.5) = 0.5 − 1.5 − (−0.5) = −0.5]. To have a negative quantity, such as −0.5, as an "amount remaining" would make interpretation difficult for some researchers. Any comparison of interaction effects would look at differences, such as, given Ralphing, the difference in interaction effects for experienced and inexperienced players is 0.5 − (−0.5) = 1.0.

Rosnow and Rosenthal (1989) chose to talk about the interaction effect in this example by saying that "(in relation to the control) the experienced ball players benefitted moderately from Ralphing to the same degree that the inexperienced ball players were harmed by it" (p. 146). But most people would examine the cell means and realize that, relative to control, Ralphing helped *both* experienced and inexperienced players. The Ralphing and experienced cell mean is 4 larger than control and experienced, and the Ralphing and inexperienced cell mean is 2 larger than control and inexperienced: Both experienced and inexperienced players improved relative to control. The problem with interpreting interaction effects is that most researchers want to examine all of the effects of a variable, not those remaining after the main effects are taken out. In terms of the example, what is desired is the effect of the Ralphing on the players *with their level of experience intact*, not "removed." Expressed another way, most researchers want to discuss the *total* impact of Ralphing, not separate pieces of Ralphing. Comparison of the cell means offers a comparison of this total impact.[5]

Cell Means Tests

Tests on cell means do not have direct correspondence to the overall test on interaction effects. In fact, the first important concept that users of tests on cell means must learn is that cell mean differences have components; that is, cell mean differences are made up of two or more parts. It is important that researchers discover that differences in cell means contain differences in interaction effects *plus* differences in at least one main effect. In the Ralphing example, for experienced players, the cell mean difference of $7 - 3 = 4$ contains not only the difference in interaction effects $[0.5 - (-0.5) = 1.0]$ but also the difference in main effect means due to Ralphing ($6 - 3 = 3$). The cell mean difference of 4 will be tested as a unit in one test for the impact of Ralphing on experienced players, but the researcher must know that it contains components of interaction effects and a main effect.

In spite of this lack of correspondence to F_{AB}, tests on cell means are easier to interpret: The 4 represents the gain compared with control induced by Ralphing for experienced players. For inexperienced players, the 2 is the gain compared with control induced by Ralphing. It must be noted that these players were not "harmed" by Ralphing, but helped by it.

The actual t statistic for comparisons on cell means is given by

$$t_{\hat{\psi}_{\text{cell means}}} = \frac{\hat{\psi} - \psi}{\sqrt{\dfrac{MS_W}{n} \displaystyle\sum_{j=1}^{J} \sum_{k=1}^{K} c_{jk}^2}} \qquad (5.12)$$

which for pairwise comparisons simplifies to

$$t_{\hat{\psi}_{\text{cell means}}} = \frac{\overline{Y}_{jk} - \overline{Y}_{j'k'}}{\sqrt{\dfrac{MS_W}{n}(2)}} \tag{5.13}$$

Whereas computation of the t statistic for cell means tests is relatively straightforward, finding critical values is more difficult. In fact, critical values for cell means tests are another facet of the controversy over MCPs in two-way ANOVAs.

Critical Values for Cell Means Tests

The focus of this aspect of tests on cell means is the *number-of-means* parameter. The number-of-means parameter is one of the values used to find a critical value for Tukey, which will be used as an example.[6] Among the symbols used as sub- or superscripts for the q, the number-of-means parameter was the first subscript and had the value of J for the one-way ANOVA. Up to this point, the number of means in a comparison in a two-way ANOVA was quite apparent because the comparisons were on main effects: For the A main effect means, the number of means is J; for the B main effect means, the number of means is K. Now the researcher is dealing with a total of JK cell means. Another way of looking at these JK means is to see them as J A means at each of the K levels of B, or as K B means at each of the J levels of A.[7] Examine Figure 5.1 for the types of comparisons that would illustrate these last two ways of considering cell mean comparisons.

Researchers may want to examine all of the pairwise comparisons of the A (or B) means at each of the levels of B (or A), but may not be interested in comparisons that vary both levels of A and B at the same time. That is, diagonal comparisons are not of interest, but comparisons within a row or column represent those desired by most researchers. If this is the case, then the researcher will not be doing all possible pairwise comparisons on the JK cell means, but a subset of these comparisons. To use JK as the number-of-means parameter would force the researcher to control α for all $JK(JK-1)/2$ pairwise comparisons. Thus to use JK as the number-of-means parameter and do a subset of these comparisons would result in overcontrol of α, giving conservative tests.

Another approach to the problem is to use as the number-of-means parameter the number of levels of the appropriate main effect. For

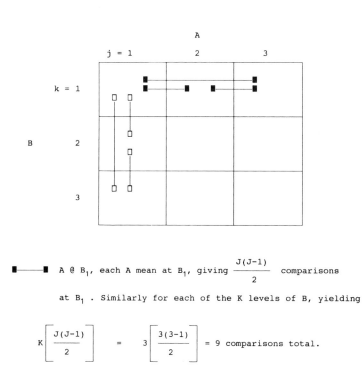

$$K \left[\frac{J(J-1)}{2} \right] = 3 \left[\frac{3(3-1)}{2} \right] = 9 \text{ comparisons total.}$$

$$J \left[\frac{K(K-1)}{2} \right] = 3 \left[\frac{3(3-1)}{2} \right] = 9 \text{ comparisons total.}$$

Figure 5.1. Cell Means, Types of Comparisons

example, if the researcher is interested in A means at each level of B, then J, the number of levels of A, might be considered as number-of-means parameter. A critical value with J as the number-of-means parameter would control α for one set of the A means, but allow p (at least one Type I error) to increase by α for each level of B at which a set of comparisons was done. Thus the researcher comparing the A means at all levels of B would end up with approximately $K\alpha$ for p(at least one Type I error). Although using JK gives conservative tests, liberal tests result from using J as number-of-means parameter (or K for comparisons on B means at each level of A).

For example, if $J = 4$ and $K = 3$, then $JK = 12$. The comparisons of the four A means at each level of B would give $J(J - 1)/2 = 4(4 - 1)/2 = 4(3)/2 = 6$ comparisons at each of the three levels of B. Thus for the $K = 3$ levels of B, there would be $6K = 6(3) = 18$ comparisons of interest. But there are $JK(JK - 1)/2 = 12(12 - 1)/2 = 12(11)/2 = 66$ pairwise comparisons that could be done on the 12 cell means. The 18 comparisons of interest represent a fairly small subset of all 66 possible pairwise comparisons on the 12 cell means. So choice of $JK = 12$ would lead to conservative tests, but $J = 4$ would lead to liberal tests. The ideal value for the number-of-means parameter is somewhere between these two extremes. For $\alpha = .05$, critical values of q with $df_W = 60$ would be $q = 3.74$ for $J = 4$ and $q = 4.81$ for $JK = 12$, so the ideal value of q lies somewhere between 3.74 and 4.81.

Cicchetti (1972) presented an easy approximate solution to the problem of the number-of-means parameter. Recognizing that the ideal value of the number-of-means parameter is associated with some number of pairwise comparisons, and that the number of comparisons being done is known as C, Cicchetti solved the equation

$$C = \frac{J' (J' - 1)}{2} \tag{5.14}$$

for J' as the approximate number-of-means parameter. In the above example, $C = 18$, so the solution for J' gives $18 = J'(J' - 1)/2$ and $36 = J'(J' - 1)$. Possible whole number values for J' are 7, which gives $7(6) = 42$, and 6, which gives $6(5) = 30$. So $J' = 7$ would be the best choice, since $7(6)/2 = 21$ is the closest to $C = 18$ without giving a value of J' that could yield a liberal test.

For tests on A means at each level of B, note that $J' = 7$ as the number-of-means parameter is between $JK = 12$, which would give conservative tests, and $J = 4$, which would give liberal tests. Using $\alpha = .05$, $J' = 7$, and $df_W = 60$ as the parameters to q in Table A.3 (Appendix A),[8] the ideal value of q is 4.31, smaller than 4.81 for the conservative tests but larger than 3.74 for the liberal tests.

If a researcher is interested in fewer than all pairwise comparisons on A means, or interested in all pairwise comparisons on A means but not for all levels of B, the Cicchetti approach still works for a simple count of the number of comparisons, C. Of course, a similar approach could be taken for tests on the B means at each level of A.

Applying the Cicchetti approach to the example of study technique and cognitive style study, we might want to see if there are significant differences between field-independent and field-dependent means for each of the four study techniques. Examining cognitive style differences for each study technique gives $C = 4$, then solving for J' gives $J' = 4$ as the number-of-means parameter. As an example, using the Tukey method on the comparison of FI to FD at STUNOTES gives

$$t = \frac{17.9231 - 15.2308}{\sqrt{(3.2131/13)\,(2)}} = 3.8293 \qquad (5.15)$$

which is compared with

$$\frac{q_{4,60}^{\alpha}}{\sqrt{2}} = \frac{3.74}{\sqrt{2}} = 2.6446 \qquad (5.16)$$

Since 3.83 is larger than 2.64, the difference in means is significant, showing that field-independent students performed better than field-dependent students in the student-notes condition. The other three pairwise comparisons of cell means between FI and FD at levels of study techniques were not significant.

We also might want to examine the differences in study technique means for each of the cognitive styles, which is simply examining the same cell means, but comparing study techniques at the different cognitive styles. There would be six pairwise comparisons at FI and six at FD, giving $C = 12$. Solving for J' gives $J' = 6$ as the number-of-means parameter. As an example, using the Tukey method on the comparison of STUNOTES to COMPOUT at FD gives

$$t = \frac{17.3846 - 15.2308}{\sqrt{(3.2131/13)\,(2)}} = 3.0634 \qquad (5.17)$$

which is compared with

$$\frac{q_{4,60}^{\alpha}}{\sqrt{2}} = \frac{4.16}{\sqrt{2}} = 2.9416 \tag{5.18}$$

Since 3.06 is larger than 2.94, the means for STUNOTES and COMPOUT at FD are significantly different. Other significant differences at FD were in agreement with main effect results found earlier: All study techniques perform better than NONOTES. Similarly, at FI, significant differences were found for all study techniques compared with NONOTES. Thus field-dependent students who take their own notes perform worse than those taking notes with a complete outline. Note that this was not found in the main effect results earlier, nor is it true for field-independent students.

MCPs for Repeated Measures Designs

Any design that measures each subject[9] $K \geq 2$ times on the same dependent variable can be called a *repeated measures design* whenever the K measurements are constituted under levels of another factor. Another way to characterize these designs is to conceptualize subject as a main effect in the model, where subject is crossed with at least one other main effect that has K levels.[10] The factor that is crossed with subject is called a *repeated factor*. The repeated factor is also called a *within-subjects factor* because the K levels of that factor are all measured "within" each subject. The K levels can be time, trials, or some treatment condition. If possible, the order of presentation of the K levels of the repeated factor is randomly assigned to each subject. This is possible if the repeated factor is a treatment, but not possible if it is time or trials.

Repeated measures designs partition the total variability into between-subjects and within-subjects variability, in contrast to between- and within-groups variability in the designs considered thus far. Since subjects are treated as a separate factor in repeated measures designs, there is always variability due to subjects (between-subjects variability). Since each subject is measured two or more times, there are always within-subjects sources of variability.

Another characteristic of repeated measures designs is that of "using the subject as its own control." That is, since each subject is measured under each level of the repeated factor, variability due to subjects is controlled, much like the function of a control group. This control of subject variability is accomplished for tests of within-subjects factors and their interactions, giving increased efficiency for these tests.

There are many different repeated measures designs, some of which have other between-subjects sources of variability in addition to subjects. Other repeated measures designs have more than one repeated factor. Repeated measures designs can be classified by the number of between- and within-subjects factors in the design. We will consider only the simple repeated measures design (subjects as the only between-subjects factor and one within-subjects factor) and the groups-by-trials repeated measures design (subjects and one additional between-subjects factor and one within-subjects factor).[11]

Simple Repeated Measures Design

The simple repeated measures design (SRMD) has only one factor in addition to subjects and that factor is repeated. The symbol S will stand for subjects and the symbol T will stand for the repeated factor. The SRMD is the basic building block for all repeated measures designs. A schematic for this design is shown in Figure 5.2.

The linear model for the SRMD is given by

$$Y_{ik} = \mu + \pi_i + \beta_k + \beta\pi_{ik} + e_{ik} \tag{5.19}$$

where μ is the grand mean, $\pi_i = \mu_i - \mu$ is the random effect of the ith subject, $\beta_k = \mu_k - \mu$ is the fixed effect of the kth level of the repeated factor, $\beta\pi_{ik} = \mu_{ik} - \mu_i - \mu_k + \mu$ is the random interaction of the ith subject and the kth level of the repeated factor, and $e_{ik} = Y_{ik} - \mu_{ik}$ is the random error of the ith subject and the kth level of the repeated factor. Note that the error and interaction are completely confounded since there is only one observation per cell, and thus there is no separate estimate of error variance.

The F test for the repeated factor T is given as

$$F = \frac{MS_T}{MS_{TS}} = \frac{SS_T/df_T}{SS_{TS}/df_{TS}} \tag{5.20}$$

where $df_T = K - 1$ and $df_{TS} = (K - 1)(n - 1)$. Note that MS_{TS} is the correct denominator for F in this design.

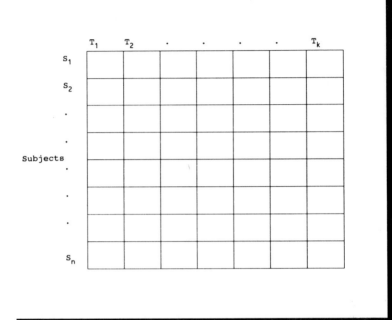

Figure 5.2. Schematic for Simple Repeated Measures Design

In addition to the usual ANOVA assumptions on e_{ik} of normality, equal variances, and independence, repeated measures designs have an assumption called *sphericity*, which is defined as equality of variances of differences of observations for all possible pairs of levels of the repeated factor. Given symbolically, sphericity is defined as follows:

$$\sigma^2_{Y_{ik} - Y_{ik'}} = \text{constant} \quad \text{for all } k \neq k' \tag{5.21}$$

The assumption of sphericity is typically not met in repeated measures designs and the effect on α is an increase of at least .05. Thus, if α is set at .05, the true α can be at least as high as .10 (see Collier, Baker, Mandeville, & Hayes, 1967). The sampling distribution of F is not well fit by the usual F distribution, and the statistic is not robust.

Because the usual F statistic is not robust, two major alternatives have been suggested. One of these is to approximate the true distribution of F by using reduced degrees of freedom. The second is to use a multivariate approach that does not assume sphericity.[12]

Multiple comparisons may be done on the means of the repeated factor in the SRMD. However, complications due to violation of the sphericity assumption eliminate all but one of the MCPs previously discussed. According to research to date, use of two-correlated-sample t tests with the Dunn critical value (Table A.4, Appendix A) with parameters $C = K(K - 1)/2$ and df $= n - 1$ gives the only MCP that has adequate control of α for all pairwise comparisons on the K means (see Maxwell, 1980; Mitzel & Games, 1981). Of course, if fewer than all possible pairwise comparisons are being computed, C would simply be the number of pairwise comparisons actually computed. Slight improvement in power can be obtained using a critical value from the Studentized maximum modulus distribution (Table A.7) with $J^* = K(K - 1)/2$ and df $= n - 1$ (see Hochberg & Tamhane, 1987, p. 215). Preliminary testing to see if the sphericity assumption has been met is discouraged (Stoline, 1984; as reported in Hochberg & Tamhane, 1987) because of problems with the preliminary test due to Mauchly (1940).

For an example of an SRMD, consider a study where each of four subjects is measured under three different treatment conditions.[13] The treatments were given one week apart to see the effect on a test of verbal skill. Data are given in Table 5.3, along with treatment means and the overall ANOVA. The overall F for treatment is significant. The three two-correlated-sample t tests are 12.08 for 1-2, 1.26 for 1-3, and 7.25 for 2-3. The Dunn critical value for $C = 3$ and df $= n - 1 = 10$ is 2.870, so comparisons 1-2 and 2-3 are significant using $\alpha = .05$.

Groups-by-Trials Repeated Measures Design

Most of the research on MCPs in repeated measures designs has been done only for the SRMD. Since the MCPs in an SRMD are done on the means of the repeated factor, the above recommendations hold for higher-order repeated measures designs *only* for the means of the main effects that are repeated. When dealing with any higher-order repeated measures design, the issue of MCPs becomes more complex because of the increased number and types of families of means. The design that is often called "groups by trials" (Winer, 1971) or "split-plot factorial, SPF-$p.q$" (Kirk, 1982) will serve as an introduction to higher-order repeated measures designs and their MCPs.

TABLE 5.3 Data, Treatment Means, Overall ANOVA, Verbal Skill Example

Subject	Treatments 1	2	3
S1	8	11	10
S2	7	10	8
S3	6	10	7
S4	4	8	3
S5	2	4	1
S6	9	12	9
S7	5	7	4
S8	10	13	9
S9	3	6	5
S10	6	9	7
S11	7	12	10
Means	6.09	9.27	6.64

Overall F Source	df	SS	MS	F	p
Subject	10	215.33333333	21.53333333		
Treatment	2	63.69696970	31.84848485	44.53	0.0001
S×T	20	14.30303030	0.71515152		

The groups-by-trials repeated measures design (GXTRMD) has one between-subjects factor in addition to subjects and one within-subjects factor. S will be used for subjects, T will be used for the within-subjects factor (trial, time, treatment, and so on), and G will be used for the between-subjects factor (group). A schematic for this design appears in Figure 5.3.

The linear model for the GXTRMD is given as

$$Y_{ijk} = \mu + \alpha_j + \pi_{i(j)} + \beta_k + \alpha\beta_{jk} + \beta\pi_{ki(j)} + e_{ijk} \qquad (5.22)$$

where μ is the grand mean, $\alpha_j = \mu_j - \mu$ is the fixed effect of the jth group, $\pi_{i(j)} = \mu_{ij} - \mu_j$ is the random effect of the ith subject in the jth group, $\beta_k = \mu_k - \mu$ is the fixed effect of trial, $\alpha\beta_{jk} = \mu_{jk} - \mu_j - \mu_k + \mu$ is the fixed interaction effect for group and trial, $\beta\pi_{ki(j)} = \mu_{ijk} - \mu_{jk} - \mu_{ij} + \mu_j$ is the random interaction effect for trial and subject, and $e_{ijk} = Y_{ijk} - \mu_{ijk}$ is the error for the ith subject in the jth group for the kth trial. Again, note that error and the highest order interaction ($\beta\pi_{ki(j)}$) are completely confounded, and thus a separate estimate of error variance is unavailable.

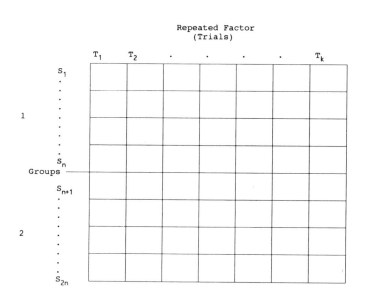

Figure 5.3. Schematic for Groups-by-Trials Repeated Measures Design

The F tests for the GXTRMD design are given as

$$F_G = \frac{\text{MS}_G}{\text{MS}_{S(G)}} = \frac{\text{SS}_G/\text{df}_G}{\text{SS}_{S(G)}/\text{df}_{S(G)}}$$

$$F_T = \frac{\text{MS}_T}{\text{MS}_{TS(G)}} = \frac{\text{SS}_T/\text{df}_T}{\text{SS}_{TS(G)}/\text{df}_{TS(G)}} \qquad (5.23)$$

$$F_{TG} = \frac{\text{MS}_{TG}}{\text{MS}_{TS(G)}} = \frac{\text{SS}_{TG}/\text{df}_{TG}}{\text{SS}_{TS(G)}/\text{df}_{TS(G)}}$$

where $\text{df}_G = J - 1$, $\text{df}_{S(G)} = J(n - 1)$, $\text{df}_T = K - 1$, $\text{df}_{TG} = (K - 1)(J - 1)$, and $\text{df}_{TS(G)} = (K - 1)J(n - 1)$. Note that the between-subject test, F_G, has a denominator different from that in the within-subject tests, F_T and F_{TG}.

In higher-order repeated measures designs, only the within-subjects tests have a sphericity assumption, and there is a separate sphericity assumption for each cluster of within-subjects tests that have the same denominator. The between-subject tests have the usual ANOVA assumptions of normality, equal variances, and independence. Thus, for the GXTRMD, there is only one sphericity assumption that affects F_T and F_{TG} but not F_G. Here, sphericity is also defined as equality of variances of differences of observations for all possible pairs of levels of the repeated factor, but is assumed for each level of the between-subjects factor, groups.[14] Likelihood of departure from sphericity and ways of dealing with the nonrobust within-subjects tests are similar to the SRMD.

Consider the following example in the area of consumer behavior.[15] A researcher investigated the effect of the presence of credit card stimuli (credit card insignias and replicas) and type of product on amount of money subjects were willing to spend on products. A total of 20 subjects were randomly assigned, 10 per group, to presence or absence of credit card stimuli. Each then was shown seven products and was asked how much he or she was willing to spend for the product. The seven products were as follows:

(1) dress
(2) dress
(3) tent
(4) man's sweater
(5) lamp
(6) electric typewriter
(7) chess set

Data and the overall ANOVA are given in Table 5.4. Both main effects were significant.

MCPs on the group means are not affected by sphericity, and thus any MCP covered in this text will suffice. For pairwise comparisons, the statistic would be

$$t_{\hat{\psi}_G} = \frac{\overline{Y}_j - \overline{Y}_{j'}}{\sqrt{\dfrac{\mathrm{MS}_{S(G)}}{nK}(2)}} \tag{5.24}$$

with $\mathrm{df}_{S(G)} = J(n-1)$. For illustration purposes only, the comparison of the groups "presence" and "absence" is given as

TABLE 5.4 Data, Cell Means, Overall ANOVA, Credit Card Example

Data		1	2	3	4	5	6	7
					Product			
	S1	40	48	67	19	74	162	50
	S2	15	16	75	24	33	118	36
	S3	50	38	105	11	40	170	40
	S4	45	45	90	31	37	160	34
Present	S5	41	13	67	40	22	145	63
	S6	12	54	88	23	40	175	33
	S7	22	52	99	20	62	131	55
	S8	64	56	90	15	23	188	46
	S9	38	30	84	47	29	152	40
	S10	40	45	65	14	38	137	41
	S11	14	38	66	20	55	128	40
	S12	20	14	82	6	11	114	36
	S13	16	30	61	12	35	110	12
	S14	35	22	71	19	20	139	68
Absent	S15	27	11	69	13	48	151	33
	S16	38	21	50	14	28	91	23
	S17	18	20	90	32	19	120	24
	S18	30	34	72	16	51	124	36
	S19	14	18	76	10	25	98	30
	S20	36	33	67	15	16	143	21

Means

	1	2	3	4	5	6	7	
				Product				
Present	36.7	39.7	83.0	24.4	39.8	153.8	43.8	60.171
Absent	24.8	24.1	70.4	15.7	30.8	121.8	32.3	45.700
	30.75	31.90	76.70	20.50	35.30	137.80	38.05	

Overall Fs

Source	df	SS	MS	F	p
Credit	1	7329.78	7329.78	25.02	.0001
S(Credit)	18	5273.79	292.99		
Product	6	206309.37	34384.90	182.63	.0001
Credit × Prod	6	1953.57	325.60	1.73	.1210
Prod × S(Credit)	108	20333.91	188.28		

$$t_{\hat{\psi}_G} = \frac{60.171 - 45.700}{\sqrt{(292.9881/70)(2)}} = 5.0016 \qquad (5.25)$$

which could be compared with a $q/\sqrt{2}$ critical value with $J = 2$ and $df_{S(G)} = 18$ of $2.97/\sqrt{2} = 2.10$. Obviously, this sole comparison of the two means is significant, $t = 5.0016$, simply because the overall F, $t^2 = F = 25.02$, is an equivalent test and was significant.

MCPs on the T means are affected by sphericity and, in the absence of research to date, would be computed like the MCPs for the repeated factor in the SRMD. Collapsing over groups, compute two-correlated-sample t tests for all possible pairs of levels of T and refer the statistics to a Dunn critical value with parameters df $= J(n - 1)$ and $C = K(K - 1)/2$ if all pairwise comparisons are computed, or C equal to the actual number of comparisons computed. To illustrate, the comparison of product 6 and product 7 is given for the credit card data. First, compute all differences, $d = Y_6 - Y_7$. Then compute the mean of the differences and the unbiased variance of the differences. The $nK = 20$ differences had mean 99.75 and variance 585.25, and

$$t = \frac{\bar{d}}{\sqrt{s_d^2/nJ}} = \frac{99.75}{\sqrt{585.25/20}} = 18.44 \qquad (5.26)$$

The $t = 18.44$ should be compared with a Dunn critical value with df $= 18$ and $C = 21$, but Table A.4 in Appendix A does not give this combination of C and df. Following the interpolation instructions given in Appendix A gives a critical value of 3.532. The difference in the means for products 6 and 7 is significant, as are the following differences: 1-3, 1-6, 2-3, 2-6, 3-4, 3-5, 3-6, 3-7, 4-6, 4-7, and 5-6.

MCPs on cell means are more complex than for the usual two-way ANOVA, due to two issues: first, the different denominators for the overall tests and, second, the sphericity assumption. As given in Kirk (1982, pp. 508-509), the MCPs of interest are often called tests for simple effects means and often cluster into two types: tests on means for groups at trials, G at T, and tests on means for trials at groups, T at G. Tests for pairwise comparisons on means for G at T use the statistic

$$t_{\hat{\psi}_{G \, \text{at} \, T}} = \frac{\bar{Y}_{jk} - \bar{Y}_{j'k}}{\sqrt{(\text{MSWCELL}/n)\,(2)}} \qquad (5.27)$$

which has a pooled variance estimate called *MSWCELL* that is given as

$$\text{MSWCELL} = \frac{\text{SS}_{S(G)} + \text{SS}_{TS(G)}}{J(n - 1) + (K - 1)J(n - 1)} \qquad (5.28)$$

Critical values for any of the MCPs can be obtained by using

$$h_\alpha = \frac{h_1 \, \mathrm{MS}_{S(G)} + h_2 \, \mathrm{MS}_{TS(G)}(K-1)}{\mathrm{MS}_{S(G)} + \mathrm{MS}_{TS(G)}(K-1)} \qquad (5.29)$$

where h_α is the critical value for an MCP, such as Tukey, and h_1 and h_2 are the α-level critical values for the MCPs with $df_{S(G)} = J(n-1)$ and $df_{TS(G)} = (K-1)J(n-1)$, respectively. If the number-of-means parameter is needed, use the value of 2. If h_1 and h_2 are values of q from the Studentized range, then h_α must be divided by $\sqrt{2}$ to obtain a critical value for t.

In the credit card example, the researcher wanted to examine the difference in presence-absence of credit card stimuli for each of the seven product types. This called for seven tests of pairwise cell mean differences of the type G at T. For example, consider the difference in the means for present versus absent at Product 2. Computation of t starts by computing MSWCELL from Equation 5.28:

$$\mathrm{MSWCELL} = \frac{5273.7857 + 20333.9143}{18 + 108} = 203.2357 \qquad (5.30)$$

Then the t statistic is computed from Equation 5.27 as

$$t_{\hat{\psi}_{G \, \mathrm{at} \, T}} = \frac{39.7 - 24.1}{\sqrt{(203.2357/10)(2)}} = 2.45 \qquad (5.31)$$

The critical value for Tukey is computed from Equation 5.29 as

$$h_\alpha = \frac{2.97(292.9881) + 2.83(188.2770)(6)}{292.9881 + 188.2770(6)} = 2.8588$$

$$t_{\mathrm{crit}} = \frac{h_\alpha}{\sqrt{2}} = \frac{2.8588}{\sqrt{2}} = 2.02 \qquad (5.32)$$

Thus the $t = 2.45$ for present versus absent at Product 2 is significant, since it exceeds the critical value of 2.02. The only other present versus absent significance is at Product 6, $t = 5.02$.

Tests for pairwise comparisons on means for T at G use the two-correlated-sample t test for two different levels of T, the kth and k'th levels, at a given level of G. This statistic can be compared with a Dunn critical value with parameters $df = n - 1$ and C. Here, C is

$K(K - 1)/2$ if all possible pairwise comparisons are computed, or the actual number of such comparisons computed.

Using the credit card example, the researcher may have been interested in product type differences at "absence of credit card stimuli." To illustrate, consider the sixth and seventh product differences. For the $n = 10$ differences, the mean is 89.5 and the variance is 376.28. The t is computed as

$$t = \frac{89.5}{\sqrt{376.2778/10}} = 14.59 \tag{5.33}$$

This $t = 14.59$ should be compared with a Dunn critical value with df $= 9$ and $C = 21$, but this combination of df and C is not given in Table A.4. Following the interpolation rules given in Appendix A, the critical value is 4.193, and the mean difference is significant. Other significant differences in means for products at "absence of credit card stimuli" were 1-3, 1-6, 2-3, 2-6, 3-4, 3-5, 3-6, 3-7, 4-6, and 5-6.

For extensive coverage of other MCP issues in repeated measures designs, such as the more general types of comparisons, a matrix approach to comparisons and their denominators, or tests for trend, see Kirk (1982).

Summary

The problem of complexity of higher-order designs complicates the computation of MCPs. The researcher must choose α control for each comparison, for each family of comparisons, or for the entire experiment. In what is called a two-way ANOVA, most researchers choose to control α for each of the three families of comparisons: the main effect means for A, the main effect means for B, and the cell means. The controversy over tests on interaction effects versus tests on cell means was discussed and resolved in favor of tests on cell means because they are easier to interpret, are closer to the original hypotheses tested by most researchers, and contain the total impact on the subjects of both main effects and interaction. Tests on main effect means are a simple extension of those for the one-way ANOVA. Tests on cell means include finding critical values with the ideal number-of-means parameter using the Cicchetti (1972) approach.

MCPs for repeated measures designs included Dunn tests for means of the repeated factor in simple and groups-by-trials repeated measures designs. Tests were also given for group means and cell means in the groups-by-trials repeated measures designs.

Notes

1. At this point, the name for the statistical procedure, *two-way ANOVA*, will be used for any experimental design that uses this procedure. Thus this generic title could stand for a factorial arrangement of two treatments, commonly called a factorial design, a randomized block design where one factor is treatment and the second is block, or a simple repeated measures design where one factor is treatment and the second is subjects. In the last section of this chapter, special emphasis will be given to the simple repeated measures design, sometimes referred to in the literature as a "one-way repeated measures design."

2. The data presented here were simulated to have exactly the same means and standard deviations as given in Frank (1984), and thus give the same results on the overall Fs.

3. For example, see Marascuilo and Levin (1970, 1976), Levin and Marascuilo (1972, 1973), Games (1973), and Rosnow and Rosenthal (1989).

4. Actually, the controversy runs much deeper than just tests on cell means versus tests on interaction effects. Marascuilo and Levin (1970) defined a Type IV error as an incorrect interpretation of a correctly rejected hypothesis. They went on to use tests on cell means as an example of a Type IV error, because the tests on cell means were not attending only to the interaction parameters. They also discussed other statistical models that might be more appropriate for the researcher who wants to test cell mean differences, notably what they call a "nested" design. It should be noted that their analysis was nested, but the actual design was crossed (for definitions of *nested* and *crossed*, see the section on repeated measures designs). Levin and Marascuilo (1972) pointed out, in the context of Type IV errors in the one-way ANOVA, that "Type IV errors of this kind may be avoided simply by bypassing the F test altogether" (p. 369). Since most researchers are ultimately interested in the cell means tests, this suggestion is quite appropriate to the two-way ANOVA also: The overall two-way ANOVA is rarely a good picture of the ultimately desired analysis. Usually it is run merely out of habit, tradition, or convenience, or to obtain some of the statistics needed for the MCPs. The reason most researchers prefer tests on cell means is that the overall ANOVA and the test of interaction do not represent the researcher's hypotheses.

5. Researchers wanting to do tests on interaction effects should see Rosnow and Rosenthal (1989) or Marascuilo and Levin (1970).

6. Similar parameters exist for the critical values for other MCPs, such as the number-of-means minus one for Scheffé, which was $J - 1$ for the one-way ANOVA. These parameters are always related to the number-of-means parameter for the Studentized range.

7. Some authors call these types of comparisons *simple-effects contrasts* (see Kirk, 1982, p. 365).

8. Some authors recommend using $\alpha = .05 + .05 = .10$ as the total α for these tests, recognizing that they are MCPs done on what are often called *simple effects* and, as such, add together the sources of variability from one main effect and the interaction. Since the original F tests on these effects are each done at the $\alpha = .05$ level, the logic is that the αs should also be added. Note that this decision is made irrespective of the decision about the number-of-means parameter.

9. The term *subject* is used here in place of the phrase *experimental unit*. Repeated measures could be taken on, for example, a city, or a class of students, or an individual subject. Repeated measures designs as used in the behavioral sciences most often have subject as the experimental unit, so this term will be used throughout this section.

10. Two variables, main effects, are said to be *crossed* if every level of one variable appears in the design with every level of the second variable. Two variables, main effects, are said to be *nested* if they are not crossed. In every repeated measures design there is at least one variable that is crossed with subjects, and there may or may not be variables in which subjects are nested.

11. Excellent coverage of repeated measures designs is given in Kirk (1982) and Winer (1971).

12. These procedures for an overall test that maintains an approximate α will not be covered in this book. They are both available in SAS using the REPEATED option in GLM and are covered in Kirk (1982, pp. 256-262) and Winer (1971, pp. 281-283). See also Rogan, Keselman, and Mendoza (1979).

13. This is similar to data in Rosenthal and Rosnow (1985), where they had only four subjects and merely measured the subjects on three different occasions to test for linear and quadratic trend. The analysis given there is both interesting and informative.

14. The sphericity assumption as stated for each of the J groups is called the "multi-sample circularity assumption" by Kirk (1982, p. 500). It is discussed in Winer (1971, p. 523) in terms of an assumption on a common population covariance matrix, with the covariance matrices for all groups assumed equal to the common covariance matrix.

15. This example is based on Feinberg (1986), with some changes: It uses fewer subjects, omits the gender variable, and only roughly simulates the data and results.

Appendix A:
Tables of Critical Values

Table A.1: Critical Values of the F Distribution

Table A.2: Critical Values of the t Distribution

Table A.3: Percentage Points of the Studentized Range

Table A.4: Percentage Points of the Dunn Multiple Comparison Test

Table A.5: Percentage Points of the Dunn-Šidák Multiple Comparison Test

Table A.6: Critical Values for Dunnett: Percentage Points for the Comparison of $J - 1$ Treatment Means with a Control

Table A.7: Critical Values for the Studentized Maximum Modulus Distribution ($\alpha = .05$)

Interpolation rules are as follows:

(1) Interpolation with respect to df should be done linearly in 1/df.
(2) Interpolation with respect to J (or C) should be done linearly in $\log_e J$ (or $\log_e C$).

TABLE A.1 Critical Values of the *F* Distribution

Degrees of Freedom: Denominator	Degrees of Freedom: Numerator														
	1	2	3	4	5	6	7	8	9	10	11	12	14	16	20
1	161	200	216	225	230	234	237	239	241	242	243	244	245	246	248
	4,052	**4,999**	**5,403**	**5,625**	**5,764**	**5,859**	**5,928**	**5,981**	**6,022**	**6,056**	**6,082**	**6,106**	**6,142**	**6,169**	**6,208**
2	18.51	19.00	19.16	19.25	19.30	19.33	19.36	19.37	19.38	19.39	19.40	19.41	19.42	19.43	19.44
	98.49	**99.00**	**99.17**	**99.25**	**99.30**	**99.33**	**99.34**	**99.36**	**99.38**	**99.40**	**99.41**	**99.42**	**99.43**	**99.44**	**99.45**
3	10.13	9.55	9.28	9.12	9.01	8.94	8.88	8.84	8.81	8.78	8.76	8.74	8.71	8.69	8.66
	34.12	**30.82**	**29.46**	**28.71**	**28.24**	**27.91**	**27.67**	**27.49**	**27.34**	**27.23**	**27.13**	**27.05**	**26.92**	**26.83**	**26.69**
4	7.71	6.94	6.59	6.39	6.26	6.16	6.09	6.04	6.00	5.96	5.93	5.91	5.87	5.84	5.80
	21.20	**18.00**	**16.69**	**15.98**	**15.52**	**15.21**	**14.98**	**14.80**	**14.66**	**14.54**	**14.45**	**14.37**	**14.24**	**14.15**	**14.02**
5	6.61	5.79	5.41	5.19	5.05	4.95	4.88	4.82	4.78	4.74	4.70	4.68	4.64	4.60	4.56
	16.26	**13.27**	**12.06**	**11.39**	**10.97**	**10.67**	**10.45**	**10.27**	**10.15**	**10.05**	**9.96**	**9.89**	**9.77**	**9.68**	**9.55**
6	5.99	5.14	4.76	4.53	4.39	4.28	4.21	4.15	4.10	4.06	4.03	4.00	3.96	3.92	3.87
	13.74	**10.92**	**9.78**	**9.15**	**8.75**	**8.47**	**8.26**	**8.10**	**7.98**	**7.87**	**7.79**	**7.72**	**7.60**	**7.52**	**7.39**
7	5.59	4.47	4.35	4.12	3.97	3.87	3.79	3.73	3.68	3.63	3.60	3.57	3.52	3.49	3.44
	12.25	**9.55**	**8.45**	**7.85**	**7.46**	**7.19**	**7.00**	**6.84**	**6.71**	**6.62**	**6.54**	**6.47**	**6.35**	**6.27**	**6.15**
8	5.32	4.46	4.07	3.84	3.69	3.58	3.50	3.44	3.39	3.34	3.31	3.28	3.23	3.20	3.15
	11.26	**8.65**	**7.59**	**7.01**	**6.63**	**6.37**	**6.19**	**6.03**	**5.91**	**5.82**	**5.74**	**5.67**	**5.56**	**5.48**	**5.36**
9	5.12	4.26	3.86	3.63	3.48	3.37	3.29	3.23	3.18	3.13	3.10	3.07	3.02	2.98	2.93
	10.56	**8.02**	**6.99**	**6.42**	**6.06**	**5.80**	**5.62**	**5.47**	**5.35**	**5.26**	**5.18**	**5.11**	**5.00**	**4.92**	**4.80**
10	4.96	4.10	3.71	3.48	3.33	3.22	3.14	3.07	3.02	2.97	2.94	2.91	2.86	2.82	2.77
	10.04	**7.56**	**6.55**	**5.99**	**5.64**	**5.39**	**5.21**	**5.06**	**4.95**	**4.85**	**4.78**	**4.71**	**4.60**	**4.52**	**4.41**
11	4.84	3.98	3.59	3.36	3.20	3.09	3.01	2.95	2.90	2.86	2.82	2.79	2.74	2.70	2.65
	9.65	**7.20**	**6.22**	**5.67**	**5.32**	**5.07**	**4.88**	**4.74**	**4.63**	**4.54**	**4.46**	**4.40**	**4.29**	**4.21**	**4.10**
12	4.75	3.88	3.49	3.26	3.11	3.00	2.92	2.85	2.80	2.76	2.72	2.69	2.64	2.60	2.54
	9.33	**6.93**	**5.95**	**5.41**	**5.06**	**4.82**	**4.65**	**4.50**	**4.39**	**4.30**	**4.22**	**4.16**	**4.05**	**3.98**	**3.86**
13	4.67	3.80	3.41	3.18	3.02	2.92	2.84	2.77	2.72	2.67	2.63	2.60	2.55	2.51	2.46
	9.07	**6.70**	**5.74**	**5.20**	**4.86**	**4.62**	**4.44**	**4.30**	**4.19**	**4.10**	**4.02**	**3.96**	**3.85**	**3.78**	**3.67**
14	4.60	3.74	3.34	3.11	2.96	2.85	2.77	2.70	2.65	2.60	2.56	2.53	2.48	2.44	2.39
	8.86	**6.51**	**5.56**	**5.03**	**4.69**	**4.46**	**4.28**	**4.14**	**4.03**	**3.94**	**3.86**	**3.80**	**3.70**	**3.62**	**3.51**
15	4.54	3.68	3.29	3.06	2.90	2.79	2.70	2.64	2.59	2.55	2.51	2.48	2.43	2.39	2.33
	8.68	**6.36**	**5.42**	**4.89**	**4.56**	**4.32**	**4.14**	**4.00**	**3.89**	**3.80**	**3.73**	**3.67**	**3.56**	**3.48**	**3.36**
16	4.49	3.63	3.24	3.01	2.85	2.74	2.66	2.59	2.54	2.49	2.45	2.42	2.37	2.33	2.28
	8.53	**6.23**	**5.29**	**4.77**	**4.44**	**4.20**	**4.03**	**3.89**	**3.78**	**3.69**	**3.61**	**3.55**	**3.45**	**3.37**	**3.25**
17	4.45	3.59	3.20	2.96	2.81	2.70	2.62	2.55	2.50	2.45	2.41	2.38	2.33	2.29	2.23
	8.40	**6.11**	**5.18**	**4.67**	**4.34**	**4.10**	**3.93**	**3.79**	**3.68**	**3.59**	**3.52**	**3.45**	**3.35**	**3.27**	**3.16**
18	4.41	3.55	3.16	2.93	2.77	2.66	2.58	2.51	2.46	2.41	2.37	2.34	2.29	2.25	2.19
	8.28	**6.01**	**5.09**	**4.58**	**4.25**	**4.01**	**3.85**	**3.71**	**3.60**	**3.51**	**3.44**	**3.37**	**3.27**	**3.19**	**3.07**
19	4.38	3.52	3.13	2.90	2.74	2.63	2.55	2.48	2.43	2.38	2.34	2.31	2.26	2.21	2.15
	8.18	**5.93**	**5.01**	**4.50**	**4.17**	**3.94**	**3.77**	**3.63**	**3.52**	**3.43**	**3.36**	**3.30**	**3.19**	**3.12**	**3.00**
20	4.35	3.49	3.10	2.87	2.71	2.60	2.52	2.45	2.40	2.35	2.31	2.28	2.23	2.18	2.12
	8.10	**5.85**	**4.94**	**4.43**	**4.10**	**3.87**	**3.71**	**3.56**	**3.45**	**3.37**	**3.30**	**3.23**	**3.13**	**3.05**	**2.94**
21	4.32	3.47	3.07	2.84	2.68	2.57	2.49	2.42	2.37	2.32	2.28	2.25	2.20	2.15	2.09
	8.02	**5.78**	**4.87**	**4.37**	**4.04**	**3.81**	**3.65**	**3.51**	**3.40**	**3.31**	**3.24**	**3.17**	**3.07**	**2.99**	**2.88**
22	4.30	3.44	3.05	2.82	2.66	2.55	2.47	2.40	2.35	2.30	2.26	2.23	2.18	2.13	2.07
	7.94	**5.72**	**4.82**	**4.31**	**3.99**	**3.76**	**3.59**	**3.45**	**3.35**	**3.26**	**3.18**	**3.12**	**3.02**	**2.94**	**2.83**
23	4.28	3.42	3.03	2.80	2.64	2.53	2.45	2.38	2.32	2.28	2.24	2.20	2.14	2.10	2.04
	7.88	**5.66**	**4.76**	**4.26**	**3.94**	**3.71**	**3.54**	**3.41**	**3.30**	**3.21**	**3.14**	**3.07**	**2.97**	**2.89**	**2.78**
24	4.26	3.40	3.01	2.78	2.62	2.51	2.43	2.36	2.30	2.26	2.22	2.18	2.13	2.09	2.02
	7.82	**5.61**	**4.72**	**4.22**	**3.90**	**3.67**	**3.50**	**3.36**	**3.25**	**3.17**	**3.09**	**3.03**	**2.93**	**2.85**	**2.74**
25	4.24	3.38	2.99	2.76	2.60	2.49	2.41	2.34	2.28	2.24	2.20	2.16	2.11	2.06	2.00
	7.77	**5.57**	**4.68**	**4.18**	**3.86**	**3.63**	**3.46**	**3.32**	**3.21**	**3.13**	**3.05**	**2.99**	**2.89**	**2.81**	**2.70**

SOURCE: From *Statistical Methods*, eighth edition, by G. W. Snedecor and W. G. Cochran, copyright © 1989 by the Iowa State University Press, Ames, Iowa, 50010, as adapted by E. W. Minium and R. B. Clarke: *Elements of Statistical Reasoning*, John Wiley & Sons, 1982. Reprinted by permission of John Wiley & Sons, Inc., and Iowa State University Press.
NOTE: The values in roman type are for $\alpha = .05$ and those in boldface type are for $\alpha = .01$.

TABLE A.1, Continued

Degrees of Freedom: Denominator	Degrees of Freedom: Numerator														
	1	2	3	4	5	6	7	8	9	10	11	12	14	16	20
26	4.22	3.37	2.98	2.74	2.59	2.47	2.39	2.32	2.27	2.22	2.18	2.15	2.10	2.05	1.99
	7.72	5.53	4.64	4.14	3.82	3.59	3.42	3.29	3.17	3.09	3.02	2.96	2.86	2.77	2.66
27	4.21	3.35	2.96	2.73	2.57	2.46	2.37	2.30	2.25	2.20	2.16	2.13	2.08	2.03	1.97
	7.68	5.49	4.60	4.11	3.79	3.56	3.39	3.26	3.14	3.06	2.98	2.93	2.83	2.74	2.63
28	4.20	3.34	2.95	2.71	2.56	2.44	2.36	2.29	2.24	2.19	2.15	2.12	2.06	2.02	1.96
	7.64	5.45	4.57	4.07	3.76	3.53	3.36	3.23	3.11	3.03	2.95	2.90	2.80	2.71	2.60
29	4.18	3.33	2.93	2.70	2.54	2.43	2.35	2.28	2.22	2.18	2.14	2.10	2.05	2.00	1.94
	7.60	5.42	4.54	4.04	3.73	3.50	3.33	3.20	3.08	3.00	2.92	2.87	2.77	2.68	2.57
30	4.17	3.32	2.92	2.69	2.53	2.42	2.34	2.27	2.21	2.16	2.12	2.09	2.04	1.99	1.93
	7.56	5.39	4.51	4.02	3.70	3.47	3.30	3.17	3.06	2.98	2.90	2.84	2.74	2.66	2.55
32	4.15	3.30	2.90	2.67	2.51	2.40	2.32	2.25	2.19	2.14	2.10	2.07	2.02	1.97	1.91
	7.50	5.34	4.46	3.97	3.66	3.42	3.25	3.12	3.01	2.94	2.86	2.80	2.70	2.62	2.51
34	4.13	3.28	2.88	2.65	2.49	2.38	2.30	2.23	2.17	2.12	2.08	2.05	2.00	1.95	1.89
	7.44	5.29	4.42	3.93	3.61	3.38	3.21	3.08	2.97	2.89	2.82	2.76	2.66	2.58	2.47
36	4.11	3.26	2.86	2.63	2.48	2.36	2.28	2.21	2.15	2.10	2.06	2.03	1.98	1.93	1.87
	7.39	5.25	4.38	3.89	3.58	3.35	3.18	3.04	2.94	2.86	2.78	2.72	2.62	2.54	2.43
38	4.10	3.25	2.85	2.62	2.46	2.35	2.26	2.19	2.14	2.09	2.05	2.02	1.96	1.92	1.85
	7.35	5.21	4.34	3.86	3.54	3.32	3.15	3.02	2.91	2.82	2.75	2.69	2.59	2.51	2.40
40	4.08	3.23	2.84	2.61	2.45	2.34	2.25	2.18	2.12	2.07	2.04	2.00	1.95	1.90	1.84
	7.31	5.18	4.31	3.83	3.51	3.29	3.12	2.99	2.88	2.80	2.73	2.66	2.56	2.49	2.37
42	4.07	3.22	2.83	2.59	2.44	2.32	2.24	2.17	2.11	2.06	2.02	1.99	1.94	1.89	1.82
	7.27	5.15	4.29	3.80	3.49	3.26	3.10	2.96	2.86	2.77	2.70	2.64	2.54	2.46	2.35
44	4.06	3.21	2.82	2.58	2.43	2.31	2.23	2.16	2.10	2.05	2.01	1.98	1.92	1.88	1.81
	7.24	5.12	4.26	3.78	3.46	3.24	3.07	2.94	2.84	2.75	2.68	2.62	2.52	2.44	2.32
46	4.05	3.20	2.81	2.57	2.42	2.30	2.22	2.14	2.09	2.04	2.00	1.97	1.91	1.87	1.80
	7.21	5.10	4.24	3.76	3.44	3.22	3.05	2.92	2.82	2.73	2.66	2.60	2.50	2.42	2.30
48	4.04	3.19	2.80	2.56	2.41	2.30	2.21	2.14	2.08	2.03	1.99	1.96	1.90	1.86	1.79
	7.19	5.08	4.22	3.74	3.42	3.20	3.04	2.90	2.80	2.71	2.64	2.58	2.48	2.40	2.28
50	4.03	3.18	2.79	2.56	2.40	2.29	2.20	2.13	2.07	2.02	1.98	1.95	1.90	1.85	1.78
	7.17	5.06	4.20	3.72	3.41	3.18	3.02	2.88	2.78	2.70	2.62	2.56	2.46	2.39	2.26
55	4.02	3.17	2.78	2.54	2.38	2.27	2.18	2.11	2.05	2.00	1.97	1.93	1.88	1.83	1.76
	7.12	5.01	4.16	3.68	3.37	3.15	2.98	2.85	2.75	2.66	2.59	2.53	2.43	2.35	2.23
60	4.00	3.15	2.76	2.52	2.37	2.25	2.17	2.10	2.04	1.99	1.95	1.92	1.86	1.81	1.75
	7.08	4.98	4.13	3.65	3.34	3.12	2.95	2.82	2.72	2.63	2.56	2.50	2.40	2.32	2.20
65	3.99	3.14	2.75	2.51	2.36	2.24	2.15	2.08	2.02	1.98	1.94	1.90	1.85	1.80	1.73
	7.04	4.95	4.10	3.62	3.31	3.09	2.93	2.79	2.70	2.61	2.54	2.47	2.37	2.30	2.18
70	3.98	3.13	2.74	2.50	2.35	2.23	2.14	2.07	2.01	1.97	1.93	1.89	1.84	1.79	1.72
	7.01	4.92	4.08	3.60	3.29	3.07	2.91	2.77	2.67	2.59	2.51	2.45	2.35	2.28	2.15
80	3.96	3.11	2.72	2.48	2.33	2.21	2.12	2.05	1.99	1.95	1.91	1.88	1.82	1.77	1.70
	6.96	4.88	4.04	3.56	3.25	3.04	2.87	2.74	2.64	2.55	2.48	2.41	2.32	2.24	2.11
100	3.94	3.09	2.70	2.46	2.30	2.19	2.10	2.03	1.97	1.92	1.88	1.85	1.79	1.75	1.68
	6.90	4.82	3.98	3.51	3.20	2.99	2.82	2.69	2.59	2.51	2.43	2.36	2.26	2.19	2.06
125	3.92	3.07	2.68	2.44	2.29	2.17	2.08	2.01	1.95	1.90	1.86	1.83	1.77	1.72	1.65
	6.84	4.78	3.94	3.47	3.17	2.95	2.79	2.65	2.56	2.47	2.40	2.33	2.23	2.15	2.03
150	3.91	3.06	2.67	2.43	2.27	2.16	2.07	2.00	1.94	1.89	1.85	1.82	1.76	1.71	1.64
	6.81	4.75	3.91	3.44	3.14	2.92	2.76	2.62	2.53	2.44	2.37	2.30	2.20	2.12	2.00
200	3.89	3.04	2.65	2.41	2.26	2.14	2.05	1.98	1.92	1.87	1.83	1.80	1.74	1.69	1.62
	6.76	4.71	3.88	3.41	3.11	2.90	2.73	2.60	2.50	2.41	2.34	2.28	2.17	2.09	1.97
400	3.86	3.02	2.62	2.39	2.23	2.12	2.03	1.96	1.90	1.85	1.81	1.78	1.72	1.67	1.60
	6.70	4.66	3.83	3.36	3.06	2.85	2.69	2.55	2.46	2.37	2.29	2.23	2.12	2.04	1.92
1000	3.85	3.00	2.61	2.38	2.22	2.10	2.02	1.95	1.89	1.84	1.80	1.76	1.70	1.65	1.58
	6.66	4.62	3.80	3.34	3.04	2.82	2.66	2.53	2.43	2.34	2.26	2.20	2.09	2.01	1.89
∞	3.84	2.99	2.60	2.37	2.21	2.09	2.01	1.94	1.88	1.83	1.79	1.75	1.69	1.64	1.57
	6.64	4.60	3.78	3.32	3.02	2.80	2.64	2.51	2.41	2.32	2.24	2.18	2.07	1.99	1.87

TABLE A.2 Critical Values of the *t* Distribution

			α for Two-Tailed Test			
	.50	.20	.10	.05	.02	.01
			α for One-Tailed Test			
df	.25	.10	.05	.025	.01	.005
1	1.000	3.078	6.314	12.706	31.821	63.657
2	0.816	1.886	2.920	4.303	6.965	9.925
3	0.765	1.638	2.353	3.182	4.541	5.841
4	0.741	1.533	2.132	2.776	3.747	4.604
5	0.727	1.476	2.015	2.571	3.365	4.032
6	0.718	1.440	1.943	2.447	3.143	3.707
7	0.711	1.415	1.895	2.365	2.998	3.499
8	0.706	1.397	1.860	2.306	2.896	3.355
9	0.703	1.383	1.833	2.262	2.821	3.250
10	0.700	1.372	1.812	2.228	2.764	3.169
11	0.697	1.363	1.796	2.201	2.718	3.106
12	0.695	1.356	1.782	2.179	2.681	3.055
13	0.694	1.350	1.771	2.160	2.650	3.012
14	0.692	1.345	1.761	2.145	2.624	2.977
15	0.691	1.341	1.753	2.132	2.602	2.947
16	0.690	1.337	1.746	2.120	2.583	2.921
17	0.689	1.333	1.740	2.110	2.567	2.898
18	0.688	1.330	1.734	2.101	2.552	2.878
19	0.688	1.328	1.729	2.093	2.539	2.861
20	0.687	1.325	1.725	2.086	2.528	2.845
21	0.686	1.323	1.721	2.080	2.518	2.831
22	0.686	1.321	1.717	2.074	2.508	2.819
23	0.685	1.319	1.714	2.069	2.500	2.807
24	0.685	1.318	1.711	2.064	2.492	2.797
25	0.684	1.316	1.708	2.060	2.485	2.787
26	0.684	1.315	1.706	2.056	2.479	2.779
27	0.684	1.314	1.703	2.052	2.473	2.771
28	0.683	1.313	1.701	2.048	2.467	2.763
29	0.683	1.311	1.699	2.045	2.462	2.756
30	0.683	1.310	1.697	2.042	2.457	2.750
40	0.681	1.303	1.684	2.021	2.423	2.704
60	0.679	1.296	1.671	2.000	2.390	2.660
120	0.677	1.289	1.658	1.980	2.358	2.617
∞	0.674	1.282	1.645	1.960	2.326	2.576

SOURCE: This table is taken from Table III of Fisher and Yates' *Statistical Tables for Biological, Agricultural and Medical Research*, published by Longman Group UK Ltd, London (previously published by Oliver and Boyd Ltd, Edinburgh), copyright © 1974 by Longman Group UK Ltd, and by permission of the authors and publishers, as adapted by E. W. Minium and R. B. Clarke: *Elements of Statistical Reasoning*, John Wiley & Sons, Inc. 1982. Reprinted by permission of John Wiley & Sons, Inc.

TABLE A.3 Percentage Points of the Studentized Range

Error df	α	Number of Means (J) or Number of Steps Between Ordered Means									
		2	3	4	5	6	7	8	9	10	11
2	.05	6.08	8.33	9.80	10.9	11.7	12.4	13.0	13.5	14.0	14.4
	.01	14.0	19.0	22.3	24.7	26.6	28.2	29.5	30.7	31.7	32.6
3	.05	4.50	5.91	6.82	7.50	8.04	8.48	8.85	9.18	9.46	9.72
	.01	8.26	10.6	12.2	13.3	14.2	15.0	15.6	16.2	16.7	17.8
4	.05	3.93	5.04	5.76	6.29	6.71	7.05	7.35	7.60	7.83	8.03
	.01	6.51	8.12	9.17	9.96	10.6	11.1	11.5	11.9	12.3	12.6
5	.05	3.64	4.60	5.22	5.67	6.03	6.33	6.58	6.80	6.99	7.17
	.01	5.70	6.98	7.80	8.42	8.91	9.32	9.67	9.97	10.24	10.48
6	.05	3.46	4.34	4.90	5.30	5.63	5.90	6.12	6.32	6.49	6.65
	.01	5.24	6.33	7.03	7.56	7.97	8.32	8.61	8.87	9.10	9.30
7	.05	3.34	4.16	4.68	5.06	5.36	5.61	5.82	6.00	6.16	6.30
	.01	4.95	5.92	6.54	7.01	7.37	7.68	7.94	8.17	8.37	8.55
8	.05	3.26	4.04	4.53	4.89	5.17	5.40	5.60	5.77	5.92	6.05
	.01	4.75	5.64	6.20	6.62	6.96	7.24	7.47	7.68	7.86	8.03
9	.05	3.20	3.95	4.41	4.76	5.02	5.24	5.43	5.59	5.74	5.87
	.01	4.60	5.43	5.96	6.35	6.66	6.91	7.13	7.33	7.49	7.65
10	.05	3.15	3.88	4.33	4.65	4.91	5.12	5.30	5.46	5.60	5.72
	.01	4.48	5.27	5.77	6.14	6.43	6.67	6.87	7.05	7.21	7.36
11	.05	3.11	3.82	4.26	4.57	4.82	5.03	5.20	5.35	5.49	5.61
	.01	4.39	5.15	5.62	5.97	6.25	6.48	6.67	6.84	6.99	7.13
12	.05	3.08	3.77	4.20	4.51	4.75	4.95	5.12	5.27	5.39	5.51
	.01	4.32	5.05	5.50	5.84	6.10	6.32	6.51	6.67	6.81	6.94
13	.05	3.06	3.73	4.15	4.45	4.69	4.88	5.05	5.19	5.32	5.43
	.01	4.26	4.96	5.40	5.73	5.98	6.19	6.37	6.53	6.67	6.79
14	.05	3.03	3.70	4.11	4.41	4.64	4.83	4.99	5.13	5.25	5.36
	.01	4.21	4.89	5.32	5.63	5.88	6.08	6.26	6.41	6.54	6.66
15	.05	3.01	3.67	4.08	4.37	4.59	4.78	4.94	5.08	5.20	5.31
	.01	4.17	4.84	5.25	5.56	5.80	5.99	6.16	6.31	6.44	6.55
16	.05	3.00	3.65	4.05	4.33	4.56	4.74	4.90	5.03	5.15	5.26
	.01	4.13	4.79	5.19	5.49	5.72	5.92	6.08	6.22	6.35	6.46
17	.05	2.98	3.63	4.02	4.30	4.52	4.70	4.86	4.99	5.11	5.21
	.01	4.10	4.74	5.14	5.43	5.66	5.85	6.01	6.15	6.27	6.38
18	.05	2.97	3.61	4.00	4.28	4.49	4.67	4.82	4.96	5.07	5.17
	.01	4.07	4.70	5.09	5.38	5.60	5.79	5.94	6.08	6.20	6.31
19	.05	2.96	3.59	3.98	4.25	4.47	4.65	4.79	4.92	5.04	5.14
	.01	4.05	4.67	5.05	5.33	5.55	5.73	5.89	6.02	6.14	6.25
20	.05	2.95	3.58	3.96	4.23	4.45	4.62	4.77	4.90	5.01	5.11
	.01	4.02	4.64	5.02	5.29	5.51	5.69	5.84	5.97	6.09	6.19
24	.05	2.92	3.53	3.90	4.17	4.37	4.54	4.68	4.81	4.92	5.01
	.01	3.96	4.55	4.91	5.17	5.37	5.54	5.69	5.81	5.92	6.02
30	.05	2.89	3.49	3.85	4.10	4.30	4.46	4.60	4.72	4.82	4.92
	.01	3.89	4.45	4.80	5.05	5.24	5.40	5.54	5.65	5.76	5.85
40	.05	2.86	3.44	3.79	4.04	4.23	4.39	4.52	4.63	4.73	4.82
	.01	3.82	4.37	4.70	4.93	5.11	5.26	5.39	5.50	5.60	5.69
60	.05	2.83	3.40	3.74	3.98	4.16	4.31	4.44	4.55	4.65	4.73
	.01	3.76	4.28	4.59	4.82	4.99	5.13	5.25	5.36	5.45	5.53
120	.05	2.80	3.36	3.68	3.92	4.10	4.24	4.36	4.47	4.56	4.64
	.01	3.70	4.20	4.50	4.71	4.87	5.01	5.12	5.21	5.30	5.37
∞	.05	2.77	3.31	3.63	3.86	4.03	4.17	4.29	4.39	4.47	4.55
	.01	3.64	4.12	4.40	4.60	4.76	4.88	4.99	5.08	5.16	5.23

 continued

TABLE A.3, Continued

12	13	14	15	16	17	18	19	20	α	Error df
\multicolumn{11}{c}{*Number of Means (J) or Number of Steps Between Ordered Means*}

12	13	14	15	16	17	18	19	20	α	Error df
14.7	15.1	15.4	15.7	15.9	16.1	16.4	16.6	16.8	.05	2
33.4	34.1	34.8	35.4	36.0	36.5	37.0	37.5	37.9	.01	
9.72	10.2	10.3	10.5	10.7	10.8	11.0	11.1	11.2	.05	3
17.5	17.9	18.2	18.5	18.8	19.1	19.3	19.5	19.8	.01	
8.21	8.37	8.52	8.66	8.79	8.91	9.03	9.13	9.23	.05	4
12.8	13.1	13.3	13.5	13.7	13.9	14.1	14.2	14.4	.01	
7.32	7.47	7.60	7.72	7.83	7.93	8.03	8.12	8.21	.05	5
10.70	10.89	11.08	11.24	11.40	11.55	11.68	11.81	11.93	.01	
6.79	6.92	7.03	7.14	7.24	7.34	7.43	7.51	7.59	.05	6
9.48	9.65	9.81	9.95	10.08	10.21	10.32	10.43	10.54	.01	
6.43	6.55	6.66	6.76	6.85	6.94	7.02	7.10	7.17	.05	7
8.71	8.86	9.00	9.12	9.24	9.35	9.46	9.55	9.65	.01	
6.18	6.29	6.39	6.48	6.57	6.65	6.73	6.80	6.87	.05	8
8.18	8.31	8.44	8.55	8.66	8.76	8.85	8.94	9.03	.01	
5.98	6.09	6.19	6.28	6.36	6.44	6.51	6.58	6.64	.05	9
7.78	7.91	8.03	8.13	8.23	8.33	8.41	8.49	8.57	.01	
5.83	5.93	6.03	6.11	6.19	6.27	6.34	6.40	6.47	.05	10
7.49	7.60	7.71	7.81	7.91	7.99	8.08	8.15	8.23	.01	
5.71	5.81	5.90	5.98	6.06	6.13	6.20	6.27	6.33	.05	11
7.25	7.36	7.46	7.56	7.65	7.73	7.81	7.88	7.95	.01	
5.61	5.71	5.80	5.88	5.95	6.02	6.09	6.15	6.21	.05	12
7.06	7.17	7.26	7.36	7.44	7.52	7.59	7.66	7.73	.01	
5.53	5.63	5.71	5.79	5.86	5.93	5.99	6.05	6.11	.05	13
6.90	7.01	7.10	7.19	7.27	7.35	7.42	7.48	7.55	.01	
5.46	5.55	5.64	5.71	5.79	5.85	5.91	5.97	6.03	.05	14
6.77	6.87	6.96	7.05	7.13	7.20	7.27	7.33	7.39	.01	
5.40	5.49	5.57	5.65	5.72	5.78	5.85	5.90	5.96	.05	15
6.66	6.76	6.84	6.93	7.00	7.07	7.14	7.20	7.26	.01	
5.35	5.44	5.52	5.59	5.66	5.73	5.79	5.84	5.90	.05	16
6.56	6.66	6.74	6.82	6.90	6.97	7.03	7.09	7.15	.01	
5.31	5.39	5.47	5.54	5.61	5.67	5.73	5.79	5.84	.05	17
6.48	6.57	6.66	6.73	6.81	6.87	6.94	7.00	7.05	.01	
5.27	5.35	5.43	5.50	5.57	5.63	5.69	5.74	5.79	.05	18
6.41	6.50	6.58	6.65	6.73	6.79	6.85	6.91	6.97	.01	
5.23	5.31	5.39	5.46	5.53	5.59	5.65	5.70	5.75	.05	19
6.34	6.43	6.51	6.58	6.65	6.72	6.78	6.84	6.89	.01	
5.20	5.28	5.36	5.43	5.49	5.55	5.61	5.66	5.71	.05	20
6.28	6.37	6.45	6.52	6.59	6.65	6.71	6.77	6.82	.01	
5.10	5.18	5.25	5.32	5.38	5.44	5.49	5.55	5.59	.05	24
6.11	6.19	6.26	6.33	6.39	6.45	6.51	6.56	6.61	.01	
5.00	5.08	5.15	5.21	5.27	5.33	5.38	5.43	5.47	.05	30
5.93	6.01	6.08	6.14	6.20	6.26	6.31	6.36	6.41	.01	
4.90	4.98	5.04	5.11	5.16	5.22	5.27	5.31	5.36	.05	40
5.76	5.83	5.90	5.96	6.02	6.07	6.12	6.16	6.21	.01	
4.81	4.88	4.94	5.00	5.06	5.11	5.15	5.20	5.24	.05	60
5.60	5.67	5.73	5.78	5.84	5.89	5.93	5.97	6.01	.01	
4.71	4.78	4.84	4.90	4.95	5.00	5.04	5.09	5.13	.05	120
5.44	5.50	5.56	5.61	5.66	5.71	5.75	5.79	5.83	.01	
4.62	4.68	4.74	4.80	4.85	4.89	4.93	4.97	5.01	.05	∞
5.29	5.35	5.40	5.45	5.49	5.54	5.57	5.61	5.65	.01	

TABLE A.4 Percentage Points of the Dunn Multiple Comparison Test

Number of Comparisons (C)	α	5	7	10	12	15	Error df 20	24	30	40	60	120	∞
2	.05	3.17	2.84	2.64	2.56	2.49	2.42	2.39	2.36	2.33	2.30	2.27	2.24
	.01	4.78	4.03	3.58	3.43	3.29	3.16	3.09	3.03	2.97	2.92	2.86	2.81
3	.05	3.54	3.13	2.87	2.78	2.69	2.61	2.58	2.54	2.50	2.47	2.43	2.39
	.01	5.25	4.36	3.83	3.65	3.48	3.33	3.26	3.19	3.12	3.06	2.99	2.94
4	.05	3.81	3.34	3.04	2.94	2.84	2.75	2.70	2.66	2.62	2.58	2.54	2.50
	.01	5.60	4.59	4.01	3.80	3.62	3.46	3.38	3.30	3.23	3.16	3.09	3.02
5	.05	4.04	3.50	3.17	3.06	2.95	2.85	2.80	2.75	2.71	2.66	2.62	2.58
	.01	5.89	4.78	4.15	3.93	3.74	3.55	3.47	3.39	3.31	3.24	3.16	3.09
6	.05	4.22	3.64	3.28	3.15	3.04	2.93	2.88	2.83	2.78	2.73	2.68	2.64
	.01	6.15	4.95	4.27	4.04	3.82	3.63	3.54	3.46	3.38	3.30	3.22	3.15
7	.05	4.38	3.76	3.37	3.24	3.11	3.00	2.94	2.89	2.84	2.79	2.74	2.69
	.01	6.36	5.09	4.37	4.13	3.90	3.70	3.61	3.52	3.43	3.34	3.27	3.19
8	.05	4.53	3.86	3.45	3.31	3.18	3.06	3.00	2.94	2.89	2.84	2.79	2.74
	.01	6.56	5.21	4.45	4.20	3.97	3.76	3.66	3.57	3.48	3.39	3.31	3.23
9	.05	4.66	3.95	3.52	3.37	3.24	3.11	3.05	2.99	2.93	2.88	2.83	2.77
	.01	6.70	5.31	4.53	4.26	4.02	3.80	3.70	3.61	3.51	3.42	3.34	3.26
10	.05	4.78	4.03	3.58	3.43	3.29	3.16	3.09	3.03	2.97	2.92	2.86	2.81
	.01	6.86	5.40	4.59	4.32	4.07	3.85	3.74	3.65	3.55	3.46	3.37	3.29
15	.05	5.25	4.36	3.83	3.65	3.48	3.33	3.26	3.19	3.12	3.06	2.99	2.94
	.01	7.51	5.79	4.86	4.56	4.29	4.03	3.91	3.80	3.70	3.59	3.50	3.40
20	.05	5.60	4.59	4.01	3.80	3.62	3.46	3.38	3.30	3.23	3.16	3.09	3.02
	.01	8.00	6.08	5.06	4.73	4.42	4.15	4.04	3.90	3.79	3.69	3.58	3.48
25	.05	5.89	4.78	4.15	3.93	3.74	3.55	3.47	3.39	3.31	3.24	3.16	3.09
	.01	8.37	6.30	5.20	4.86	4.53	4.25	4.1*	3.98	3.88	3.76	3.64	3.54
30	.05	6.15	4.95	4.27	4.04	3.82	3.63	3.54	3.46	3.38	3.30	3.22	3.15
	.01	8.68	6.49	5.33	4.95	4.61	4.33	4.2*	4.13	3.93	3.81	3.69	3.59
35	.05	6.36	5.09	4.37	4.13	3.90	3.70	3.61	3.52	3.43	3.34	3.27	3.19
	.01	8.95	6.67	5.44	5.04	4.71	4.39	4.3*	4.26	3.97	3.84	3.73	3.63
40	.05	6.56	5.21	4.45	4.20	3.97	3.76	3.66	3.57	3.48	3.39	3.31	3.23
	.01	9.19	6.83	5.52	5.12	4.78	4.46	4.3*	4.1*	4.01	3.89	3.77	3.66
45	.05	6.70	5.31	4.53	4.26	4.02	3.80	3.70	3.61	3.51	3.42	3.34	3.26
	.01	9.41	6.93	5.60	5.20	4.84	4.52	4.3*	4.2*	4.1*	3.93	3.80	3.69
50	.05	6.86	5.40	4.59	4.32	4.07	3.85	3.74	3.65	3.55	3.46	3.37	3.29
	.01	9.68	7.06	5.70	5.27	4.90	4.56	4.4*	4.2*	4.1*	3.97	3.83	3.72
100	.05	8.00	6.08	5.06	4.73	4.42	4.15	4.04	3.90	3.79	3.69	3.58	3.48
	.01	11.04	7.80	6.20	5.70	5.20	4.80	4.7*	4.4*	4.5*		4.00	3.89
250	.05	9.68	7.06	5.70	5.27	4.90	4.56	4.4*	4.2*	4.1*	3.97	3.83	3.72
	.01	13.26	8.83	6.9*	6.3*	5.8*	5.2*	5.0*	4.9*	4.8*			4.11

SOURCE: From "Multiple Comparisons Among Means," *Journal of the American Statistical Association*, 1961, *56*, 52-64, by O. J. Dunn, copyright © 1961 by the American Statistical Association, as adapted by R. E. Kirk: *Experimental Design: Procedures for the Behavioral Sciences*, Brooks/Cole Publishing Company, 1982. Used by permission of Brooks/Cole Publishing Company and the American Statistical Association.
*Obtained by graphical interpolation.

TABLE A.5 Percentage Points of the Dunn-Šidák Multiple Comparison Test

Error df	α	Number of Comparisons (C)												
		2	3	4	5	6	7	8	9	10	15	20	25	30
2	.10	4.243	5.243	6.081	6.816	7.480	8.090	8.656	9.188	9.691	11.890	13.741	15.371	16.845
	.05	6.164	7.582	8.774	9.823	10.769	11.639	12.449	13.208	13.927	17.072	19.721	22.054	24.163
	.01	14.071	17.248	19.925	22.282	24.413	26.372	28.196	29.908	31.528	38.620	44.598	49.865	54.626
3	.10	3.149	3.690	4.115	4.471	4.780	5.055	5.304	5.532	5.744	6.627	7.326	7.914	8.427
	.05	4.156	4.826	5.355	5.799	6.185	6.529	6.842	7.128	7.394	8.505	9.387	10.129	10.778
	.01	7.447	8.565	9.453	10.201	10.853	11.436	11.966	12.453	12.904	14.796	16.300	17.569	18.678
4	.10	2.751	3.150	3.452	3.699	3.909	4.093	4.257	4.406	4.542	5.097	5.521	5.870	6.169
	.05	3.481	3.941	4.290	4.577	4.822	5.036	5.228	5.402	5.562	6.214	6.714	7.127	7.480
	.01	5.594	6.248	6.751	7.166	7.520	7.832	8.112	8.367	8.600	9.556	10.294	10.902	11.424
5	.10	2.549	2.882	3.129	3.327	3.493	3.638	3.765	3.880	3.985	4.403	4.718	4.972	5.187
	.05	3.152	3.518	3.791	4.012	4.197	4.358	4.501	4.630	4.747	5.219	5.573	5.861	6.105
	.01	4.771	5.243	5.599	5.888	6.133	6.346	6.535	6.706	6.862	7.491	7.968	8.355	8.684
6	.10	2.428	2.723	2.939	3.110	3.253	3.376	3.484	3.580	3.668	4.015	4.272	4.477	4.649
	.05	2.959	3.274	3.505	3.690	3.845	3.978	4.095	4.200	4.296	4.675	4.956	5.182	5.372
	.01	4.315	4.695	4.977	5.203	5.394	5.559	5.704	5.835	5.954	6.428	6.782	7.068	7.308
7	.10	2.347	2.618	2.814	2.969	3.097	3.206	3.302	3.388	3.465	3.768	3.990	4.167	4.314
	.05	2.832	3.115	3.321	3.484	3.620	3.736	3.838	3.929	4.011	4.336	4.574	4.764	4.923
	.01	4.027	4.353	4.591	4.782	4.941	5.078	5.198	5.306	5.404	5.791	6.077	6.306	6.497
8	.10	2.289	2.544	2.726	2.869	2.987	3.088	3.176	3.254	3.324	3.598	3.798	3.955	4.086
	.05	2.743	3.005	3.193	3.342	3.464	3.569	3.661	3.743	3.816	4.105	4.316	4.482	4.621
	.01	3.831	4.120	4.331	4.498	4.637	4.756	4.860	4.953	5.038	5.370	5.613	5.807	5.969
9	.10	2.246	2.488	2.661	2.796	2.907	3.001	3.083	3.155	3.221	3.474	3.658	3.802	3.921
	.05	2.677	2.923	3.099	3.237	3.351	3.448	3.532	3.607	3.675	3.938	4.129	4.280	4.405
	.01	3.688	3.952	4.143	4.294	4.419	4.526	4.619	4.703	4.778	5.072	5.287	5.457	5.598

continued

Error df	α	2	3	4	5	6	7	8	9	10	15	20	25	30
							Number of Comparisons (C)							
10	.10	2.213	2.446	2.611	2.739	2.845	2.934	3.012	3.080	3.142	3.380	3.552	3.686	3.796
	.05	2.626	2.860	3.027	3.157	3.264	3.355	3.434	3.505	3.568	3.813	3.989	4.128	4.243
	.01	3.580	3.825	4.002	4.141	4.256	4.354	4.439	4.515	4.584	4.852	5.046	5.199	5.326
11	.10	2.186	2.412	2.571	2.695	2.796	2.881	2.955	3.021	3.079	3.306	3.468	3.595	3.699
	.05	2.586	2.811	2.970	3.094	3.196	3.283	3.358	3.424	3.484	3.715	3.880	4.010	4.117
	.01	3.495	3.726	3.892	4.022	4.129	4.221	4.300	4.371	4.434	4.682	4.860	5.001	5.117
12	.10	2.164	2.384	2.539	2.658	2.756	2.838	2.910	2.973	3.029	3.247	3.402	3.522	3.621
	.05	2.553	2.770	2.924	3.044	3.141	3.224	3.296	3.359	3.416	3.636	3.793	3.916	4.017
	.01	3.427	3.647	3.804	3.927	4.029	4.114	4.189	4.256	4.315	4.547	4.714	4.845	4.953
13	.10	2.146	2.361	2.512	2.628	2.723	2.803	2.872	2.933	2.988	3.196	3.347	3.463	3.557
	.05	2.526	2.737	2.886	3.002	3.096	3.176	3.245	3.306	3.361	3.571	3.722	3.839	3.935
	.01	3.371	3.582	3.733	3.850	3.946	4.028	4.099	4.162	4.218	4.438	4.595	4.718	4.819
14	.10	2.131	2.342	2.489	2.603	2.696	2.774	2.841	2.900	2.953	3.157	3.301	3.413	3.504
	.05	2.503	2.709	2.854	2.967	3.058	3.135	3.202	3.261	3.314	3.518	3.662	3.775	3.867
	.01	3.324	3.528	3.673	3.785	3.878	3.956	4.024	4.084	4.138	4.347	4.497	4.614	4.710
15	.10	2.118	2.325	2.470	2.582	2.672	2.748	2.814	2.872	2.924	3.122	3.262	3.370	3.459
	.05	2.483	2.685	2.827	2.937	3.026	3.101	3.166	3.224	3.275	3.472	3.612	3.721	3.810
	.01	3.285	3.482	3.622	3.731	3.820	3.895	3.961	4.019	4.071	4.271	4.414	4.526	4.618
16	.10	2.106	2.311	2.453	2.563	2.652	2.726	2.791	2.848	2.898	3.092	3.228	3.334	3.420
	.05	2.467	2.665	2.804	2.911	2.998	3.072	3.135	3.191	3.241	3.433	3.569	3.675	3.761
	.01	3.251	3.443	3.579	3.684	3.771	3.844	3.907	3.963	4.013	4.206	4.344	4.451	4.540

TABLE A.5, Continued

df	α													
18	.10	2.088	2.287	2.426	2.532	2.619	2.691	2.753	2.808	2.857	3.043	3.174	3.275	3.358
	.05	2.439	2.631	2.766	2.869	2.953	3.024	3.085	3.138	3.186	3.370	3.499	3.599	3.681
	.01	3.195	3.379	3.508	3.609	3.691	3.760	3.820	3.872	3.920	4.102	4.231	4.332	4.414
20	.10	2.073	2.269	2.405	2.508	2.593	2.663	2.724	2.777	2.824	3.005	3.132	3.229	3.309
	.05	2.417	2.605	2.736	2.836	2.918	2.986	3.045	3.097	3.143	3.320	3.445	3.541	3.620
	.01	3.152	3.329	3.454	3.550	3.629	3.695	3.752	3.802	3.848	4.021	4.144	4.239	4.317
25	.10	2.047	2.236	2.367	2.466	2.547	2.614	2.672	2.722	2.767	2.938	3.058	3.149	3.224
	.05	2.379	2.558	2.683	2.779	2.856	2.921	2.976	3.025	3.069	3.235	3.351	3.440	3.513
	.01	3.077	3.243	3.359	3.449	3.521	3.583	3.635	3.682	3.723	3.882	3.995	4.081	4.152
30	.10	2.030	2.215	2.342	2.439	2.517	2.582	2.638	2.687	2.731	2.895	3.010	3.098	3.169
	.05	2.354	2.528	2.649	2.742	2.816	2.878	2.932	2.979	3.021	3.180	3.291	3.376	3.445
	.01	3.029	3.188	3.298	3.384	3.453	3.511	3.561	3.605	3.644	3.794	3.900	3.981	4.048
40	.10	2.009	2.189	2.312	2.406	2.481	2.544	2.597	2.644	2.686	2.843	2.952	3.036	3.103
	.05	2.323	2.492	2.608	2.696	2.768	2.827	2.878	2.923	2.963	3.113	3.218	3.298	3.363
	.01	2.970	3.121	3.225	3.305	3.370	3.425	3.472	3.513	3.549	3.689	3.787	3.862	3.923
60	.10	1.989	2.163	2.283	2.373	2.446	2.506	2.558	2.603	2.643	2.793	2.897	2.976	3.040
	.05	2.294	2.456	2.568	2.653	2.721	2.777	2.826	2.869	2.906	3.049	3.148	3.223	3.284
	.01	2.914	3.056	3.155	3.230	3.291	3.342	3.386	3.425	3.459	3.589	3.679	3.749	3.805
120	.10	1.968	2.138	2.254	2.342	2.411	2.469	2.519	2.562	2.600	2.744	2.843	2.918	2.978
	.05	2.265	2.422	2.529	2.610	2.675	2.729	2.776	2.816	2.852	2.987	3.081	3.152	3.209
	.01	2.859	2.994	3.087	3.158	3.215	3.263	3.304	3.340	3.372	3.493	3.577	3.641	3.693
∞	.10	1.949	2.114	2.226	2.311	2.378	2.434	2.482	2.523	2.560	2.697	2.791	2.862	2.920
	.05	2.237	2.388	2.491	2.569	2.631	2.683	2.727	2.766	2.300	2.928	3.016	3.083	3.137
	.01	2.806	2.934	3.022	3.089	3.143	3.186	3.226	3.260	3.289	3.402	3.480	3.539	3.587

SOURCE: From Table 1 in "An Improved t Table for Simultaneous Control on g Contrasts," *Journal of the American Statistical Association*, 1977, 72, 531–534, by P. A. Games, copyright © 1977 by the American Statistical Association, as adapted by R. E. Kirk: *Experimental Design: Procedures for the Behavioral Sciences*, Brooks/Cole Publishing Company, 1982. Used by permission of Brooks/Cole Publishing Company and the American Statistical Association.

TABLE A.6 Critical Values for Dunnett: Percentage Points for the Comparison of *J* - 1 Treatment Means with a Control

One-Tailed Comparisons

Error df	α	Number of Treatment Means, Including Control (J)								
		2	3	4	5	6	7	8	9	10
5	.05	2.02	2.44	2.68	2.85	2.98	3.08	3.16	3.24	3.30
	.01	3.37	3.90	4.21	4.43	4.60	4.73	4.85	4.94	5.03
6	.05	1.94	2.34	2.56	2.71	2.83	2.92	3.00	3.07	3.12
	.01	3.14	3.61	3.88	4.07	4.21	4.33	4.43	4.51	4.59
7	.05	1.89	2.27	2.48	2.62	2.73	2.82	2.89	2.95	3.01
	.01	3.00	3.42	3.66	3.83	3.96	4.07	4.15	4.23	4.30
8	.05	1.86	2.22	2.42	2.55	2.66	2.74	2.81	2.87	2.92
	.01	2.90	3.29	3.51	3.67	3.79	3.88	3.96	4.03	4.09
9	.05	1.83	2.18	2.37	2.50	2.60	2.68	2.75	2.81	2.86
	.01	2.82	3.19	3.40	3.55	3.66	3.75	3.82	3.89	3.94
10	.05	1.81	2.15	2.34	2.47	2.56	2.64	2.70	2.76	2.81
	.01	2.76	3.11	3.31	3.45	3.56	3.64	3.71	3.78	3.83
11	.05	1.80	2.13	2.31	2.44	2.53	2.60	2.67	2.72	2.77
	.01	2.72	3.06	3.25	3.38	3.48	3.56	3.63	3.69	3.74
12	.05	1.78	2.11	2.29	2.41	2.50	2.58	2.64	2.69	2.74
	.01	2.68	3.01	3.19	3.32	3.42	3.50	3.56	3.62	3.67
13	.05	1.77	2.09	2.27	2.39	2.48	2.55	2.61	2.66	2.71
	.01	2.65	2.97	3.15	3.27	3.37	3.44	3.51	3.56	3.61
14	.05	1.76	2.08	2.25	2.37	2.46	2.53	2.59	2.64	2.69
	.01	2.62	2.94	3.11	3.23	3.32	3.40	3.46	3.51	3.56
15	.05	1.75	2.07	2.24	2.36	2.44	2.51	2.57	2.62	2.67
	.01	2.60	2.91	3.08	3.20	3.29	3.36	3.42	3.47	3.52
16	.05	1.75	2.06	2.23	2.34	2.43	2.50	2.56	2.61	2.65
	.01	2.58	2.88	3.05	3.17	3.26	3.33	3.39	3.44	3.48
17	.05	1.74	2.05	2.22	2.33	2.42	2.49	2.54	2.59	2.64
	.01	2.57	2.86	3.03	3.14	3.23	3.30	3.36	3.41	3.45
18	.05	1.73	2.05	2.21	2.32	2.41	2.48	2.53	2.58	2.62
	.01	2.55	2.84	3.01	3.12	3.21	3.27	3.33	3.38	3.42
19	.05	1.73	2.03	2.20	2.31	2.40	2.47	2.52	2.57	2.61
	.01	2.54	2.83	2.99	3.10	3.18	3.25	3.31	3.36	3.40
20	.05	1.72	2.03	2.19	2.30	2.39	2.46	2.51	2.56	2.60
	.01	2.53	2.81	2.97	3.08	3.17	3.23	3.29	3.34	3.38
24	.05	1.71	2.01	2.17	2.28	2.36	2.43	2.48	2.53	2.57
	.01	2.49	2.77	2.92	3.03	3.11	3.17	3.22	3.27	3.31
30	.05	1.70	1.99	2.15	2.25	2.33	2.40	2.45	2.50	2.54
	.01	2.46	2.72	2.87	2.97	3.05	3.11	3.16	3.21	3.24
40	.05	1.68	1.97	2.13	2.23	2.31	2.37	2.42	2.47	2.51
	.01	2.42	2.68	2.82	2.92	2.99	3.05	3.10	3.14	3.18
60	.05	1.67	1.95	2.10	2.21	2.28	2.35	2.39	2.44	2.48
	.01	2.39	2.64	2.78	2.87	2.94	3.00	3.04	3.08	3.12
120	.05	1.66	1.93	2.08	2.18	2.26	2.32	2.37	2.41	2.45
	.01	2.36	2.60	2.73	2.82	2.89	2.94	2.99	3.03	3.06
∞	.05	1.64	1.92	2.06	2.16	2.23	2.29	2.34	2.38	2.42
	.01	2.33	2.56	2.68	2.77	2.84	2.89	2.93	2.97	3.00

SOURCE: The part of this table presenting one-tailed comparisons is from "A Multiple Comparison Procedure for Comparing Several Treatments with a Control," *Journal of the American Statistical Association*, 1955, 50, 1096-1121, by C. W. Dunnett, copyright © 1955 by the American Statistical Association, as adapted by R. E. Kirk: *Experimental Design: Procedures for the Behavioral Sciences,*

continued

TABLE A.6, Continued

Error df	α	Number of Treatment Means, Including Control (J)								
		2	3	4	5	6	7	8	9	10
5	.05	2.57	3.03	3.29	3.48	3.62	3.73	3.82	3.90	3.97
	.01	4.03	4.63	4.98	5.22	5.41	5.56	5.69	5.80	5.89
6	.05	2.45	2.86	3.10	3.26	3.39	3.49	3.57	3.64	3.71
	.01	3.71	4.21	4.51	4.71	4.87	5.00	5.10	5.20	5.28
7	.05	2.36	2.75	2.97	3.12	3.24	3.33	3.41	3.47	3.53
	.01	3.50	3.95	4.21	4.39	4.53	4.64	4.74	4.82	4.89
8	.05	2.31	2.67	2.88	3.02	3.13	3.22	3.29	3.35	3.41
	.01	3.36	3.77	4.00	4.17	4.29	4.40	4.48	4.56	4.62
9	.05	2.26	2.61	2.81	2.95	3.05	3.14	3.20	3.26	3.32
	.01	3.25	3.63	3.85	4.01	4.12	4.22	4.30	4.37	4.43
10	.05	2.23	2.57	2.76	2.89	2.99	3.07	3.14	3.19	3.24
	.01	3.17	3.53	3.74	3.88	3.99	4.08	4.16	4.22	4.28
11	.05	2.20	2.53	2.72	2.84	2.94	3.02	3.08	3.14	3.19
	.01	3.11	3.45	3.65	3.79	3.89	3.98	4.05	4.11	4.16
12	.05	2.18	2.50	2.68	2.81	2.90	2.98	3.04	3.09	3.14
	.01	3.05	3.39	3.58	3.71	3.81	3.89	3.96	4.02	4.07
13	.05	2.16	2.48	2.65	2.78	2.87	2.94	3.00	3.06	3.10
	.01	3.01	3.33	3.52	3.65	3.74	3.82	3.89	3.94	3.99
14	.05	2.14	2.46	2.63	2.75	2.84	2.91	2.97	3.02	3.07
	.01	2.98	3.29	3.47	3.59	3.69	3.76	3.83	3.88	3.93
15	.05	2.13	2.44	2.61	2.73	2.82	2.89	2.95	3.00	3.04
	.01	2.95	3.25	3.43	3.55	3.64	3.71	3.78	3.83	3.88
16	.05	2.12	2.42	2.59	2.71	2.80	2.87	2.92	2.97	3.02
	.01	2.92	3.22	3.39	3.51	3.60	3.67	3.73	3.78	3.83
17	.05	2.11	2.41	2.58	2.69	2.78	2.85	2.90	2.95	3.00
	.01	2.90	3.19	3.36	3.47	3.56	3.63	3.69	3.74	3.79
18	.05	2.10	2.40	2.56	2.68	2.76	2.83	2.89	2.94	2.98
	.01	2.88	3.17	3.33	3.44	3.53	3.60	3.66	3.71	3.75
19	.05	2.09	2.39	2.55	2.66	2.75	2.81	2.87	2.92	2.96
	.01	2.86	3.15	3.31	3.42	3.50	3.57	3.63	3.68	3.72
20	.05	2.09	2.38	2.54	2.65	2.73	2.80	2.86	2.90	2.95
	.01	2.85	3.13	3.29	3.40	3.48	3.55	3.60	3.65	3.69
24	.05	2.06	2.35	2.51	2.61	2.70	2.76	2.81	2.86	2.90
	.01	2.80	3.07	3.22	3.32	3.40	3.47	3.52	3.57	3.61
30	.05	2.04	2.32	2.47	2.58	2.66	2.72	2.77	2.82	2.86
	.01	2.75	3.01	3.15	3.25	3.33	3.39	3.44	3.49	3.52
40	.05	2.02	2.29	2.44	2.54	2.62	2.68	2.73	2.77	2.81
	.01	2.70	2.95	3.09	3.19	3.26	3.32	3.37	3.41	3.44
60	.05	2.00	2.27	2.41	2.51	2.58	2.64	2.69	2.73	2.77
	.01	2.66	2.90	3.03	3.12	3.19	3.25	3.29	3.33	3.37
120	.05	1.98	2.24	2.38	2.47	2.55	2.60	2.65	2.69	2.73
	.01	2.62	2.85	2.97	3.06	3.12	3.18	3.22	3.26	3.29
∞	.05	1.96	2.21	2.35	2.44	2.51	2.57	2.61	2.65	2.69
	.01	2.58	2.79	2.92	3.00	3.06	3.11	3.15	3.19	3.22

Brooks/Cole Publishing Company, 1982. Used by permission of Brooks/Cole Publishing Company and the American Statistical Association. The part of the table presenting two-tailed comparisons is from "New Tables for Multiple Comparisons with a Control," *Biometrics*, 1964, *20*, 482-491, by C. W. Dunnett, copyright © 1964 by the Biometric Society, as adapted by R. E. Kirk: *Experimental Design: Procedures for the Behavioral Sciences*, Brooks/Cole Publishing Company, 1982. Used by permission of Brooks/Cole Publishing Company and the Biometric Society.

TABLE A.7 Critical Values for the Studentized Maximum Modulus Distribution ($\alpha = .05$)

df\J*	2	3	4	5	6	7	8	9	10	11	12	13	14	15	16	18	20
2	5.57	6.34	6.89	7.31	7.65	7.93	8.17	8.38	8.57	8.74	8.89	9.03	9.16	9.28	9.39	9.59	9.77
3	3.96	4.43	4.76	5.02	5.23	5.41	5.56	5.69	5.81	5.92	6.01	6.10	6.18	6.26	6.33	6.45	6.57
4	3.38	3.74	4.00	4.20	4.37	4.50	4.62	4.72	4.82	4.90	4.97	5.04	5.11	5.17	5.22	5.32	5.41
5	3.09	3.40	3.62	3.79	3.93	4.04	4.14	4.23	4.31	4.38	4.45	4.51	4.56	4.61	4.66	4.74	4.82
6	2.92	3.19	3.39	3.54	3.66	3.77	3.86	3.94	4.01	4.07	4.13	4.18	4.23	4.28	4.32	4.39	4.46
7	2.80	3.06	3.24	3.38	3.49	3.59	3.67	3.74	3.80	3.86	3.92	3.96	4.01	4.05	4.09	4.16	4.22
8	2.72	2.96	3.13	3.26	3.36	3.45	3.53	3.60	3.66	3.71	3.76	3.81	3.85	3.89	3.93	3.99	4.05
9	2.66	2.89	3.05	3.17	3.27	3.36	3.43	3.49	3.55	3.60	3.65	3.69	3.73	3.77	3.80	3.87	3.92
10	2.61	2.83	2.98	3.10	3.20	3.28	3.35	3.41	3.47	3.52	3.56	3.60	3.64	3.68	3.71	3.77	3.82
11	2.57	2.78	2.93	3.05	3.14	3.22	3.29	3.35	3.40	3.45	3.49	3.53	3.57	3.60	3.63	3.69	3.74
12	2.54	2.75	2.89	3.00	3.09	3.17	3.24	3.29	3.35	3.39	3.43	3.47	3.51	3.54	3.57	3.63	3.68
13	2.51	2.72	2.86	2.97	3.06	3.13	3.19	3.25	3.30	3.34	3.39	3.42	3.46	3.49	3.52	3.57	3.62
14	2.49	2.69	2.83	2.94	3.02	3.09	3.16	3.21	3.26	3.30	3.34	3.38	3.41	3.45	3.48	3.53	3.58
15	2.47	2.67	2.81	2.91	2.99	3.06	3.13	3.18	3.23	3.27	3.31	3.35	3.38	3.41	3.44	3.49	3.54
16	2.46	2.65	2.78	2.89	2.97	3.04	3.10	3.15	3.20	3.24	3.28	3.31	3.35	3.38	3.40	3.46	3.50
17	2.44	2.63	2.77	2.87	2.95	3.02	3.08	3.13	3.17	3.21	3.25	3.29	3.32	3.35	3.38	3.43	3.47
18	2.43	2.62	2.75	2.85	2.93	3.00	3.05	3.11	3.15	3.19	3.23	3.26	3.29	3.32	3.35	3.40	3.44
19	2.42	2.61	2.73	2.83	2.91	2.98	3.04	3.09	3.13	3.17	3.21	3.24	3.27	3.30	3.33	3.38	3.42
20	2.41	2.59	2.72	2.82	2.90	2.96	3.02	3.07	3.11	3.15	3.19	3.22	3.25	3.28	3.31	3.36	3.40
21	2.40	2.58	2.71	2.81	2.88	2.95	3.01	3.05	3.10	3.14	3.17	3.21	3.24	3.26	3.29	3.34	3.38
22	2.39	2.57	2.70	2.79	2.87	2.94	2.99	3.04	3.08	3.12	3.16	3.19	3.22	3.25	3.27	3.32	3.36
23	2.39	2.57	2.69	2.78	2.86	2.92	2.98	3.03	3.07	3.11	3.14	3.18	3.21	3.23	3.26	3.31	3.35
24	2.38	2.56	2.68	2.77	2.85	2.91	2.97	3.02	3.06	3.10	3.13	3.16	3.19	3.22	3.25	3.29	3.33
25	2.37	2.55	2.67	2.77	2.84	2.90	2.96	3.01	3.05	3.09	3.12	3.15	3.18	3.21	3.23	3.28	3.32
26	2.37	2.54	2.67	2.76	2.83	2.90	2.95	3.00	3.04	3.08	3.11	3.14	3.17	3.20	3.22	3.27	3.31
27	2.36	2.54	2.66	2.75	2.83	2.89	2.94	2.99	3.03	3.07	3.10	3.13	3.16	3.19	3.21	3.26	3.30
28	2.36	2.53	2.65	2.74	2.82	2.88	2.93	2.98	3.02	3.06	3.09	3.12	3.15	3.18	3.20	3.25	3.29
29	2.35	2.53	2.65	2.74	2.81	2.87	2.93	2.97	3.01	3.05	3.08	3.11	3.14	3.17	3.19	3.24	3.28
30	2.35	2.52	2.64	2.73	2.80	2.87	2.92	2.96	3.00	3.04	3.07	3.11	3.13	3.16	3.18	3.23	3.27
35	2.33	2.50	2.62	2.71	2.78	2.84	2.89	2.93	2.97	3.01	3.04	3.07	3.10	3.13	3.15	3.19	3.23
40	2.32	2.49	2.60	2.69	2.76	2.82	2.87	2.91	2.95	2.99	3.02	3.05	3.08	3.10	3.12	3.17	3.20
45	2.31	2.48	2.59	2.68	2.75	2.80	2.85	2.90	2.93	2.97	3.00	3.03	3.06	3.08	3.10	3.14	3.18
50	2.30	2.47	2.58	2.66	2.73	2.79	2.84	2.88	2.92	2.95	2.99	3.01	3.04	3.06	3.09	3.13	3.16
60	2.29	2.45	2.56	2.65	2.72	2.77	2.82	2.86	2.90	2.93	2.96	2.99	3.02	3.04	3.06	3.10	3.14
80	2.28	2.44	2.55	2.63	2.69	2.75	2.80	2.84	2.87	2.91	2.94	2.96	2.99	3.01	3.03	3.07	3.11
100	2.27	2.43	2.53	2.62	2.68	2.74	2.78	2.82	2.86	2.89	2.92	2.95	2.97	3.00	3.02	3.06	3.09
120	2.26	2.42	2.53	2.61	2.67	2.73	2.77	2.81	2.85	2.88	2.91	2.94	2.96	2.98	3.01	3.04	3.08
200	2.25	2.41	2.51	2.59	2.66	2.71	2.75	2.79	2.83	2.86	2.89	2.92	2.94	2.96	2.98	3.02	3.05
∞	2.24	2.39	2.49	2.57	2.63	2.68	2.73	2.77	2.80	2.83	2.86	2.88	2.91	2.93	2.95	2.98	3.02

SOURCE: From *Multiple Comparison Procedures*, by Y. Hochberg and A. C. Tamhane. Copyright © 1987 by John Wiley & Sons, Inc. Reprinted by permission of John Wiley & Sons, Inc.

Appendix B: Peritz Program

PERITZ: A FORTRAN program for performing multiple comparisons of means using the Peritz Q method

SAMUEL A. MARTIN and LARRY E. TOOTHAKER
University of Oklahoma, Norman, Oklahoma

Several methods have been proposed for the comparison of means (see Miller, 1981; or Hochberg & Tamhane, 1987). Multiple comparison procedures for the completely randomized univariate design are available in commercial statistics packages such as SAS, SPSS^x, and BMDP. However, the analysis of mean differences in a design more sophisticated than the completely randomized univariate design requires extra programming in these packages—when it is at all possible. In two-way and higher order ANOVA designs, the most frequent approach to hypothesis testing is to test for overall significance by using the ANOVA followed by a comparison of cell means when there is a significant interaction, or by a comparison of marginal means when a main effect is significant. Cell mean comparisons are not handled in a straightforward manner in these packages. In addition, empirical research into the performance of multiple comparison procedures (Einot & Gabriel, 1975; Ramsey, 1978, 1981) indicates that most range procedures available in the statistics packages either are too liberal in attempting to control for Type I errors or are lacking in power. (See Jaccard, Becker, & Wood, 1984, for a review of Monte Carlo analysis of multiple comparison procedures.)

All statistics used in hypothesis testing similar to multiple comparison procedures seek to establish the following properties: First, the Type I error rate (probability of falsely rejecting at least one hypothesis of equality of means in an experiment) should not exceed the nominal alpha rate. Second, the multiple comparison procedure should detect as many true differences as possible (power), given that it meets the first criterion of controlling the Type I error rate. Fisher's *LSD*, Duncan's multiple range test, and the Newman-Keuls procedure violate the first requirement, while Scheffé's S procedure and Tukey's *HSD* protect against Type I errors at the expense of power. The RMP procedure proposed by Ryan (1960) and modified by Einot and Gabriel (1975) and Welsch (1977) (SAS's REGWQ procedure) changes the alpha rate of the Newman-Keuls procedure to protect against the type of configuration where the nominal alpha rate is exceeded (multiple equality of means in an experiment in which the full null condition is not true). Where Newman-Keuls uses the studentized range value at level α for each stretch in a stepdown fashion, Ryan's modified procedure allocates

Correspondence may be addressed to Samuel A. Martin, Department of Psychology, 455 West Lindsey, Room 705, Norman, Oklahoma 73019.

α among k means for any stretch size p at $1 - (1-\alpha)^{p/k}$ for all stretches of means from size $p = 2$ to size $k - 2$, and at α for $k-1$ and k stretches. Peritz (Peritz, 1970; see also Begun & Gabriel, 1981) proposed a method to take advantage of the power of the Newman-Keuls while protecting against the type of mean configuration that provides a problem for this procedure. The Peritz logic involves a stepdown procedure that (1) accepts as nonsignificant any mean difference that Newman-Keuls fails to reject, (2) declares significant any mean difference that is significant at the RMP's alpha level and (3) declares any mean comparison not handled by (1) or (2) as contentious. Contentious sets of means are declared significant if all complementary sets of means are significant using the RMP's alpha level; otherwise, the set is stepdown accepted. Stepdown acceptance involves implicitly declaring as nonsignificant all comparisons of means contained within the stretch of a comparison that has been explicitly declared nonsignificant. Since α rates for stretch sizes k and $k-1$ are equal for both the Newman-Keuls and the RMP procedures, all three procedures are equivalent for a comparison of three means.

The obtaining of critical values at the Ryan's alpha level and the performing of tests on complements of sets of means make the Peritz technique very difficult to compute by hand, and thus it is problematic as a useful method. The program discussed in this paper performs a Peritz pairwise comparison of means. Input to the program (see Appendix A for a sample run) includes the number of groups or cells, the mean square within (error) term, the degrees of freedom within (error), the alpha rate to use for the comparisons, a label for each group to provide group or cell information on the printout, the means to be compared, and the number of subjects per group or cell. By allowing the user to enter the error term and degrees of freedom, this program can be used for repeated measures designs, between-within designs, analysis of covariance designs, and randomized blocks designs. Designs involving unequal numbers of subjects per group or cell use the Tukey-Kramer adjustment procedure (Kramer, 1956; Tukey, 1953), since it has been demonstrated that using harmonic means (as done in SAS, SPSS^x, and BMDP) can result in a liberal (i.e., excessive Type I error rate) test (Keselman, Toothaker, & Shooter, 1975).

The program uses a routine published by Dunlap, Powell, and Konnerth (1977) to provide for calculation of exact probabilities for studentized range values. This program supplements the POSTHOC program (Cooksey, 1979) by providing the Peritz procedure as well as removing the requirement that the user enter studentized range values.

The Peritz program was written for a VAX 8600 computer using the VAX/VMS operating system. The program is written in the VAX-FORTRAN implementation of the FORTRAN-77 language standard and should be fully compatible with any FORTRAN-77 level compiler. The listing for this program may be found in Appendix B.

REFERENCES

BEGUN, J., & GABRIEL, K. R. (1981). Closure of the Newman-Keuls multiple comparisons procedure. *Journal of the American Statistical Association*, **76**, 241-245.

COOKSEY, R. W. (1979). POSTHOC: A FORTRAN program for conducting post hoc multiple comparisons among means. *Behavior Research Methods & Instrumentation*, **11**, 601.

DUNLAP, W. P., POWELL, R. S., & KONNERTH, T. K. (1977). A FORTRAN IV function for calculating probabilities associated with the studentized range statistic. *Behavior Research Methods & Instrumentation*, **9**, 373-375.

EINOT, I., & GABRIEL, K. R. (1975). A study of the power of several methods in multiple comparisons. *Journal of the American Statistical Association*, **70**, 574-583.

HOCHBERG, Y., & TAMHANE, A. C. (1987). *Multiple comparison procedures*. New York: Wiley.

JACCARD, J., BECKER, M. A., & WOOD, G. (1984). Pairwise multiple comparison procedures: A review. *Psychological Bulletin*, **96**, 589-596.

KESELMAN, H. J., TOOTHAKER, L. E., & SHOOTER, M. (1975). An evaluation of two unequal n_k forms of the Tukey multiple comparison statistic. *Journal of the American Statistical Association*, **70**, 584-587.

KRAMER, C. Y. (1956). Extension of multiple range test to group means with unequal numbers of replications. *Biometrics*, **13**, 307-310.

MILLER, R. G. (1981). *Simultaneous statistical inference* (2nd ed.). New York: McGraw-Hill.

PERITZ, E. (1970). *A note on multiple comparisons*. Unpublished manuscript, Hebrew University, Jerusalem.

RAMSEY, P. H. (1978). Power differences between pairwise multiple comparisons. *Journal of the American Statistical Association*, **73**, 479-485.

RAMSEY, P. H. (1981). Power of univariate pairwise multiple comparisons procedures. *Psychological Bulletin*, **90**, 352-366.

RYAN, T. A. (1960). Significance tests for multiple comparisons, variances, and other statistics. *Psychological Bulletin*, **57**, 318-328.

TUKEY, J. W. (1953). The problem of multiple comparisons. Unpublished manuscript, Princeton University, Princeton, NJ.

WELSCH, R. E. (1977). Stepwise multiple comparison procedures. *Journal of the American Statistical Association*, **72**, 566-575.

APPENDIX A
Sample Run of Peritz Program

```
Please enter the following information:

Number of Groups: 5

Mean Square Within (Error): 7.669

Degrees of Freedom Within (Error): 20

Alpha Rate: .05

You will now be prompted for the 5 means and a label for each mean.  If you
don't want to enter a specific treatment label, enter <return> and a default
label of "Mean nn" (nn = Group Number) will be provided.

NOTE: Labels can be up to 16 characters in length.

Enter the group 1 label (default: Mean 01): A1
         Mean for group 1 (A1): 16.1
         Number of subjects for group 1 (A1): 5

Enter the group 2 label (default: Mean 02): A2
         Mean for group 2 (A2): 17
         Number of subjects for group 2 (A2): 5

Enter the group 3 label (default: Mean 03): A3
         Mean for group 3 (A3): 20.7
         Number of subjects for group 3 (A3): 5

Enter the group 4 label (default: Mean 04): A4
         Mean for group 4 (A4): 21.1
         Number of subjects for group 4 (A4): 5

Enter the group 5 label (default: Mean 05): A5
         Mean for group 5 (A5): 26.5
         Number of subjects for group 5 (A5): 5


                        (Program Output)

   Number of groups: 5              Degrees of Freedom Within: 20

   Mean Square Within:    7.66900        Set Alpha: 0.050


                                                       Mean
Comparison       Mean         N           Q         Difference
A1            16.10000        5                      0.90000
A2            17.00000        5        0.72670
                                    Non-significant
```

APPENDIX A (Continued)

A1	16.10000	5	3.71427	4.60000
A3	20.70000	5	Significant	
A1	16.10000	5	4.03725	5.00000
A4	21.10000	5	Significant	
A1	16.10000	5	8.39748	10.40000
A5	26.50000	5	Significant	
A2	17.00000	5	2.98756	3.70000
A3	20.70000	5	Non-significant	
A2	17.00000	5	3.31054	4.10000
A4	21.10000	5	Non-significant	
A2	17.00000	5	7.67077	9.50000
A5	26.50000	5	Significant	
A3	20.70000	5	0.32298	0.40000
A4	21.10000	5	Non-significant	
A3	20.70000	5	4.68321	5.80000
A5	26.50000	5	Significant	
A4	21.10000	5	4.36023	5.40000
A5	26.50000	5	Significant	

APPENDIX B
Program Peritz

```
C
C Program to perform PERITZ MCP test
C
        IMPLICIT NONE
C
        INTEGER*2       MAX_GROUPS
        PARAMETER       (MAX_GROUPS = 50)
        INTEGER*2       GROUPS,N(MAX_GROUPS),DFW
        REAL*8          MEANS(MAX_GROUPS),MSW,ALPHA
        CHARACTER*16    LABELS(MAX_GROUPS)
        LOGICAL*1       PERITZ_TEST(MAX_GROUPS,MAX_GROUPS)
C
C get data from user
C
        CALL READ_PARAMS (GROUPS,DFW,N,MEANS,MSW,ALPHA,LABELS)
C
C sort data into ordered set of means
C
        CALL QUICK_SORT (GROUPS,MEANS,LABELS)
C
C perform Peritz MCP procedure
C
        CALL DO_PERITZ (GROUPS,DFW,N,MEANS,MSW,ALPHA,PERITZ_TEST)
C
C print output from analysis
C
        CALL PRINT_PERITZ (GROUPS,DFW,N,MEANS,MSW,ALPHA,LABELS,PERITZ_TEST)
C
        END

        SUBROUTINE READ_PARAMS (GROUPS,DFW,N,MEANS,MSW,ALPHA,LABELS)
C
C Subroutine to get parameters for pairwise mean comparisons
C
C       GROUPS: Number of Means (Minimum: 3, Maximum: 50)
C       N:      Number of Subjects per Group
C       MEANS:  Vector of Means
C       MSW:    Mean Square Within
C       ALPHA:  Set alpha for comparison
C       LABELS: Vector of Treatment Labels (Default:  Mean ##)
C
        IMPLICIT NONE
C
```

APPENDIX B (Continued)

```
      INTEGER*2     MAX_GROUPS
      PARAMETER     (MAX_GROUPS = 50)
      INTEGER*2     GROUPS,DFW,N(MAX_GROUPS),I,LEN
      REAL*0        MEANS(MAX_GROUPS), MSW, ALPHA
      CHARACTER*16  LABELS(MAX_GROUPS),TEMP
      CHARACTER*47  PROMPT
C
      WRITE (6,1000)
      GROUPS = 0
      DO WHILE ((GROUPS .LT. 3) .OR. (GROUPS .GT. MAX_GROUPS))
          WRITE (6,1001) 'Number of Groups:  '
          READ (5,*,ERR=10) GROUPS
10        IF ((GROUPS .LT. 3) .OR. (GROUPS .GT. MAX_GROUPS)) THEN
              WRITE (6,2001) 7,MAX_GROUPS
          END IF
      END DO
C
      MSW = 0.0
      DO WHILE (MSW .LE. 0.0)
          WRITE (6,1001) 'Mean Square Within (Error):  '
          READ (5,*,ERR=30) MSW
30        IF (MSW .LE. 0.0) THEN
              WRITE (6,2002) 7,0
          END IF
      END DO
C
      DFW = 0
      DO WHILE (DFW .LT. 2*GROUPS)
          WRITE (6,1001) 'Degrees of Freedom Within (Error):  '
          READ (5,*,ERR=20) DFW
20        IF (DFW .LT. 2*GROUPS) THEN
              WRITE (6,2002) 7,2*GROUPS
          END IF
      END DO
C
      ALPHA = 0.0
      DO WHILE ((ALPHA .LT. 0.001) .OR. (ALPHA .GT. .25))
          WRITE (6,1001) 'Alpha Rate:  '
          READ (5,*,ERR=35) ALPHA
35        IF ((ALPHA .LT. 0.001) .OR. (ALPHA .GT. .25)) THEN
              WRITE (6,4002) 7
          END IF
      END DO
C
      WRITE (6,3000) GROUPS
      DO I=1,GROUPS
          WRITE (6,*)
          WRITE (LABELS(I),3001) I
          WRITE (PROMPT,3002)I,LABELS(I)
          CALL LIB$GET_INPUT(TEMP,PROMPT,LEN)
          IF (LEN .GT. 0) THEN
              LABELS(I)=TEMP
          ELSE
              LEN = 7
          END IF
40        WRITE (6,3003) I,LABELS(I) (1:LEN)
          READ (5,*,ERR=40) MEANS(I)
          N(I) = 0
          DO WHILE (N(I) .LT. 2)
50            WRITE (6,3004) I,LABELS(I) (1:LEN)
              READ (5,*,ERR=50) N(I)
              IF (N(I) .LT.-2) THEN
                  WRITE (6,2002) 7,2
              END IF
          END DO
      END DO
1000  FORMAT ('0Please enter the following information:')
1001  FORMAT (//'+',A,$)
2001  FORMAT (1X,A1,'Please enter a number between 3 and',I3)
2002  FORMAT (1X,A1,'Please enter a number larger than',I4)
3000  FORMAT (//1X,'You will now be prompted for the',I3,' means'
     1        ' and a label for each mean.  If you'/
     2        ' don''t want to enter a specific treatment label,'
     3        ' enter <return> and a default'/
     4        ' label of "Mean nn" (nn = Group Number) will be provided.'//
     5        ' NOTE:  Labels can be up to 16 characters in length.')
3001  FORMAT ('Mean ',I2.2)
3002  FORMAT ('Enter the group',I3,' label (default:  ',A7,'):  ')
3003  FORMAT (11X,'Mean for group',I3,' (',A,'):  ',$)
```

APPENDIX B (Continued)

```
C
C Calculate Ryan's Alpha for each stretch size
C
          RYAN_ALPHA(GROUPS) = ALPHA
          RYAN_ALPHA(GROUPS-1) = ALPHA
          DO I=2,GROUPS-2
                RYAN_ALPHA(I)=1-(1-ALPHA)**(FLOAT(I)/FLOAT(GROUPS))
          END DO
C
C Set up test matrix to initially show that all comparisons are Peritz reject
C Set up status matrix to indicate that all comparisons are NK-reject
C Set up matrix to indicate if any pw-comparison is Ryan-significant
C
          DO I=1,GROUPS
                DO J=1,GROUPS
                      TESTS(I,J)=.TRUE.
                      STATUS(I,J)='C'
                      RYAN_REJECT(I,J)='R'
                END DO
          END DO
C
C Do STP comparison of all means to test if Ryan critical
C
          DO I=1,GROUPS-1
                DO J=I+1,GROUPS
                STRETCH=J-I+1
                Q = ABS(MEAN(J)-MEAN(I))/SQRT((MSW/N(I)+MSW/N(J))/2.)
                PROB=Q_PROB(Q,STRETCH,DFW)
                PROB_MTX(I,J)=PROB
                IF (PROB .GT. RYAN_ALPHA(STRETCH)) RYAN_REJECT(I,J) = 'A'
                END DO
          END DO
C
C Perform the Newman-Keuls stepdown procedure
C Note:  An NK accept is an automatic Peritz accept
C
          STRETCH = GROUPS
          DO WHILE (STRETCH .GE. 2)
                DO I=1,GROUPS-STRETCH+1
                P=I+STRETCH-1
                IF (TESTS(I,P)) THEN
C
C If not NK-critical, stepdown accept
C
                      IF (PROB_MTX(I,P).GT.ALPHA) THEN
                          DO J=I,P-1
                            DO K=J+1,P
                              TESTS(J,K)=.FALSE.
                              STATUS(J,K)='A'
                            END DO
                          END DO
C
C If Ryan-critical, reject
C
                      ELSE IF (RYAN_REJECT(I,P).EQ.'R') THEN
                          STATUS(I,P)='R'
C
C Otherwise, perform the Peritz procedure
C
                      ELSE
C
C Test the complements to the left
C
                          IF (STATUS(I,P).EQ.'C') THEN
                            DO IQ=1,I-2
                              DO JQ=IQ+1,I-1
                                IF (RYAN_REJECT(IQ,JQ).EQ.'A') STATUS(I,P)='A
                              END DO
                            END DO
                          END IF
C
C Test the complements to the right
C
                          IF (STATUS(I,P).EQ.'C') THEN
                            DO IQ=P+1,GROUPS-1
                              DO JQ=IQ+1,GROUPS
                                IF (RYAN_REJECT(IQ,JQ).EQ.'A') STATUS(I,P)='A'
                              END DO
                            END DO
                          END IF
```

APPENDIX B (Continued)

```
C
C Test the complements surrounding
C
                        IF (STATUS(I,P).EQ.'C') THEN
                          DO IQ=1,I-1
                            DO JQ=P+1,GROUPS
                              IF (RYAN_REJECT(IQ,JQ).EQ.'A') STATUS(I,P)='A'
                            END DO
                          END DO
                        END IF
C
C If STATUS has not been set to 'A' on the complements, do a PERITZ reject
C Otherwise, stepdown accept
C
                        IF (STATUS(I,P) .EQ. 'A') THEN
                          DO J=I,P-1
                            DO K=J+1,P
                              TESTS(J,K)=.FALSE.
                            END DO
                          END DO
                        END IF
                      END IF
                    END IF
                  END DO
                STRETCH = STRETCH-1
              END DO
              END
              REAL*8 FUNCTION Q_PROB(R,S,DF)
C
C Calculate probability for Studentized Range Statistic
C        Adapted from:   Dunlap, Powell, & Konnerth, 1977
C
C        R:      For a stretch, (largest mean-smallest mean)/(MSW/n)
C        S:      Number of groups in the stretch
C        DF:     Degrees of Freedom Within
C
        IMPLICIT NONE
C
        REAL*8          R,ZP(2),COEFF(33),EMAX/89./,XDF,DG,G,XI,C,DT,DMAX,BI,
       1                RI,UI,SI,SRA,BR,SR,RA,XJ,X,Z,BZ,T,P,RH,H,PR,D,SRH,Q,XS
        INTEGER*2       S,DF,I,IDG,J,K
C
        DATA COEFF /1.,4.,2.,4.,2.,4.,2.,4.,2.,4.,2.,4.,2.,4.,2.,4.,2.,
       1            4.,2.,4.,2.,4.,2.,4.,2.,4.,2.,4.,2.,4.,2.,4.,1./
C
        IF (R .LE. 0) THEN
          Q_PROB=1.0
          RETURN
        END IF
        XDF=DF
        DG=XDF/2.-1.
        IDG=DG
        XS=S
        G=0.0
        IF (DG .LT. 0.) THEN
          G=.572364943
        ELSE IF (DG .EQ. 5.) THEN
          G=G-.120782238
        ELSE IF (DG .GT. 0.) THEN
          DO I=1,IDG
            XI=I
            G=G+LOG(DG-XI+1.)
          END DO
          IF (MOD(DF,2).NE.0) G=G-.120782238
        END IF
        C=EXP(.693147181+LOG(.196349541*XDF)*XDF/2.-G)
C
        DT=LOG(R+1.)*100.
        DMAX=MAX(DT,XDF)
        RI=5.2+R*.5-LOG(DMAX)-1./SQRT(R)
        IF (RI.LT.0.15) RI=.15
        BI=R-RI
        IF (BI.LT.0.0) BI=0.
        UI=R+RI
        SI=(UI-BI)/32.
C
        SRA=0.0
        DO I=2,33
          XI=I-1
          BR=BI+SI*XI
          SR=(-.918938533-BR*BR/(R*R*2.)+LOG(4.*BR/R))*XDF
```

APPENDIX B (Continued)

```
3004      FORMAT (11X,'Number of subjects for group',I3. ( ,A. ):   ,$)
4002      FORMAT (1X,A1,'Please enter a number between .001 and .25')
          END

          SUBROUTINE QUICK_SORT(GROUPS,MEANS,LABELS)
C
C Use Quicksort routine to sort means and labels into ascending order
C
          IMPLICIT NONE
          INTEGER*2 GROUPS
          REAL*8 MEANS(GROUPS),MIDDLE,TEMP1
          CHARACTER*16 LABELS(GROUPS),TEMP2
          INTEGER*2 LEFT_STACK(50),RIGHT_STACK(50),LEFT,RIGHT,I,J,POINTER
          POINTER=1
          LEFT_STACK(1)=1
          RIGHT_STACK(1)=GROUPS
          DO WHILE (POINTER .GT. 0)
                  LEFT=LEFT_STACK(POINTER)
                  RIGHT=RIGHT_STACK(POINTER)
                  POINTER=POINTER-1
                  DO WHILE (LEFT .LT. RIGHT)
                          I=LEFT
                          J=RIGHT
                          MIDDLE=MEANS((LEFT+RIGHT)/2)
                          DO WHILE (I .LE. J)
                                  DO WHILE (MEANS(I).LT.MIDDLE)
                                          I=I+1
                                  END DO
                                  DO WHILE (MIDDLE .LT. MEANS(J))
                                          J=J-1
                                  END DO
                                  IF (I .LE. J) THEN
                                          TEMP1=MEANS(I)
                                          MEANS(I)=MEANS(J)
                                          MEANS(J)=TEMP1
                                          TEMP2=LABELS(I)
                                          LABELS(I)=LABELS(J)
                                          LABELS(J)=TEMP2
                                          I=I+1
                                          J=J-1
                                  END IF
                          END DO
                          IF (I .LT. RIGHT) THEN
                                  POINTER=POINTER+1
                                  LEFT_STACK(POINTER)=I
                                  RIGHT_STACK(POINTER)=RIGHT
                          END IF
                          RIGHT=J
                  END DO
          END DO
          END

          SUBROUTINE DO_PERITZ (GROUPS,DFW,N,MEAN,MSW,ALPHA,TESTS)
C
C Peritz routine
C
C         MEAN:           sorted vector of group means
C         TESTS:          matrix to indicate peritz-reject for a comparison
C         GROUPS:         Number of means to be compared
C         N:              vector of subjects per group
C         MSW:            Error term - Mean Square Within
C         DFW:            Degrees of freedom for error term
C         ALPHA:          User-defined set alpha
C
          IMPLICIT NONE
C
C Parameters passed in the subroutine call
C
          INTEGER*2       GROUPS,N(50),DFW
          REAL*8          MEAN(GROUPS),MSW,ALPHA
          LOGICAL*1       TESTS(50,50)
C
C Local variables
C
          INTEGER*2       I,J,K,P,STRETCH,IQ,JQ
          REAL*8          Q,RYAN_ALPHA(49),PROB,Q_PROB,PROB_MTX(50,50)
          CHARACTER       STATUS(50,50),RYAN_REJECT(50,50)
```

APPENDIX B (Continued)

```
C
                RA=0.0
                DO J=1,33
                        XJ=J-1
                        BZ=XJ*.34375-7.
                        Z=BR+BZ
                        DO K=1,2
                                IF (K.EQ.2) Z=BZ
                                X=ABS(Z)
                                Q=.39894228*EXP(-X*X/2.)
                                IF (X .GT. 3.7) THEN
                                        ZP(K)=Q*(SQRT(4.+X*X)-X)/2.
                                ELSE
                                        T=1./(1.+.2316419*X)
                                        P=.31938153*T
                                        P=P-.356563782*T**2
                                        P=P+1.78147937*T**3
                                        P=P-1.821255978*T**4
                                        P=P+1.330274429*T**5
                                        ZP(K)=Q*P
                                END IF
                                IF (Z .GT. 0.) ZP(K)=1.-ZP(K)
                        END DO
                        RH=0.
                        D=ZP(1)-ZP(2)
                        IF (D .GT. 0) THEN
                                H=LOG(D)
                                PR=-.918938533-BZ*BZ/2.+H*(XS-1.)+LOG(XS)
                                IF (PR+EMAX.GT.0) RH=EXP(PR)
                        END IF
                        RA=RA+COEFF(J)*RH
                END DO
                RA=.34375*RA/3.
                SRH=0.
                D=(1.-RA)/BR
                IF (D .GT. 0.) THEN
                        SR=SR+LOG(D)
                        IF (SR+EMAX.GT.0) SRH=EXP(SR)
                END IF
                SRA=SRA+COEFF(I)*SRH
        END DO
        Q_PROB=SI*SRA/3.*C
        END

        SUBROUTINE PRINT_PERITZ(GROUPS,DFW,N,MEANS,MSW,ALPHA,LABELS,PERITZ_TEST)
C
C Subroutine to print results from PERITZ MCP analysis
C
        IMPLICIT NONE
C
        INTEGER*2       MAX_GROUPS
        PARAMETER       (MAX_GROUPS = 50)
        INTEGER*2       GROUPS,DFW,N(MAX_GROUPS),I,J
        REAL*8          MEANS(MAX_GROUPS),MSW,ALPHA,Q
        CHARACTER*16    LABELS(MAX_GROUPS),SIGNIFICANCE
        LOGICAL*1       PERITZ_TEST(MAX_GROUPS,MAX_GROUPS)
        WRITE (6,1000) GROUPS,DFW,MSW,ALPHA
        WRITE (6,1002)
        DO I=1,GROUPS-1
                DO J=I+1,GROUPS
                        IF (PERITZ_TEST(I,J)) THEN
                                SIGNIFICANCE='    Significant'
                        ELSE
                                SIGNIFICANCE='Non-significant'
                        END IF
                        Q = ABS(MEANS(I)-MEANS(J))/SQRT((MSW/N(I)+MSW/N(J))/2.)

                        WRITE (6,1001)  LABELS(I),MEANS(I),N(I),Q,
     1                                  MEANS(J)-MEANS(I),LABELS(J),MEANS(J),
     2                                  N(J),SIGNIFICANCE
                END DO
        END DO
1000    FORMAT (/5X,'Number of groups:',I3,21X,'Degrees of Freedom Within:',I4//
     1          5X,'Mean Square Within:',F15.5,21X,'Set Alpha:',F6.3/)
1001    FORMAT (1X,A,F16.5,I6,8X,2F16.5/1X,A,F16.5,I6,9X,A/)
1002    FORMAT (75X,'Mean'/
     1          1X,'Comparison',16X,'Mean',7X,'N',18X,'Q',11X,'Difference'/)
        END
```

SOURCE: From "PERITZ: A FORTRAN Program for Performing Multiple Comparison of Means Using the Peritz Q Method," *Behavior Research Methods, Instruments, & Computers*, 1989, *21*, 465-472, copyright © 1989 by the Psychonomic Society, Inc. Reprinted by permission of the publisher.

References

Box, G. E. P. (1953). Nonnormality and tests on variances. *Biometrika, 40*, 318-335.

Box, G. E. P. (1954). Some theorems on quadratic forms applied in the study of analysis of variance problems, I: Effect of inequality of variance in the one-way classification. *Annals of Mathematical Statistics, 25*, 290-302.

Bradley, J. V. (1978). Robustness? *British Journal of Mathematical and Statistical Psychology, 31*, 144-152.

Carmer, S. G., & Swanson, M. R. (1973). An evaluation of ten multiple comparison procedures by Monte Carlo methods. *Journal of the American Statistical Association, 68*, 66-74.

Cicchetti, D. V. (1972). Extension of multiple-range tests to interaction tables in the analysis of variance: A rapid approximate solution. *Psychological Bulletin, 77*, 405-408.

Cochran, W. G. (1954). Some methods for strengthening the common χ^2 tests. *Biometrics, 10*, 417-451.

Cochran, W. G. (1964). Approximate significance levels of the Behrens-Fisher test. *Biometrics, 20*, 191-195.

Cohen, J. (1969). *Statistical power analysis for the behavioral sciences.* New York: Academic Press.

Collier, R. O., Baker, F. B., Mandeville, G. K., & Hayes, T. F. (1967). Estimates of test size for several test procedures based on conventional variance ratios in the repeated measures design. *Psychometrika, 32*, 339-353.

Conover, W. J., & Iman, R. L. (1981). Rank transformations as a bridge between parametric and nonparametric statistics. *American Statistician, 35*, 124-133.

Duncan, D. B. (1955). Multiple range and multiple *F* tests. *Biometrics, 11*, 1-42.

Dunn, O. J. (1958). Estimation of the means of dependent variables. *Annals of Mathematical Statistics, 29*, 1095-1111.

Dunn, O. J. (1961). Multiple comparisons among means. *Journal of the American Statistical Association, 56*, 52-64.

Dunn, O. J. (1964). Multiple comparisons using rank sums. *Technometrics, 6*, 241-252.

Dunnett, C. W. (1955). A multiple comparison procedure for comparing several treatments with a control. *Journal of the American Statistical Association, 50*, 1096-1121.

Dunnett, C. W. (1980a). Pairwise multiple comparisons in the homogeneous variance, unequal sample size case. *Journal of the American Statistical Association, 75*, 789-795.

Dunnett, C. W. (1980b). Pairwise multiple comparisons in the unequal variance case. *Journal of the American Statistical Association, 75*, 796-800.

160

Dunnett, C. W. (1982). Robust multiple comparisons. *Communications in Statistics, 11*, 2611-2629.

Dwass, M. (1960). Some *k*-sample rank-order tests. In I. Olkin et al. (Eds.), *Contributions to probability and statistics* (pp. 198-202). Stanford, CA: Stanford University Press.

Einot, I., & Gabriel, K. R. (1975). A study of the powers of several methods of multiple comparisons. *Journal of the American Statistical Association, 70*, 574-583.

Elkin, I., Shea, M. T., Watkins, J. T., Imber, S. D., Sotsky, S. M., Collins, J. F., Glass, D. R., Pilkonis, P. A., Leber, W. R., Docherty, J. P., Fiester, S. J., & Parloff, M. B. (1989). National Institute of Mental Health treatment of depression collaborative research program. *Archives of General Psychiatry, 46*, 971-982.

Feinberg, R. A. (1986). Credit cards as spending facilitating stimuli: A conditioning interpretation. *Journal of Consumer Research, 13*, 348-356.

Fisher, R. A. (1935). *The design of experiments.* Edinburgh: Oliver & Boyd.

Frank, B. M. (1984). Effect of field independence-dependence and study technique on learning from a lecture. *American Educational Research Journal, 21*, 669-678.

French, J. W., Ekstrom, R. B., & Price, L. A. (1963). *Manual for kit of reference tests for cognitive factors.* Princeton, NJ: Educational Testing Service.

Games, P. A. (1973). Type IV errors revisited. *Psychological Bulletin, 80*, 304-307.

Games, P. A., & Howell, J. F. (1976). Pairwise multiple comparison procedures with unequal *n*'s and/or variances. *Journal of Educational Statistics, 1*, 113-125.

Hamilton, M. A. (1967). Development of a rating scale for primary depressive illness. *British Journal of Social and Clinical Psychology, 6*, 278-296.

Hayter, A. J. (1986). The maximum familywise error rate of Fisher's least significant difference test. *Journal of the American Statistical Association, 81*, 1000-1004.

Hochberg, Y. (1974). Some generalizations of the T-method in simultaneous inference. *Journal of Multivariate Analysis, 4*, 224-234.

Hochberg, Y., & Tamhane, A. C. (1987). *Multiple comparison procedures.* New York: John Wiley.

Holm, S. (1979). A simple sequentially rejective multiple test procedure. *Scandinavian Journal of Statistics, 6*, 65-70.

Howell, J. F., & Games, P. A. (1973). The effects of variance heterogeneity on simultaneous multiple-comparison procedures with equal sample size. *British Journal of Mathematical and Statistical Psychology, 27*, 72-81.

Keselman, H. J., Games, P. A., & Rogan, J. C. (1979). An addendum to "A comparison of modified-Tukey and Scheffé methods of multiple comparisons for pairwise contrasts." *Journal of the American Statistical Association, 74*, 626-627.

Keselman, H. J., & Rogan, J. C. (1978). A comparison of modified-Tukey and Scheffé methods of multiple comparisons for pairwise contrasts. *Journal of the American Statistical Association, 73*, 47-51.

Keselman, H. J., & Toothaker, L. E. (1973). An empirical comparison of the Marascuilo and normal scores nonparametric tests and the Scheffé and Tukey parametric tests for pairwise comparisons. In *Proceedings of the 81st Annual Convention.* Washington, DC: American Psychological Association.

Keselman, H. J., & Toothaker, L. E. (1974). Comparison of Tukey's T-method and Scheffé's S-method for various numbers of all possible differences of averages contrasts under violation of assumptions. *Educational and Psychological Measurement, 34*, 511-519.

Keselman, H. J., Toothaker, L. E., & Shooter M. (1975). An evaluation of two unequal n_k forms of the Tukey multiple comparison statistic. *Journal of the American Statistical Association, 70*, 584-587.

Keuls, M. (1952). The use of the "Studentized range" in connection with an analysis of variance. *Euphytica, 1*, 112-122.

Kirk, R. E. (1982). *Experimental design: Procedures for the behavioral sciences.* Belmont, CA: Brooks/Cole.

Kramer, C. Y. (1956). Extension of multiple range test to group means with unequal numbers of replications. *Biometrics, 12,* 307-310.

Kramer, C. Y. (1957). Extension of multiple range tests to group correlated adjusted means. *Biometrics, 13,* 13-18.

Levin, J. R., & Marascuilo, L. A. (1972). Type IV errors and interactions. *Psychological Bulletin, 78,* 368-374.

Levin, J. R., & Marascuilo, L. A. (1973). Type IV errors and Games. *Psychological Bulletin, 80,* 308-309.

Marascuilo, L. A., & Levin, J. R. (1970). Appropriate post hoc comparisons for interaction and nested hypotheses in analysis of variance designs: The elimination of Type IV errors. *American Educational Research Journal, 7,* 397-421.

Marascuilo, L. A., & Levin, J. R. (1976). The simultaneous investigation of interaction and nested hypotheses in two-factor analysis of variance designs. *American Educational Research Journal, 13,* 61-65.

Martin, S. A., & Toothaker, L. E. (1989). PERITZ: A FORTRAN program for performing multiple comparisons of means using the Peritz Q method. *Behavior Research Methods, Instruments, & Computers, 21,* 465-472.

Martin, S. A., Toothaker, L. E., & Nixon, S. J. (1989, April). *A Monte Carlo comparison of multiple comparison procedures under optimal and nonoptimal conditions.* Paper presented at the annual meeting of the Southwestern Psychological Association, Houston.

Mauchly, J. W. (1940). Significance test for sphericity of a normal n-variate distribution. *Annals of Mathematical Statistics, 11,* 204-209.

Maxwell, S. E. (1980). Pairwise multiple comparisons in repeated measures designs. *Journal of Educational Statistics, 5,* 269-287.

Miller, R. G. (1981). *Simultaneous statistical inference* (2nd ed.). New York: Springer-Verlag.

Mitzel, H. C., & Games, P. A. (1981). Circularity and multiple comparisons in repeated measures designs. *British Journal of Mathematical and Statistical Psychology, 34,* 253-259.

Nemenyi, P. (1963). *Distribution-free multiple comparisons.* Unpublished doctoral dissertation, Princeton University.

Newman, D. (1939). The distribution of the range in samples from a normal population, expressed in terms of an independent estimate of standard deviation. *Biometrika, 31,* 20-30.

Peritz, E. (1970). *A note on multiple comparisons.* Unpublished manuscript, Hebrew University, Israel.

Petrinovich, L. F., & Hardyck, C. D. (1969). Error rates for multiple comparison methods. *Psychological Bulletin, 71,* 43-54.

Ramsey, P. H. (1978a). Power differences between pairwise multiple comparisons. *Journal of the American Statistical Association, 73,* 479-485.

Ramsey, P. H. (1978b). Rejoinder to "Comment on 'Power differences between pairwise multiple comparisons.' " *Journal of the American Statistical Association, 73,* 487.

Ramsey, P. H. (1980). Exact Type I error rates for robustness of Student's t test with unequal variances. *Journal of Educational Statistics, 5,* 337-349.

Ramsey, P. H. (1981). Power of univariate pairwise multiple comparison procedures. *Psychological Bulletin, 90,* 352-366.

Ringland, J. T. (1983). Robust multiple comparisons. *Journal of the American Statistical Association, 78,* 145-151.

Rodgers, J. L., Nicewander, W. A., & Toothaker, L. E. (1984). Linearly independent, orthogonal, and uncorrelated variables. *American Statistician, 38,* 133-134.

Rogan, J. C., Keselman, H. J., & Mendoza, J. L. (1979). Analysis of repeated measurements. *British Journal of Mathematical and Statistical Psychology, 32*, 269-286.

Rosenthal, R., & Rosnow, R. (1985). *Contrast analysis: Focused comparisons in the analysis of variance.* Cambridge, U.K.: Cambridge University Press.

Rosnow, R., & Rosenthal, R. (1989). Definition and interpretation of interaction effects. *Psychological Bulletin, 105*, 143-146.

Ryan, T. A. (1960). Significance tests for multiple comparison of proportions, variance, and other statistics. *Psychological Bulletin, 57*, 318-328.

SAS Institute, Inc. (1990). *SAS/STAT user's guide* (Vol. 1). Cary, NC: Author.

Sawilowsky, S. S., Blair, R. C., & Higgins, J. J. (1989). An investigation of the Type I error and power properties of the rank transform procedure in factorial ANOVA. *Journal of Educational Statistics, 14*, 255-267.

Scheffé, H. (1953). A method for judging all contrasts in analysis of variance. *Biometrika, 40*, 87-104.

Scheffé, H. (1959). *The analysis of variance.* New York: John Wiley.

Shaffer, J. P. (1979). Comparison of means: An *F* test followed by a modified multiple range procedure. *Journal of Educational Statistics, 4*, 14-23.

Shaffer, J. P. (1986). Modified sequentially rejective multiple test procedures. *Journal of the American Statistical Association, 81*, 826-831.

Šidák, Z. (1967). Rectangular confidence regions for the means of multivariate normal distributions. *Journal of the American Statistical Association, 62*, 626-633.

SPSS, Inc. (1990). *SPSS reference guide.* Chicago: Author.

Steel, R. G. D. (1960). A rank sum test for comparing all pairs of treatments. *Technometrics, 2*, 197-207.

Stoline, M. R. (1984). *Preliminary tests to determine variance-covariance structure incorporated into one-way repeated measurement design tests for means.* Unpublished manuscript.

Tamhane, A. C. (1979). A comparison of procedures for multiple comparisons of means with unequal variances. *Journal of the American Statistical Association, 74*, 471-480.

Toothaker, L. E. (1986). *Introductory statistics for the behavioral sciences.* New York: McGraw-Hill.

Tukey, J. W. (1953). *The problem of multiple comparisons.* Mimeographed monograph.

Welch, B. L. (1949). Further note on Mrs. Aspin's tables and on certain approximations to the tabled functions. *Biometrika, 36*, 293-296.

Welsch, R. E. (1977a). Stepwise multiple comparison procedures. *Journal of the American Statistical Association, 72*, 566-575.

Welsch, R. E. (1977b). *Tables for stepwise multiple comparison procedures.* Unpublished manuscript, Massachusetts Institute of Technology.

Winer, B. J. (1971). *Statistical principles in experimental design* (2nd ed.). New York: McGraw-Hill.

Index

About the Author

Larry E. Toothaker is currently Professor of Psychology at the University of Oklahoma, Norman, where he has taught since 1968. His research interests include multiple comparison procedures, repeated measures designs, robustness, outlier-resistant tests, and nonparametric methods. He has published articles in the *Journal of the American Statistical Association, Journal of Educational Statistics, Psychological Bulletin,* and other journals. He is author of Introductory Statistics for the Behavioral Sciences, and is an award-winning teacher of statistics and experimental design. In 1988, he was chosen as the best professor in Oklahoma as the winner of the Gold Medal of Excellence in Teaching. He trained to be a high school mathematics teacher during his undergraduate work at the University of Nebraska, and his graduate work was in educational psychology at the University of Wisconsin. He and his wife, Nietzie, have two children, Lori and Brady, who are currently college students. Larry is an avid runner and competes in local road races and master's track meets. The family is active in their local church, where Larry and Nietzie teach Bible classes and Larry is a deacon.